MW00642002

CHANGE THE WALLPAPER

CHANGE THE WALLPAPER

CHANGE
THE
WALLPAPER

Transforming Cultural Patterns
to Build More Just Communities

NILANJANA DASGUPTA

Yale

UNIVERSITY PRESS

New Haven and London

Yale University Press books may be purchased in quantity for educational,
business, or promotional use. For information, please e-mail
sales.press@yale.edu (U.S. office) or sales@yaleup.co.uk (U.K. office).

Designed by Vera Villanueva.
Set in Calluna and Quasimoda type by Motto Publishing Services.
Printed in the United States of America.

Library of Congress Control Number: 2024937446
ISBN 978-0-300-27022-8 (hardcover : alk. paper)

A catalogue record for this book is available from the British Library.

This paper meets the requirements of
ANSI/NISO Z39.48-1992 (Permanence of Paper).

10 9 8 7 6 5 4 3 2 1

To my parents, Shakuntala and Kajal Dasgupta,
the scientist and engineer

To my grandparents, Ashoka and Saibal Gupta,
Indian freedom fighters

To my great grandmother, Jyotirmoyee Devi Sen,
a feminist writer before her time

And to my husband, Al Simon,
who saw the Wallpaper *before I did*

CONTENTS

PREFACE

I've given countless presentations on the science of diversity, equity, inclusion, and belonging to students, educators, leaders of schools, universities, businesses, nonprofits, federal and state policymakers, legal audiences, and various other groups over the past twenty-five years. As an academic scientist whose research is on implicit bias— rapid assumptions about people based on group membership—and social psychological interventions to promote belonging and thriving, this topic is important to me. In talking about my work on diversity science to varied audiences my goal is to raise awareness about these issues using an evidence-based scientific approach. Billions of dollars are spent on education and training in diversity, equity, and inclusion in organizations, a few of which are grounded in science, but most are not.[1] Despite prodigious spending, there's surprisingly little consistent evidence to suggest that such trainings produce changes in individuals or organizations. Although some studies reveal that attendees report more self-awareness and self-knowledge after attending diversity training, such cognitive benefits dissipate quickly over time with little evidence of measured behavior change in the workplace. And these trainings haven't moved the needle in such organizational metrics as the diversity of people hired or promoted, people in leadership roles, fairness in decision-making, or the feelings of belonging among those with less power. Moreover, some studies show that diversity training may backfire by creating resistance and resentment among some participants. In short, appealing to individual hearts and minds through diversity trainings has not produced greater social justice in organizations.[2] Why?

Change the Wallpaper is my answer: we're approaching the problem in the wrong way. One reason this approach doesn't work is that diversity training programs often assume that accurate information and good intentions are enough to change individual attitudes and beliefs—that attitudes and beliefs are freely and consciously chosen. However, my research and that of many colleagues show that we often don't choose our attitudes and beliefs. Just like learning a new language through immersion, attitudes take root in our minds based on what we see and hear in a local culture. And they grow quietly without our attention.

Second, diversity training programs assume that behavior change will follow from changes in individual attitudes and beliefs. But a fundamental lesson from social psychology is that attitudes and beliefs do not move behavior consistently. Behavior is shaped by many factors unrelated to personal attitudes and beliefs: the role we occupy when making decisions, other people's opinions, decisions, and actions around us, and the norms and conventions of that space, among other influences. Each of these situational considerations exerts invisible nudges toward action that may or may not fit with our personal opinions. Think of these situational forces as the metaphorical wallpaper that surrounds us in a local environment. This wallpaper, always in the background, hardly noticed, quietly shapes our experiences, our understanding of local expectations, and our action. While diversity training appeals to individual attitudes and opinions, it doesn't touch the situational forces that influence individual behavior.

A third reason diversity training programs have not yielded a significant impact on the ground is that individual behavior change, even if it were to occur, is not sufficient to create culture change. Although in individualistic cultures such as ours we conceive of individuals as agents of change whose actions somehow trickle up to change organizations and even systems, in reality individuals acting alone are powerless when the wallpaper is sticky and old. In many cases the wallpaper was installed generations ago by people in power who built the room to benefit themselves and others like them. Its norms and traditions started in a way that seemed natural, not imposed or coercive. Subsequent occupants of the room came to accept the status quo without question. But when people begin to notice unfair practices and inequalities in the local environment, begin to ask questions, to share their reactions with peers and colleagues, and step forward to speak up collectively, the momentum becomes a force with the potential to challenge the wallpaper status quo. To be sure, whether collective action will change local culture is not a given, and change is often slow, but it is more likely than when actions are taken by individuals without the backing of a coalition.

A distinctive quality of *Change the Wallpaper* is that it shows how individual action informs interpersonal relationships, which, in turn, gives rise to coordination and collective action—for good or for ill—that defines distinctive local cultures. Most books about bias, inequality, and social change focus on either *individual* bias in attitudes and behavior or *societal* bias in culture and policies, not both. In *Change the Wallpaper* I make connections to illustrate how the local spaces we inhabit shift our everyday behavior to create or reinforce small inequalities that go unnoticed. Such behaviors accumulate over time to yield consistently unequal outcomes in teams, organizations, social groups, community groups, neighborhoods, cities, and towns. Multiply these behaviors and outcomes across many settings and we have a systemic problem. In the space in between the individual and society is the local culture where individuals live; that is a sweet spot for social change through coordinated action.

Change the Wallpaper is solutions oriented. It doesn't stop at identifying the problems; it offers specific approaches and actions. Noticing the wallpaper creates opportunities to change behavior and gather with others to promote social justice and equality. I integrate a wide range of research from across academic fields and apply it to everyday human behavior in order to isolate specific forces that can be levers to move the culture. I weave together science with stories of real people and events to ground abstract research findings in vivid reality.

Readers of *Change the Wallpaper* may come from various walks of life, but three groups stand out in my mind as people who may be particularly interested in this topic. First, leaders, managers, coaches, trainers, consultants, and other professionals who want to be more inclusive and members of work teams and organizations. Second, socially conscious people who are looking for science-informed approaches to actions that bring about culture change in their local sphere. And most broadly, readers interested in big ideas about the human mind, behavior, and society. Many people are frustrated by the failure of good intentions to bring progress toward diversity, equity, and inclusion in organizations and in our larger society. They are looking for new insights and concrete methods to make culture change where they live and work. *Change the Wallpaper* is for them.

ACKNOWLEDGMENTS

H is wallpaper changed," remarked my husband, telling me of our son's first impression as he set foot on the campus of a private liberal arts college whose student body was starkly different from his diverse public high school. That sentence struck me as the perfect metaphor for the power of situations that silently shape what appears normal to us. We don't notice the wallpaper and its impacts on our mind and behavior until it changes.

This book is the product of a twenty-five-year career in social psychological research blended with many conversations and debates with my husband, Al Simon, about the history and politics of societal inequality—and about the challenge of acting as individuals to make a dent in the structures upholding that inequality. What can ordinary individuals do to make a difference if they are not policymakers or organizational leaders? The result is this book, more expansive and illuminating than if I had written solely from the perspective of social psychology. Thank you, Al, for enriching this book and my life.

Having big ideas is all well and good, but to convert them into tangible form requires protected time and mental space. I am indebted to the Samuel F. Conti Faculty Fellowship from the Uni-

versity of Massachusetts Amherst for awarding me a precious year
to focus solely on book writing free from teaching and service responsibilities. I couldn't have written this book without a yearlong
leave with full pay. I am very grateful to Leila Campoli, my agent,
who came into my life at the right time, at the beginning of the
COVID-19 pandemic. She was the guide who demystified the book-
writing process and provided incisive and extensive feedback that
made my manuscript better. Thank you to Dolly Chugh, for introducing us. I feel lucky to have found an excellent editor in Jean
Thomson Black at Yale University Press, who, with her editorial assistant Elizabeth Sylvia, championed the book throughout the pub-
lication process. They were responsive and conscientious in their
feedback and guidance. Dan Heaton, with his meticulous editing,
candid feedback, and humorous sidebars made the final review of
the manuscript fun. In all, I couldn't have asked for a better pub-
lisher to bring this book to fruition. Many thanks to Priyankar
Gupta for translating my abstract ideas into beautiful illustrations.

Stories of real people bring this book alive in a way that science
by itself often cannot. For their generosity in sharing their personal
stories, I'm grateful to Randy Le, Jacqueline Zeimbekakis, Elaine
Wolfson, Elisa Vega-Burns, Patrick Chettri, Sayra, Noor Jahan,
Pappu, Iqbal, Al Simon, Alex Simon, and Conner Morgan. Thank
you, Urvi Saviel, for introducing me to Patrick and the Mazdurpara slum.

A small cadre of friends, family, and students read the whole
manuscript and provided multiple valuable perspectives. I'm immensely grateful for their time and input: my husband and sister,
Al Simon and Srirupa Dasgupta; friends Ellen and Robert Meero-
pol, Madeleine Hertz, and Adam Eichen; and students in my implicit social cognition research lab—Hector Sosa, Aanchal Setia,
Tiani Perkins, Liora Morhayim, Trisha Dehrone, Samantha Mc-
Caughan, Savana Giurleo, David Clulk Le, Alice Lin, Anika Ma-

haraj, Jennifer Nadig, Sophia Nguyen, Bianca Palestis, Stephanie Silva, and Priya Darshankar. Other friends commented on a couple of early chapters—thank you all: Jill Jackson Jenkins, Romita Ray, Kim Reed, Wendy Varner, Hannah Varner, Max Monn, Janet Nelson, and Linda Baker.

For being my research partners during a twenty-five-year quest to understand the nature of implicit bias, prejudice, and stereotypes, and to design and test interventions that can change the course of people's lives, I am grateful to my current and former graduate students and postdoctoral fellows: Shaki Asgari, Luis Rivera, Jane Stout, Melissa McManus Scircle, Matthew Hunsinger, Levi Adelman, Deborah Wu, Kelsey Thiem, Kumar Yogeeswaran, Adrian Rivera-Rodriguez, Aanchal Setia, Hector Sosa, Tara Dennehy, Jacqueline Smith, Marielena Barbieri, Chelsea Moore, James Rae, Greg Larsen, Ahrona Chand Matzke, Celesti Colds Fechter, Randall Richardson, and Cade McCall.

Pursuing a research career in social psychology became possible because of mentorship from Mahzarin Banaji, my PhD adviser at Yale University, and Tony Greenwald, my postdoctoral adviser at the University of Washington in Seattle. Thank you for being my intellectual sherpas for so many decades. You taught me to put my faith in data while searching for answers to difficult questions and to believe the data even when the results surprise and contradict prior beliefs. To Brenda Allen and Fletcher Blanchard at Smith College: thank you for being my first academic mentors and for modeling what supportive mentoring looks like.

The convergence of science and social justice, the overarching theme of this book, is inspired by my multigenerational family whose actions were my wallpaper growing up. I am deeply grateful to them. Shakuntala and Kajal, my parents, instilled in me a thirst for knowledge, especially scientific knowledge. Ashoka and Saibal, my grandparents, who were heavily involved in India's struggle for independence from British occupation and worked closely with Mahatma Gandhi, modeled for their children and grandchildren social justice as a core value—standing up for what is right in whatever way possible. The writings by my great grandmother Jyotirmoyee Devi, a feminist writer in early-twentieth-century India, showed me that individuals can act with agency despite powerful constraints.

Thank you to members of my extended family in the United States, who bring me joy, sustenance, teasing, and good humor, and whose presence plucks me out of work and deposits me into the real world: Al, Olivia and Alex, Julian and Javier, Srirupa and Pablo, Anirban and Irina, Robi and Raka.

CHANGE THE WALLPAPER

CHANGE THE WALLPAPER

INTRODUCTION

Yewande Komolafe and Sue Li, both immigrant women of color, were trying to gain a foothold in the culinary world of New York. Yewande grew up in Lagos, Nigeria. She came to the United States as a sixteen-year-old. Many generations of women in her family were in food-oriented careers; her mother was a food scientist. Yewande knew she wanted to pursue a culinary career. Sue Li started as a student at Barnard College in Manhattan after immigrating to the United States from Taipei, Taiwan. Although she studied statistics in college, she quickly veered toward food styling after a job assisting with a cookbook connected to a Manhattan restaurant. By 2010, both Yewande and Sue had built up years of experience freelancing as recipe developers, testers, and food stylists and were looking to take the next step in their careers. Yewande and Sue didn't know each other. When an opportunity came up to become freelance staff at *Bon Appétit*, the preeminent food magazine of the day, both women jumped at the chance. This was the beginning of a better life.[1]

Bon Appétit was looking to change its image. It had just hired Adam Rapoport as editor in chief. Rapoport was young, cool, and hip.[2] The newly reinvented *Bon Appétit* seemed full of promise.

Rapoport had free rein to hire a new team of editors and creative directors to fill top decision-making roles. All his hires were white and trendy. Although delicious food was an important anchor of *Bon Appétit,* it was selling something more: a fantasy lifestyle, stylish, wealthy, and white. These attributes embodied the culture at *Bon Appétit*—its wallpaper. Top-tier editors, when they met for pitch meetings to select recipes and stories for the magazine, convened in a sunlit, open space on the fifth floor of a midtown Manhattan office building.

Below, on the fourth floor, Yewande, Sue, and other freelance cooks worked in the test kitchen as temps. They tested recipes pitched by the people upstairs. The test kitchen had no windows and no sunlight; each temp worked in isolation in a siloed bay. Yewande and Sue wanted to pitch their own recipes and be considered for permanent positions, but the path to success was unclear. Nobody invited them to pitch recipes. Nobody brought them into the fold. They were permanently stuck on the bottom rung of *Bon Appétit*—almost always alone in a sea of stylish white folk. Both felt isolated and filled with self-doubt.

Once in a great while, a temp would succeed in moving upstairs as a permanent employee. Alison Roman was one such lucky person. She started in the test kitchen in 2011. Alison and Yewande had similar work experience. Although Yewande had worked at *Bon Appétit* longer, Alison quickly gained a foothold at the company. She developed a rapport with the people upstairs, got good recipe assignments, and had opportunities to pitch food stories. Alison looked like the editorial team. She fit the wallpaper.

Yewande and Sue didn't realize at first that being noticed at *Bon Appétit* required conforming to a certain style, both in the persona they conveyed and the recipes they pitched. Over time, the magazine's wallpaper came to shape employees' beliefs about themselves and their colleagues. After attempting to climb the *Bon Appétit* ladder several times and being told that they were not a good fit, Yewande and Sue started to doubt their work. Both women left the magazine soon after.

The *Bon Appétit* story has many layers that became public during and after summer 2020, when the murder of George Floyd accelerated a new chapter of racial reckoning in the United States. Accusations of structural racism came to light, not only at *Bon Appétit* but in the food world more broadly.[3] Rapoport resigned as *Bon Appétit's* chief editor on June 8, 2020, after a 2013 photo of him dressed in a Halloween costume that caricatured Puerto Ricans was reposted on Twitter. His downfall wasn't because of one embarrassing photo. Instead, it was an inevitable product of the house he had built within *Bon Appétit* that belied his socially conscious, thoughtful, and empathetic persona he presented to the outside world. Inside the *Bon Appétit* house, the wallpaper was toxic. His staff reported race disparities in compensation, interpersonal slights tinged with stereotypes, and an all-white editorial team of gatekeepers who saw little value in ethnic recipes and stories pitched by Black and Brown chefs. Rapoport's resignation is part of a bigger conversation about deeprooted biases related to race, ethnicity, and global cuisine within the culture of American food media.

The *Bon Appétit* story highlights how organizational wallpaper shapes people's beliefs, behavior, and experiences; how it defines the organization's culture. The wallpaper takes its design from senior leaders entrusted with decision-making, in this case an all-white editorial team. The few people of color at *Bon Appétit* were at the bottom of the organizational hierarchy. Some, like Yewande and Sue, were not even permanent employees. The uneven racial representation across the organization confirmed an unspoken racial hierarchy. Moreover, the physical design of the office building and location of employees' workspaces created an "upstairs-downstairs" segregation that reinforced status differences among the staff and minimized professional interactions between the ranks. The decision makers upstairs had few conversations with the people in the test kitchen downstairs, and the groups remained strangers to each other.

Once hired, *Bon Appétit*'s editorial team installed a wallpaper in their image. This included the value they assigned to different types of cuisine, types of food stories they tagged as most interesting, chefs they identified as most talented, and decisions about who was a "good fit" for the magazine and who wasn't. Through informal norms and gatekeeping, cuisines that originated in Europe and recipes proposed by white chefs were promoted. The leadership team invited mostly white chefs and freelancers to pitch their ideas, mostly disregarding ideas and people who clashed with the wallpaper. Freelancers and midlevel editors began to pitch recipes and food stories that fit this vision to improve their chances of success. Employees noticed who received recognition and who did not. These observations shaped their implicit beliefs about what constituted culinary talent, which influenced their feelings of belonging at *Bon Appétit*, based on whether they fit (or failed to fit) the magazine's definition of talent. All this was done in a way that seemed natural, not explicitly imposed, so employees at the magazine found it easy to believe that their colleagues accepted the editorial decisions as legitimate. Few resisted what seemed the natural order. The *Bon Appétit* story illustrates the power of a social structure to quietly shape the quality of people's attitudes, a theme that is consistent with my research.[4] These local values encourage unequal work assignments, talent development opportunities, and employment.

Powerful social norms make people conform. One of the central lessons from social psychology is that people who find themselves among others who are acting in the same way tend to behave similarly even if they have private doubts.[5] At *Bon Appétit* this meant that while some employees were privately dissatisfied, most did not express their misgivings. And with few explicit dissenters, there was no coordinated action. Change happened when an external shocking event—George Floyd's murder and Black Lives Matter protests—made people at *Bon Appétit* start to see the wallpaper of their organization in a way they had not before. Employees started to speak up, sharing previously private concerns and complaints. These conversations sparked solidarity and mobilized collective action that tore down the old wallpaper, toppled the old leadership, and sparked culture change at *Bon Appétit.*

To get from the level of individuals to organizational change, we first need to see the wallpaper, notice its quiet influences on us and others, and understand its consequences. We then need to talk to others, share our insights, assess others' degree of agreement and willingness to speak up, and mobilize a group to act collectively in the interest of a group of people who are affected and their allies. When greater awareness and understanding arouse empathy and anger, those who had lived with the wallpaper become more likely to act.[6] That is what happened at *Bon Appétit.* Awareness of inequality without emotions like anger and empathy is not enough to galvanize people into action, and collective action is essential. Individual action alone is rarely effective against an entrenched system.

Different Types of Wallpaper

The metaphorical wallpaper at the heart of this book comes in four varieties. First are the group identities of people in influential roles who are respected and admired, and their relationships with one another. In Figure 1 (see Chapter 1) this variety of wallpaper takes the form of a boardroom with portraits on the wall of individuals who are clearly respected and admired in this environment—and all look much the same. The similarity of their appearance and of their identity groups sends the message that these groups are important in shaping the culture of the boardroom. By extension, groups not represented among the portraits must be less important. The portraits are in the background and might even escape notice of the people around the boardroom table, yet their presence on the wall conveys a compelling message about social hierarchy to those present.

A second variety of wallpaper hangs from material culture: physical objects, products and technology, architecture, and the spatial design of neighborhoods, towns, and cities. Material objects give physical form to the local culture, signal that either equality or inequality is normal, and quietly encourage individuals to behave in ways that fit with that norm. *Bon Appétit*'s upstairs-downstairs office arrangement is one example of material culture that normalized inequality. Figure 2 (see Chapter 2), showing two neighborhoods separated by a highway, illustrates this type of wallpaper. One neighborhood has tightly packed apartment buildings where people live in close quarters, while across the highway the other neighborhood has single-family homes with spacious yards, suggesting differences in social class between the two communities. People within each neighborhood know one another; they are interconnected in a web of relationships. But they are disconnected from people across the highway in the other neighborhood. The physical separation gets in the way of social relationships, resulting in two segregated social networks, one more affluent than the other. Like wallpaper, the impact of architecture and landscape design on the segregation of human relationships is not the focus of attention for people living in each neighborhood. They are going about their lives and forming relationships with some, but not others, based on proximity. They are not thinking about how the design of their city influences whom they get to know and whom they don't.

Third is symbolic or nonmaterial culture, especially stories that popularize a set of values and ideology in a local culture, conveyed through word of mouth and in material form in books, media, technology, and symbolic objects. Through the repetition of stories, the values conveyed in them either habituate us to social hierarchy, rendering it normal and deserved, or question the morality of inequality. Figure 3 (see Chapter 3) illustrating a mountain with several climbers conveys some common values in American culture that are told and retold through children's books, advice from parents, teachers, coaches, and managers, and speeches from leaders of all stripes. One such value captured by a climber nearing the top of the mountain is that hard work always pays off, implying that someone who does not succeed must not have worked hard enough. A related value captured by another climber who has taken a tumble, often conveyed through stories and word-of-mouth, is that stumbles and falls in life are the result of bad personal choices. The unspoken implication is that individuals are responsible for tripping and falling; it is not caused by external barriers or impediments in their environment. A climber on top of the mountain captures another common value—the belief that talent is inborn. People who are innately talented get to the top of the mountain fairly easily, implying that struggles on the mountain trail indicate inadequate talent.

The fourth variety of wallpaper constitutes everyday behavioral norms, customs, and conventions—the way things are done by default. These norms and conventions are learned through cultural immersion, observation, and imitation; they may not be explicitly taught. People who know them navigate the local culture easily and accomplish their goals; those who don't know the norms get stuck. Figure 4 (see Chapter 4) illustrates this concept in the form of a maze: some people have successfully navigated the maze and are approaching the reward—a shining light—while others are lost in the maze, unable to find their way forward.

Each variety of wallpaper interacts with the others, amplifying the impact on the local culture, much like the colors, textures, and patterns of real wallpaper work together to affect the esthetics of an interior space. Some people, for example, create books, television programming, movies, art, or architecture to give physical form to symbolic values and ideologies. These objects of material culture communicate social norms, values, rituals, and desirable behavior. Some products, like technology and physical architecture, assist or limit social interactions. Norms, values, and other ideas spread from people in influential roles to others who are socially connected to them.

In Part I, I show how different varieties of wallpaper create inequality in small but cumulative ways. You will see how to notice them, name them, and understand the ways they operate. In Part II I show how these varieties of wallpaper can be changed to nudge the local culture toward greater justice and equality. My expertise is in social and behavioral sciences, so you will find that science is prominent in the book. You will read thumbnail sketches of numerous studies. But equally important are stories of people who make the science come alive. Some are people I interviewed, while others are people whose stories have been told in public forums. Some types of wallpaper discussed in the book can be changed by ordinary people acting collectively and strategically, while other types require actions by formal leaders. Although you will see examples of both here, I am particularly attentive to actions that are within the reach of ordinary people in their local communities, social circles, and workplaces, and less to those that require high-level leaders and policymakers in organizations and government (for the latter, see the extensive work of behavioral economists Iris Bohnet, Richard Thaler, Cass Sunstein, Raj Chetty, and others).[7] At the end of each chapter, I summarize the main takeaways—what you may want to carry with you as you turn the page to the next chapter.

In the world of interior design, professionals use real wallpaper of varying colors, textures, and patterns to set the tone of interior spaces, making them appear contemporary or traditional, casual or sophisticated, warmly inviting or coolly aloof, feminine or masculine. The esthetics signal who the room is built for—who belongs—which makes some people walk into the room while others stay away or step in for a moment only to walk out. Through the intentional use of colors, textures, motifs, and symbols, wallpaper conveys values that either fit with traditions or defy them. A room's wallpaper, together with the material objects in that space, create a mood and communicate norms and expectations—it guides social interactions within the space.

There are many parallels between the impacts of real wallpaper and those of its metaphorical cousin. My four varieties of metaphorical wallpaper shape individual behavior and then spread to groups to influence cultures. Often the result is inequality. But there's also hope. Once you recognize varieties of wallpaper and understand how they work individually and collectively, you will grow to recognize what you can do individually and as part of a group to effect positive social change. In this book you will find the science to support this approach, stories of people who illustrate the science, and solutions that you can use in your life. If you are interested in equality and social justice, frustrated by the lack of progress, and looking for fresh solutions, read *Change the Wallpaper.*

PART I

TYPES OF WALLPAPER AND HOW TO NOTICE THEM

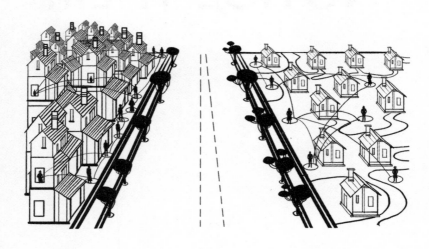

Talent is inborn

Hard work always pays off

Bad choices

1

THE ROOMS IN WHICH WE LIVE

Vibe, Value, and Belonging

When I was in college, the portraits in campus buildings were mostly of older white people who looked wealthy. They were important figures in the college's history, but to me, an eighteen-year-old Indian student, they couldn't have looked more different from the faces I grew up with. Even now, when I'm in a boardroom or the hallway of an organization, I notice the portraits on the wall and the people in the room. I've become finely attuned to this type of wallpaper, which is also reflected in the demographics of people in the room who are highly regarded. Overwhelmingly the portraits show old white men in expensive suits who are revered by the organization. As I notice their sameness, I am reminded of my difference. I wonder whether others notice the sameness. And whether they value people who look different.

We learn what "great" looks like by noticing who is respected, deferred to, and seen as worthy in our local culture, as illustrated by the portraits in the boardroom in Figure 1. We infer that they must have deserved respect because of their special qualities. Attributes embodied by these highly regarded individuals get associated with the groups to which they belong—including their most obvious identities, race, class, and gender. Then we make another in-

1. The successes of powerful individuals are celebrated while the accomplishments of others remain invisible.

ferential leap: we assume that other people who belong to the same group also possess the same attributes and have the potential to be great. Conversely, people from different groups have less of these attributes and less greatness potential.

Greatness is a marker of social status. Our beliefs about social status are assumptions about who is better, more competent, and more deserving of symbolic resources (respect, influence, power) and material resources (jobs, opportunities, income). Status matters because we all care about being valued by others and having others publicly acknowledge our worth. Status beliefs influence how we rank people on a symbolic ladder. People on higher rungs are assumed to possess more of the qualities that are deemed markers of merit than those on lower rungs. These beliefs are culturally shared. They influence whom we seek out for relationships and with whom we share information and opportunities. People all along the status continuum—those who benefit from assumptions of merit and those who are disadvantaged by them—are aware of status beliefs. Some accept these beliefs as legitimate while others don't subscribe to them personally but concede their social reality.

Arbitrary Behaviors as Status Markers

Some years ago, I did some consulting work with a prestigious bio-medical organization and witnessed firsthand how trivial observable differences between people become interpreted in ways that legitimize status hierarchy. In this organization bold and extroverted behavior was admired and was consistent with the personality of its top leaders. Organizational leaders treated public forums as places for vigorous spontaneous debate of ideas. They tacitly assumed that extroverted behavior demonstrated talent and entrepreneurialism more than quieter reflective thinking and decision-making. In a group interview with me, one employee (I'll call her Aisha to protect her identity) described her experience at work. When Aisha attended group meetings and a new issue came up for discussion, she preferred to reflect on it and respond later. Other colleagues at the same meeting who were extroverted and talkative would jump in quickly with their opinions. Aisha observed that over time her colleagues who were extroverted and quick to step in garnered more recognition and status and were treated as more talented than others like her who were quieter and more reflective. This created a two-tier system where one group—the verbal, extroverted type—gained influence while the other group—the quieter, introverted type—got sidelined. As they heard her story, several of Aisha's co-workers present at the interview nodded in agreement. Rewarding extroversion disadvantaged people with quieter personalities, as well as other employees from working-class backgrounds and people of color. Aisha had a quiet personality; she was also a woman of color. Another colleague of hers present at this group interview, also a Black woman, said she felt cautious about jumping in with her opinions in group meetings at a predominantly white workplace because of concerns about confirming racial stereotypes of loudness.[1] By implicitly favoring extroverted employees, this organization created a dilemma for employees of color, who were wary of being outspoken lest they be branded as being pushy.[2]

Status differences can be created by the most trivial distinctions among people. Imagine that you take a personality test in which you are asked to estimate the frequency of various events. For example, how many people ride the New York subway every day? After you complete the test, your results are computed, and you learn that you have an "overestimator" personality. Among other people who take the same personality test some, like you, are also overestimators, while others are identified as "underestimators." You're told that overestimator and underestimator personalities are stable characteristics, and most people around the world can be grouped into one or the other personality type. You get assigned to a team with a person who is an underestimator to play a knowledge quiz on a topic that is unfamiliar to both of you. This is a competition, and the best team will get a prize. Each of you gets paid for your work on the team. For reasons that aren't clear, you are paid more than your underestimator partner. Their behavior during the quiz seems somewhat hesitant. You each take turns answering the questions and sharing your responses with each other. You must guess whose answer is likely to be correct and whether you should switch your answer to correspond to that of your partner to maximize your team's chance of winning. What do you do? Do you feel more knowledgeable and confident than your partner? Do you stick to your answer or defer to your partner? How might other people watching the two of you evaluate your influence on the team relative to your underestimator partner's?

These are questions that Cecilia Ridgeway, a sociologist at Stanford University, and her colleagues asked in their research.[3] They grouped people into two fictitious personality categories, then put them in two-person teams—one from each "personality type"—to work on an unfamiliar task. Sometimes, without explanation, one partner was paid less than the other and seemed hesitant during the interaction, and conversely, sometimes the partner who was paid more appeared confident. The unexplained difference in pay and confidence created a subtle hierarchy between the two people on the team. Participants in the study tended to believe that the person who was paid more and appeared confident was more knowledgeable and of higher status than the lower-paid partner, even though it was made clear that the task was completely unfamiliar to everyone, and the pay difference seemed arbitrary. Participants regarded as high status assumed that their knowledge must be superior and their status deserved. Ostensibly low-status participants, even if they didn't personally accept the status distinction, conceded that others would see the status distinction as meaningful. Having a third person observe the interaction and praise the person who appeared confident reinforced the status hierarchy, legitimizing its truth.[4] Repeated rounds of this task slowly started pressuring "low-status" participants to accept the arbitrary difference that disadvantaged them as meaningful indicators of their lower standing. When arbitrary differences between people become seen as objective measures of competence, a status difference emerges that justifies material inequalities by implying that higher status people won their standing legitimately on the basis of superior merit.

In Ridgeway's experiments, arbitrary differences in confidence and pay between team members encouraged false assumptions about one person's superior knowledge elevating their status. Similarly, in Aisha's organization personality differences in extroversion led her bosses to incorrectly assume that extroverted behavior was an observable indicator of underlying talent, which elevated the status of extroverted employees compared to Aisha and others who were quieter in public meetings. If, because of differences in socialization, extroversion is unevenly distributed across groups (race, class, gender, national origin), people from some groups gain unfair advantages over other groups, which is the beginning of illegitimate inequality. When this type of inequality is interpreted as the product of legitimate merit, it replicates itself and becomes common and entrenched over time.[5]

Accent as a Status Marker

Saadia Khan, a Pakistani immigrant in the United States, human rights activist, and social entrepreneur, had an illuminating experience at a high-end store in Greenwich, Connecticut.

A salesperson approached her, offering her help. Where was Saadia from, the person asked. New York, Saadia replied. No, no, where are you really from? The salesperson wanted to know. Upon learning that Saadia was born and raised in Pakistan and immigrated to the United States almost twenty years ago, the salesperson remarked pointedly, "Oh, but that accent is still there."[6]

Saadia suspects the conversation may have gone differently if she had spoken with a British or French accent. The salesperson might have been more admiring of her accent instead of making a snarky remark. English accents enjoy an elevated hierarchical position in the cultural wallpaper. That hierarchy is ubiquitous in the United States and other countries colonized by the British, where English culture and language were imposed on Indigenous populations. English, spoken with a certain accent, became a marker of elite social class, success, and intelligence, and it marked the pathway to social mobility through white-collar professions within the colonial power structure. That accent hierarchy still prevails in English-speaking countries. In the American version of the accent hierarchy, the high-status default accent, presumed to be neutral, is called Standard American, General American, or Broadcast English. Regional accents are lower in status. Some foreign accents are admired while others are not. A British accent is accorded superiority among foreign accents, while African and Asian accents are at the bottom of the hierarchy.

Because accent is associated with social status, it is used as a proxy for the speaker's competence and intelligence much like extroversion in the earlier example. Accent, pronunciation, and speech cadence are assigned social class instantly. Once someone's presumptive social class is detected, that assumption biases listeners' inferences about the speaker's intelligence and ability, which in turn bias decisions about hiring, compensation, and other privileges and opportunities. Michael Kraus, a social psychologist, and his research team had participants listen to brief audio recordings of people speaking.[7] They didn't give listeners any additional information about the speakers or the context of their speeches. Despite the bare-bones information, the researchers found that listeners could tell whether the speaker was a college graduate with above-chance accuracy after hearing only seven spoken words. Accuracy got better when listeners heard thirty seconds of spontaneous speech. And college-educated listeners picked up the class-based cues embedded in speech more effectively than listeners who had not attended college. When Kraus's team compared the recorded speech to the spoken English on digital mass media websites hosted by Google, Amazon, and other retailers, they found significantly more similarity between the Standard American English spoken on these websites and the speech of affluent people with college degrees in prestigious occupations than with the speech of people without college degrees in less prestigious occupations. In other words, Standard American English is upper-class speech.[8]

Does accent influence a person's likelihood of getting a job? Kraus and his team invited a group of almost three hundred people with prior experience in hiring to listen to and evaluate the hirability of prospective job applicants from varying social-class backgrounds in the greater New Haven, Connecticut, area. Evaluators only heard applicants' response to the preinterview question "How would you describe yourself?" They didn't receive any substantive information about the candidates—no résumé, work experience, or interview responses. Evaluators were asked to judge the candidate's professional qualities, make a recommendation of starting salary and signing bonus, and guess the candidate's social class. Candidates' accents in this preinterview conversation had a big impact on these judgments. Evaluators assumed candidates who spoke with an accent associated with upper classes were more competent, a better fit for the job, and more hirable; they proposed bigger signing bonuses for these candidates than for others whose accents suggested lower-class origins, without knowing anything about the real qualifications of any of the applicants. Evaluators also reported feeling more similar to candidates who sounded upper-class. The unchecked assumption—that accent and the social class it signals translate into real ability that makes someone a good fit for jobs—presents a significant obstacle to fairness and economic mobility.

Taken together, these studies and stories show that observable attributes like someone's accent and level of confidence are arbitrarily assumed to be proxies for unobservable attributes that are important—talent, ability, and potential to be successful in a job. Often people are not aware that they are using observable characteristics to make inferences about unobserved talent and potential. Or they might be vaguely aware of their inferences without questioning their accuracy. These inferences remain at the back of the mind and the culture—like wallpaper.

Nationality as a Status Marker: Will the Real American Please Stand Up?

Being American is a marker of high status around the world. But who is the authentic American? Two representations compete in our national imagination. Sometimes Americanness is defined in terms of a set of deeply shared values—reverence for individual freedom and democracy and the willingness to sacrifice for one's community and nation (real Americans are civically engaged patriots), while at other times it is defined in terms of ethnocultural ancestry originating in Europe (real Americans are white). Whichever representation is dominant in our imagination is learned from the wallpaper of material culture around us—by noticing who is respected, deferred to, and seen as worthy of being memorialized in national portraits, statues, dollar bills, and stamps. Are their special qualities their contributions to, and sacrifices for, this nation? Or is it their ethnoracial ancestral roots?[9]

A growing body of social psychological research shows that observable attributes like race are assumed to constitute a proxy for unobservable attributes such as patriotism, including loyalty to and willingness to sacrifice for the United States. Although the U.S. Constitution eschews race and religion in its definition of citizenship, the psychological boundary separating American from foreign is often influenced by race. People assume that white people are more American than Black, Asian, and Hispanic people, even if the latter were born and raised in the United States. These beliefs are evident when measured unobtrusively with implicit measurement tools, but they also emerge when people are directly asked who is American and who is not.[10] The "American-equals-white" stereotype leads to misattribution of American nationality to foreign celebrities who are white Europeans and the exclusion of American celebrities who are Black.[11] This racialized stereotype of Americanness exists despite the ubiquity of multiculturalism in the United States and the long history of immigration that created this nation and continues to feed its population.[12]

If whiteness is a presumed marker of true Americanness, does it bias hiring decisions for professional roles that are supposed to protect the safety and security of the United States? I wondered aloud with my former graduate student Kumar Yogeeswaran, who is now a professor in New Zealand. Our curiosity was jointly inspired by the burgeoning social psychological research on national belonging and by the high-profile case of Dr. Wen Ho Lee, an American nuclear scientist of Taiwanese descent, who worked at the Los Alamos National Laboratory in New Mexico from 1978 to 1999, where he conducted research on the safety of the U.S. nuclear arsenal. In 1999 Dr. Lee was accused of stealing secrets about the U.S. nuclear arsenal for China. For five years, Lee was interrogated, threatened, polygraphed, indicted for spying, and incarcerated, much of it in solitary confinement. But federal prosecutors were never able to produce hard evidence to connect him to espionage. As the case dragged on, there was growing criticism of the U.S. government and the national press for mishandling the case. In the aftermath, the *New York Times* reexamined all documents and interviewed or reinterviewed many people involved in this case. Their new review revealed that investigators took fragmentary and often ambiguous evidence and wove it into a grand narrative of espionage that was so weak that it eventually collapsed. Wen Ho Lee was released. He filed a civil suit against the federal government and several media organizations and won a $1.6 million settlement. The federal judge in charge of the case publicly apologized to Lee for denying him bail and relegating him to a long period of solitary confinement.[13]

Motivated by this disturbing case, Kumar and I conducted a study to investigate whether people's implicit views of Americanness would influence hiring decisions in a national security job in a lab simulation. We brought research volunteers into our lab and measured the extent to which they implicitly associated Americanness with race using the Implicit Association Test (IAT). How quickly did they respond to quintessential American symbols (for example, the national flag, the Statue of Liberty, the symbol of the bald eagle) when paired with white or East Asian faces during this rapid computerized task? After a few other unrelated tasks, we asked participants how much they viewed various ethnic groups as patriotic and loyal to the United States. One week later we invited the same participants back to a different location, allegedly for a different study on hiring decisions, conducted by a different experimenter. Here, they were asked to evaluate five job candidates for an important job in the U.S. National Security Agency (NSA) based on a forensic investigator job description. Most elements of the job description were curated from actual jobs listed on the NSA website. We created a set of five equally qualified résumés that ostensibly belonged to a shortlist of finalists. Each résumé included the applicant's demographic information, education, and employment history. They were matched in age, education, and prior work experience. Applicants' places of birth in the United States and citizenship were printed on the résumés to ensure that participants knew that all finalists were American. We systematically varied applicants' race through their names: two of the candidates had Chinese-sounding names (Sung Chang and Meilin Huang) and three had European-sounding names (for example, Allen McMillan and Susan Cutting). Our results revealed that the faster participants implicitly associated American symbols with white faces, the more they doubted the patriotism and national loyalty of Asian Americans as a group, which in turn was significantly associated with their rejection of qualified Asian American job candidates and preference to hire white candidates instead. A second study confirmed this finding and additionally showed that the hiring bias occurred only for the national security version of the job but not for a forensics position in the corporate world with a virtually identical job description, suggesting that the employment discrimination we uncovered was driven by doubts about Asian Americans' patriotism and loyalty to the nation, not a form of generalized discrimination for any job.[14]

Can the image of Americans be made more inclusive? For example, would the status of Americanness be granted to an American person of color whose civic engagement had helped their local community or the nation? Kumar and I predicted that biographical stories of individual Americans engaging in public service might expand the psychological boundary of "real Americans." In contrast, stories of individual Americans practicing their (non-European) ethnic culture might contract the psychological boundary of Americanness by mentally priming the American-equals-white stereotype.

To test our predictions, we conducted a series of experiments in which we showed research volunteers a series of short life stories of several admired Americans (all Hispanic Americans). The stories emphasized the protagonists' civic engagement in one of two ways—we described them as serving the nation or serving their local community. This allowed us to explore whether any type of public service works or whether national service is required to be acknowledged as authentically American and to overcome people's suspicions about inadequate patriotism. Independently, the stories also described the protagonists either as attached to their ethnic heritage or made no mention of their ethnicity. After having each research volunteer read one of four versions of these stories, we measured the implicit beliefs about how much Hispanic Americans count as "real Americans" in the same way as in our previous studies. We found that emphasizing Hispanic American protagonists' national service (rather than their local service) made their entire ethnic group be seen as more American. However, emphasizing Hispanic American individuals' ethnic identity made their entire group appear more foreign compared with not mentioning ethnicity at all. A later study explained the reason why this happened. Highlighting ethnic identity in these stories increased participants' concern that the uniqueness of the United States was being diluted by "foreign influences," which in turn strengthened their implicit bias that American equals white. In contrast, highlighting protagonists' public service to the nation increased pride in American uniqueness, which in turn weakened the American-equals-white bias.[15]

Not all expressions of ethnic identity are the same. Ethnic identity expressions are accepted more readily when practiced in the privacy of one's home than when practiced in public. Consider, for example, situations in which people express their ethnic identity by speaking a language other than English. Do they speak their ethnic language only in the privacy of their homes or also in public places with friends and family? We found that people were viewed as less American if they were heard speaking a language other than English in a public place than if they speak their language at home. Whereas the former situation challenges mainstream "English only" norms, the latter does not. Moreover, not all ethnic groups are held to the same standard. Nonwhite groups (Native Americans and Chinese Americans) were implicitly viewed as less American if they spoke an ethnic language publicly whereas white ethnics (Polish Americans) were accepted as legitimate Americans even if they spoke Polish publicly.[16]

In sum, observable forms of ethnic identity are used as proxies for American nationality. People may or may not be aware that they are using other people's observable characteristics to make inferences about their unobserved citizenship. These inferences bestow on some a special status of being authentically American while denying that status to others.

Names as a Status Marker

Another observable attribute that signals social status is someone's name: names carry cultural associations. Like accents, names also bias recruiters' judgments of who is meritorious and worthy of hire.

In the early 2000s, economists Marianne Bertrand and Sendhil Mullainathan sent multiple résumés from phantom job seekers to 1,300 help-wanted ads in Boston and Chicago newspapers.[17] For each job posting they sent résumés that were virtually identical in content, with one critical difference. Some résumés were assigned names popular among white Americans (think Emily Walsh and Greg Baker), while others were assigned names popular among African Americans (such as Jamal Jones and Lakisha Washington). They then waited to see which of these phantom candidates would get invited for job interviews. The results were disturbing. Greg, Emily, and other applicants with white-sounding names received 50 percent more callbacks for job interviews than Jamal, Lakisha, and others with Black-sounding names. If these had been real applicants, individuals with white-sounding names would have to send out ten résumés to get one callback while those with Black-sounding names would have to send out fifteen résumés to get one callback. Because all these phantom applicants had identical qualifications except for their alleged race, systematic differences in call-back rates for interviews were clearly driven by racial stereotypes, not actual merit.

Is race bias lessened when job candidates' résumés are of very high quality? Bertrand and Mullainathan systematically varied résumé quality: high-quality résumés claimed more work experience, more skills, more honors and awards, and fewer gaps in employment than did lower-quality résumés. Far from reducing the disparity of hiring managers' responses, high-quality résumés encountered increased race bias in invitations to interview. White candidates received 61 percent more callbacks for job interviews than Black candidates when both had high-quality résumés. In contrast, white candidates received 38 percent more callbacks than Black candidates when both had lower-quality résumés. Companies whose ads that stated that they were "equal opportunity employers" discriminated as much as those that made no such claim. The researchers speculated that hiring managers were probably unaware that their call-back decisions were racially biased. Whether aware or not, these gatekeepers ushered more white job applicants into interviews than Black applicants.[18] This is not just one study, and it doesn't end there. Aggregating multiple studies that encompass more than thirteen thousand job applicants, sociologist Lincoln Quillian and his colleagues found considerable follow-on discrimination in actual job offers, not just interviews. White applicants received 53 percent more callbacks for interviews than people of color with comparable qualifications, and they received a whopping 145 percent more actual job offers than people of color with similar skills.[19]

This type of hiring bias and resulting employment inequality is a global phenomenon. As in the United States, job candidates' names spark stereotypic assumptions in other countries as well, leading some candidates to be systematically favored over others without objective merit. Of course, the specific groups assumed to be more and less qualified depend on the status hierarchy in each country. Dan-Olof Rooth, a Swedish economist, wondered—do the names of job applicants and their implied religion influence who gets called back for job interviews? And do call-back decisions depend on the hiring managers' implicit ethnic attitudes? With these questions in mind, Rooth sent applications to approximately 1,500 job postings in Sweden for a range of jobs.[20] He submitted to each job posting two résumés that were virtually identical except that one in each pair bore a native Swedish name while the other bore a Muslim name. Rooth also measured hiring managers' implicit attitudes toward Muslims versus native Swedes using the Implicit Association Test.[21] He found that hiring managers who showed more implicit bias against Muslims and relative preference for native-born Swedes were less likely to call back candidates with Muslim names for job interviews. Every one unit increase in implicit bias reduced the callback rate for Muslim job applicants by 5 percent.

As is evident from these examples, by conveying rich cultural information about a person's gender, race, and religion, names are observable attributes that can become proxies for individuals' position within a societal hierarchy. In India, names denote not only religion but also caste. Caste is a fixed social hierarchy with roots in ancient Hinduism that shaped Hindu Indian society through centuries, giving each person a designated place in the social hierarchy that guided their lifestyle, occupation, marital relationships, and more. Although discrimination based on caste is prohibited by the Indian constitution, its residue remains in contemporary Indian society, much like racism remains in the United States despite constitutional amendments. To determine whether people's caste has an impact on employment in modern India, economist Abhijit Banerjee and his colleagues used the résumé paradigm to conduct a study in New Delhi. In the résumés they constructed, job candidates' last names signaled caste. Most Hindus raised in India would recognize Ashok Gupta and Anita Arora as upper-caste names and know that Ashok Paswan and Anita Mandal are lower-caste names. The researchers tested whether applicants' caste would shape inferences about their professional skills and affect their chances of receiving job interviews for two types of jobs: software engineering and customer service.[22] Banerjee and colleagues found no caste bias for software engineering jobs. Candidates were called back at equal rates regardless of caste when they had equal technical qualifications, perhaps because those can be evaluated based on objective credentials in résumés. But caste-based bias emerged clearly for customer-service jobs that required communication and verbal skills. Candidates with lower-caste last names were called back at substantially lower rates than candidates with upper-caste last names for customer-service job interviews, suggesting that hiring managers were influenced by caste stereotypes when making inferences about professional "polish" and communication skills that are harder to identify from formal credentials in résumés.

You might be thinking the job market has changed a lot since these résumé studies were conducted. You're right. Nowadays, the initial screening of applicants for many jobs is done by automated algorithms. If you've applied for a job lately, chances are your application was reviewed by an artificial intelligence tool before it got to a human decision maker. Many large companies use AI to target particular types of prospective employees, screen résumés, conduct job interviews, and use games to infer personality, as well as cognitive, social, and emotional skills. Does the use of technology reduce human bias? Unfortunately, often no. While software accelerates the process of sifting through job applications, algorithms have a history of biasing the opportunities presented to people by gender, race, and other characteristics. According to an audit done by Basileal Imana and his colleagues at the University of Southern California, Facebook's advertisement delivery algorithm shows different job ads to women compared with men even though the jobs require the same qualifications. Facebook's algorithm appears to be picking up the demographic distribution of people in these jobs in the real world and reproduces that sex distribution when it places the ads in front of viewers, even though there is no reason to do so based on qualifications. In fact, this is considered sex-based discrimination under United States equal employment opportunity law, which bans ad targeting based on protected characteristics.[23]

In addition, there is a growing number of AI tools that companies use to screen job applicants. These automated systems decide which smaller set of applicants from a large pool will reach a human hiring manager. The AI tool analyzes video interviews for content, word choice, facial expressions, and so on, assigning each interviewee an "employability score," which is compared to those of other applicants. But the validity of these tools is dubious; in fact, there is no evidence that these scores accurately predict job performance. Critics worry that algorithms trained on limited data will be more likely to give higher employability scores to typical applicants who are more frequently represented in the current workforce and give lower scores to those who appear atypical because they are less frequently represented in the current workforce. The result would be to reinforce current demographic imbalances instead of building a diverse workforce.[24] Put differently, these automated technological tools seem to be reproducing biased wallpaper in hiring decisions. And, in fact, the technology may even be magnifying bias in new ways.

People with Status Are Presumed Competent

There's another subtle way in which unearned credentials work. Imagine you are supervising someone at work. Your supervisee's performance is a mixed bag: some instances of good performance and some mistakes. How would you evaluate the performance on the whole? Would you want to keep the employee or let them go? When social psychologists Monica Biernat, Kathleen Fuegen, and Diane Kobrynowicz researched these questions, they found that evaluators give more benefit of the doubt to white and male employees compared to Black and female employees. Mistakes and average performance were given a pass or not weighed as heavily in evaluations for white and male employees, but the same behavior was given more weight in evaluations for Black or female employees. What this means is that visible attributes advantage people in high-status groups in two ways: first, by giving them a boost through a presumption of competence based on group membership (independent of objective skills), and second, by giving them the benefit of the doubt if their performance is mediocre.[25]

Even when people of color graduate from highly prestigious educational institutions, the status of their alma mater may not protect them. Stephen Sauer, a management scientist, and his business school colleagues varied the representation of top-tier executives at companies, then asked financial analysts to predict the performance of the company.[26] They found that analysts made lower stock price projections when firms were led by African American executives from highly prestigious educational backgrounds than when they were led by white American executives from the same backgrounds. There was less race difference in stock price projections when the Black and white executives were educated at public universities. Sauer and colleagues suspect that analysts assumed that African American executives who graduated from high-prestige universities were admitted through preferential treatment, whereas the white managers were admitted because of actual merit. As a result, whiteness gave some business executives a leg up because of undeserved credentials, while Blackness obscured deserved credentials.

A common thread across all these studies and stories is that whiteness, high caste, high social class, religious majority status, and maleness are implicit credentials. They make up the wallpaper that frames some people, making them appear more talented and deserving, bringing them more opportunities and resources than other people not framed by these unearned credentials. People with these positive frames appear more competent and hirable in the eyes of hiring managers, bosses, and supervisors, even when their objective qualifications are the same as those of people from racial or religious minority groups, lower socioeconomic classes, lower castes, or women. When individuals who lack these alleged "credentials" break through barriers and manage to become successful, their success is sometimes seen as the product of unfair advantage.

Low-Status Markers and Self-Doubt

Randy Le moved from Texas to Massachusetts for college, which is where I met him. As the child of Vietnamese immigrants, he had grown up quickly. Randy and his sister were translators for their parents and the English-speaking world around them. His parents worked at the corner 7-Eleven, a grocery store, a nail salon, and a florist shop, hustling to give their children a better life. Not having finished high school, Randy's parents were determined to have their children go to college, find their own path, and live a better life. Encouraged by them, Randy ventured far from home to study. Coming from Texas, he assumed that the University of Massachusetts Amherst campus would be racially diverse. To his surprise it didn't feel diverse at all. He joined the marching band, which helped him make some friends. But as he said to me, "There was always something blocking me from opening up to them." All his bandmates were from middle- and upper-middle-class college-educated families. Randy felt embarrassed to tell them that his parents had not graduated high school and that his family was poor. Randy was experiencing what social psychologists call social identity threat. He was in an environment where his identity as a low-income student was hidden, like a secret he couldn't share. Immersed among students with college-educated parents and economically comfortable families, he felt that he didn't belong. Very quickly, that uncertainty about belonging sapped his motivation, persistence, and aspirations. He grew homesick. And he struggled to adjust socially. Even though academically he was doing fine, over the course of his first year in college he slowly stopped caring about school. He wondered whether he should go home to Texas.

This is the experience of many low-income students and students of color at predominantly white campuses. It is also the experience of numerous professional people of color and women on upward career trajectories in professions where they are the only person from their identity group or one of very few in that environment.[27] Being from an identity group that is a numeric minority in high-achieving environments increases some people's vulnerability to imposter fears. They are inclined to attribute good performance to luck, personal charm, or other external forces, and downplay their personal ability.[28] For example, some African American students at predominantly white universities experience imposter fear, which is associated with lower academic confidence. Likewise, for some women in engineering, academic failure shakes their self-esteem, but academic success doesn't strengthen self-esteem. Self-suspected imposters also tend to be more cautious and speak up less in work contexts where they are in a minority. In one study, for instance, we randomly assigned some women to engineering teams that otherwise comprised all men, while assigning other women to teams with equal numbers of women and men, and yet others to teams where women were the majority. On average, a lone woman on a team with all male colleagues rarely spoke even when she had good ideas that would have advanced their team project. When she was in the majority, however, a woman was far more likely to be verbally active and engage with the team project. These examples show how the experience of being a numeric minority in a high-stakes achievement environment can shake individuals' confidence especially when they face difficulty, even if their actual performance is objectively as good as that of others.[29]

How do people who are "onlys" or one of few respond in their environments? Sometimes they get burned out, leave, and opt for a different path.[30] Although leaving may look like a free choice, in reality the available options are invisibly shaped by stereotypes that signal who naturally belongs in this environment and is likely to succeed and whose success is in doubt.[31] Those who don't opt out sometimes form informal communities—both virtual and in-person—of colleagues who share their identities to support one another, expand networks, and create a sense of belonging.[32] Some stick it out through sheer grit regardless of setbacks, adapting to stressors and adversity in their single-minded pursuit of long-term goals.[33] Many people "codeswitch," adjusting their self-presentation in homogeneous environments to fit in by mirroring the norms, behaviors, and attributes of the majority. People of color codeswitch in mostly white spaces, as do women in mostly male spaces, and gay, lesbian, and queer people in mostly heterosexual spaces. Sometimes codeswitching involves dressing differently, changing one's way of speaking, or adopting specific hobbies and conversation topics to mirror those of the high-status group. People switch back to a different, more authentic self-presentation in environments shared with others from their own identity group. Codeswitching is a double-edged sword. Although it allows people from the historically marginalized group to fit in, it also reaffirms the expectation that the norms and informal rules of the game set by the majority group are appropriate and right and that everyone should assimilate. People may feel pressured to codeswitch and fear penalties if they don't.[34] Grit, resilience, and codeswitching are survival tactics of the "onlys" in an unequal system. Relying on individual strategies to "make it" shifts the focus away from the need to critically examine and change structural barriers in organizations and other local cultures.

If we invite into the room people with prestige-linked attributes, elevate their status with resources and recognition, and screen out equally worthy individuals lacking perceived prestige, the room remains homogeneous. Occasionally, a few individuals who are different make it into the room and survive through individualized struggle. But many more never enter the room or leave it through the revolving door because the local norms, culture, rewards, and networks favor prestige.

Low-Status Markers, Property Values, and Wealth Disparities

Status markers are attached not only to people but also to places—houses, neighborhoods, and other gathering spots. In the early days of the coronavirus pandemic, interest rates were at rock bottom. Abena and Alex Horton decided to refinance their four-bedroom, four-bath house in Jacksonville, Florida. The going price for homes in their predominantly white neighborhood was between $350,000 and $550,000. The Hortons expected their home to appraise for approximately $450,000. To their surprise, the appraiser valued their house at $330,000. Ms. Horton, who is Black, immediately suspected discrimination and requested a second appraisal. The couple's bank agreed that the price was off. In anticipation of the second appraisal, the Hortons did an informal experiment. Before the appraiser arrived, Abena Horton removed all family photographs from the mantle, replacing them with oil paintings of Alex Horton, her husband, who is white. She also removed books by Zora Neale Hurston and Toni Morrison from the shelves. Sifting through holiday photo cards sent by friends, she kept on display only photos of white friends and their families. On the day of the appraisal, Ms. Horton and the couple's six-year-old son went on a shopping trip, leaving Mr. Horton alone at home to greet the appraiser. The new appraiser valued their home at $465,000, 41 percent higher than the first appraisal.[35]

A similar experience happened to Stephen Richmond, an aerospace engineer, who owned a home in an affluent suburb of Hartford, Connecticut. He too was hoping to refinance his home. The value of his house jumped after he had a white neighbor stand in for him during a second appraisal, having removed family photographs and posters of Black-themed movies from the walls. The second appraisal of his home was $40,000 more than the first, just a few weeks earlier.[36]

The Horton and Richmond families are not isolated cases. Black-owned homes are consistently appraised lower than similar homes in similar neighborhoods, preventing Black homeowners from growing wealth through home equity at the same rate as their white peers to pass it down to their children.[37] The subjectivity of home appraisals leaves room for racial stereotypes to bias appraisers' judgments of property value.

Home appraisers are not the only people affected by status stereotypes that distort the value of properties. Imagine you're a prospective homebuyer. You spend a lot of time checking out houses for sale on Zillow in several middle-class neighborhoods. Sometimes you see pictures of the family who currently owns the house in some of the rooms. Is it possible that the picture of the family living in the house could affect how valuable the property appears to you and your eagerness to buy? Could it affect how you view the neighborhood around the house? The answers are yes and yes. Social psychologists Courtney Bonam, Hilary Bergsieker, and Jennifer Eberhardt asked a racially diverse sample of Americans to evaluate a house for sale. As on a real estate website, the property profile included photos and descriptions of the house and its amenities. Visible in one of the photos was a picture of the family currently living in the house. The picture showed an attractive well-dressed family. Some viewers saw a Black family while others saw a white family. Other than that, they saw all the same information about the house. Viewers' reaction to the same house was significantly different depending on the race of the current homeowners. People who saw a home that seemed to be owned by a Black family concluded that the surrounding neighborhood would be less safe and less well maintained, with lower-quality schools and municipal services, and less access to retail and financial institutions, while viewers who saw the identical house with a picture of a white family were unlikely to assume such drawbacks to the neighborhood. Viewers of the Black-owned home were less eager to move into the neighborhood than others who viewed the same, white-owned, home. Research participants seemed unaware that the race of the current homeowners had biased their impression of the house, its surrounding neighborhood, and their interest in living there.[38] In this study racial status became a proxy for property value. People who noticed the current homeowners' race, an attribute objectively unrelated to their purchasing decision, made inferences about the environment and monetary value of the property based on status stereotypes.

Why? Partly because racial stereotypes include assumptions about neighborhood disorder. Sometimes these stereotypes influence people's judgments regardless of their own race and ethnicity. When neighborhoods have more Black residents, Americans who are white, Black, and Latino allegedly "see" more neighborhood disorder, even after objective markers of disorder measured by video cameras and trained observers are statistically adjusted.[39] Does Blackness lead people to infer lower property values and offer lower bids because they assume the neighborhood is working class? Sociologist Maria Krysan at the University of Illinois Chicago and her colleagues conducted an ingenious study to distinguish the impacts of race and class stereotypes on prospective buyers' housing preferences.[40] They showed Chicago and Detroit residents short drive-through videos of real neighborhoods, simulating what people do when searching for a home—they drive around and look at neighborhoods. Some videos showed neighborhoods that appeared to be working class, others appeared to be middle class, and yet others were upper-middle class. To signal the racial composition of each neighborhood in a casual, unobtrusive manner, they planted people in each video—some taking a walk through the neighborhood, some picking up a newspaper from the sidewalk, some working under the hood of a car. The race of these individuals subtly signaled whether the neighborhood was all-white, racially mixed, or all-Black. Within each grouping, there was an equal number of working-class, middle-class, and upper-middle-class neighborhoods. Viewers only saw one version of each video to prevent suspicion. When asked how desirable each neighborhood was, white (but not Black) viewers evaluated all-white neighborhoods to be most desirable, followed by racially mixed ones, with all-Black neighborhoods deemed the least desirable, regardless of the neighborhoods' social class. In other words, for white viewers, Blackness was an implicit proxy for lower property value even in an affluent neighborhood.

To what extent are people reluctant to purchase a home owned by a Black family because of an implicit or explicit desire to avoid interracial interactions? Esther Havekeas and her collaborators found that even when white prospective buyers express a preference for a neighborhood with diversity, they end up searching in less diverse areas. In contrast, African Americans—and to a lesser extent Latinos—search in neighborhoods that correspond to their stated preferences, but they end up buying in neighborhoods with a larger percentage of their own group.[41]

Avoidance of interracial interactions is also evident when researchers look at how white people navigate neighborhoods through their choices and actions. Eric Anicich, an organizational psychologist, and his team showed people a map of a fictitious city that was either highly diverse or more racially homogeneous, then asked them to imagine living there, choose their preferred local amenities, and recommend governing rules for those amenities.[42] When shown the racially diverse neighborhood map, people preferred that the local country club be private rather than public, suggesting an impulse to restrict club access to people deemed desirable. This didn't happen when they were shown a less diverse neighborhood map. More participants also indicated a preference to send their children to a private school in a racially diverse city than in a less diverse one. And they reported anticipating a stressful commute to work if the city map was highly diverse than if it was less diverse. These results suggest that white Americans associated neighborhood-level racial diversity with greater stress, which in turn predicted a tendency to avoid interracial interactions by choosing private schools and private clubs.

From Individual Behavior to Structural Inequality

Collectively, this research shows that the racial composition of neighborhoods and the race of homeowners function as wallpaper, activating in viewers' minds stereotypes about order or disorder, safety or crime, desirability or undesirability of neighborhood conditions, all of which affect the subjective and material value they attach to homes and neighborhoods. Actions of ordinary individuals accumulate to create and magnify race and class disparities in wealth and residential segregation. Buyers and renters choose where they want to live and how much they are willing to pay for housing, thus influencing demand and affecting property prices and rental value. Appraisers estimate property values that affect the buying and selling prices of homes, as well as tax rates and access to credit. Sellers, landlords, and rental agencies select among prospective buyers and tenants. Individuals in local government decide where to locate amenities and services (such as parks, parking, streetlights, libraries, and grocery stores) and whether and where to allow polluting land uses (such as factories and highways). Individuals and organizations control and invest in properties, deciding what use to make of a property (liquor store or grocery store) and how much money to put into improvements.[43] These individual actions cumulatively shape structural inequality. Individual choices to avoid places that are diverse in race and class impoverish people's knowledge of systemic inequality and keep their social relationships insular.

In addition to individual choices about neighborhoods, consider all the other circumstances in which individual decision makers evaluate people for college, internships, jobs, and other opportunities. If these choices are even slightly biased by the faulty inference that observable status markers (names, accent, confidence, extroversion) reflect real merit, they will result in people being sorted by superficial criteria unrelated to real merit. Many slightly faulty individual choices aggregated across a population yield a structural hierarchy based on an illusion of merit, not the real thing.

To see how all this may be relevant to you, ask yourself the following questions:

- What quick inferences do you draw about people when you hear their names or accent, observe their confidence or insecurity, or see their extroverted or introverted behavior? Do you assume something about their skills, ability, or "fit" based on these observables?

- If you've had a choice to decide where to live, did neighborhood diversity have any impact on your decision? Did you hope to live in a diverse place but end up in one that was less diverse? If so, why did that happen?

- If you own your home, do you think neighborhood diversity (or lack thereof) had any effect on the price you paid for it?

- How often are you in places where many people are different from you based on their social identities? How often are you in other places where most people are similar to you based on their social identities? Are these numbers unequal—if so, why?

2

CHUTES AND LADDERS

Access to Networks and Opportunities

When I was a child my favorite board game was Chutes and Ladders. My cousins and I would compete to win by the roll of dice. Sometimes I would roll a lucky number, land on a ladder, and surge closer to the finish line. At other times, I would roll an unlucky number, land on a long chute, and slide to the bottom. Life is like chutes and ladders, except that life's players aren't all subject to the same rules. The accident of birth propels some players toward ladders and others toward chutes. The game may look fair from the outside, but the dice are rigged. Real life has invisible chutes and ladders. Resource-rich social networks lift some people up, while resource-poor networks drag others down.

I saw the power of social networks in action in my student Sabrina's experience. Sabrina was a business major, a working-class student, the daughter of Vietnamese immigrants. She needed a paid summer internship and had applied for more than forty positions without a single callback. Then a senior executive I know at a large tech company mentioned an internship opportunity shared by a colleague at another company. I recommended Sabrina. Within a few days Sabrina landed a job interview. In less than two weeks, she had a paid internship that converted into a full-time job after she graduated from college. Would this have happened without the connection? Probably not. What made the difference was someone in a trusted position vouching for Sabrina. This is the power of social networks.

We are advised to network, network, network, because social and professional connections increase access to resources and opportunities through formal and informal channels that can lead to educational or professional advances. Jobs are often filled without a formal hiring process. By some estimates, approximately 50 percent of jobs in the United States are filled through informal referrals, not formal advertisements.[1] Even when a formal hiring process exists, the influence of social connections can be strong.[2] In a study on the transition from college to career, Elena Obukhova and George Lan followed the employment search processes of 291 graduates of multiple colleges and universities in the northeast United States.[3] Using data from 3,112 contemporaneous job searches, the researchers measured the impact of personal contacts on individuals' success in securing full-time jobs after college graduation. They found that contacts carry a clear advantage. Job applications identified through contacts were 11 percent more likely to lead to interviews and 13 percent more likely to lead to job offers than applications through formal job ads without contacts. Individuals who received an offer were 21 percent more likely to accept it if the job opportunity was identified through contacts than if they had responded to a formal ad without contacts. One might be tempted to interpret these results to mean that if only everyone put in sincere effort to network when they search for professional opportunities, their effort would pay off and equalize access to good jobs. Unfortunately, the truth is motivation and effort to network don't yield equal opportunity because people's networks vary in social capital—a fancy term that means the extent to which favors, information, and other resources are available from personal connections to which others don't have access.

Who You Know and What They Do for You

Finding a job, a professional development opportunity, a leadership role, increased salary, and other benefits depends a great deal on the quality of our social networks.[4] People who are more educated, more affluent, or associated with elite institutions are privileged in two ways. First, they have access to more contacts who are of higher status, located in strategic positions within organizations, and privy to useful information. Second, they are privileged in terms of network returns, which means that some people's contacts are more willing than others to share useful information and actively mobilize their resources to assist the advice seeker by putting in a good word, writing a letter of recommendation, or coaching. Together, differential advantage in network access and network returns creates disparities in employment, other professional opportunities, and formal and informal modes of social mobility.

As an example, consider a study by Steve McDonald, who analyzed a representative survey of three thousand people in the United States, ages twenty-two to sixty-five, who were previously employed or employed at the time of the survey.[5] Among other questions, the survey asked respondents about unsolicited job leads they received from others in the past year. "During the last twelve months did someone mention job possibilities, openings, or opportunities to you, without your asking, in casual conversations?" McDonald was interested in testing whether access to employment-based information was shaped by the gender, race, and status of individuals who offered job information to survey respondents. Several findings stand out. First, people in white male–dominated networks received 103 percent more unsolicited job leads than those in networks without any white men. Second, people in all-female networks received 47 percent fewer job leads than others in all-male networks. Third, white male–dominated networks provided greatest access to job leads; their benefits accrued equally to everyone within those networks including women and racial minorities if they could get into those circles. Fourth, when women and people of color were in mostly same-race or same-gender networks, the individuals they were connected to tended to be of lower status, whereas those who were in racially diverse and gender-diverse networks had more high-status connections. The conclusion is that the gender and racial composition of social networks directly predicts how much social capital people can access. Networks with a majority of white men provide significantly greater access to job information and high-status contacts than female- and racial minority–dominated networks. Gender and racial segregation of social networks helps consolidate resource advantages of white men, while also limiting access to these resources for women and people of color.

Beyond network access, gaps in network returns also loom large. In a U.S. study, sociologists David Pedulla and Devah Pager investigated racial gaps in network returns.[6] Over an eighteen-month period they followed a nationally representative sample of 2,060 job seekers who were applying for a broad array of jobs including management, sales, and business administration. Survey respondents were asked what jobs they had applied for, whether they had heard about these openings through their personal networks or formal job ads, whether someone in their network had mobilized resources on their behalf, whether they knew someone at the company to which they applied, and whether the application resulted in a job offer. Pedulla and Pager discovered that, among network-based applications, white job seekers were significantly more likely to know someone at the companies to which they had applied than were Black job seekers (65 percent compared with 56 percent). In addition, people connected to white job seekers were more likely to contact potential employers on their behalf, to make a formal referral or informally put in a good word, than those connected to Black job seekers, which accounted for almost 16 percent of the Black-white gap in job offers among network-based applications. This is what racial disparity in network returns looks like.

These findings echo the experience of my student Sabrina. When Sabrina was applying for internships through formal channels, none of them yielded any interviews. But the door opened when a senior technology executive, who was indirectly connected to Sabrina through me, referred Sabrina to her colleague. Pedulla and Pager also observed that, while using one's network yielded more job offers than formal applications for everybody, this effect was twice as large for white job seekers than for Black ones. To get the same number of job offers, Black job seekers would have to go through roughly twice as many network contacts as white job seekers.

Network-driven disparities can be subtle. Even when people have access to the same professional networks, in industries that rely on referrals for business growth and career advancement, members of majority groups receive more referrals. Mabel Abraham, a business professor at Columbia University, illuminated this process by tracking how entrepreneurs within business networks refer one another to potential new clients.[7] She found that even when men and women entrepreneurs had access to the same network, female entrepreneurs received fewer business referrals to clients from network colleagues, friends, and family members of those colleagues than did male entrepreneurs. This gender gap in third-party referrals was most pronounced for women entrepreneurs in male-dominated occupations, who received 27 percent fewer referrals to potential new clients than men in the same network. Fewer referrals translated into lost revenue. Abraham's speculation was that network members referred fewer women-owned businesses because they were responding to the perceived gender preferences or expectations of others.

What this research tells us is that individuals' effort to network to advance their professional outcomes isn't enough to overcome group-based inequality in who they know, what resources their contacts have, and whether those contacts are willing to use their resources to help. A person's social network is the wallpaper in their room that influences whether their potential is recognized, which in turn affects whether they get invited into the next room. Like wallpaper, social networks work subtly in the background. Their influence is informal. It's about getting an introduction to the right person at the right time, having someone praise you to the right person who can open the door to new opportunity, being informally coached, held up as someone with promise despite lack of relevant work experience, or being given the benefit of doubt.

Organizational Practices Magnify the Impact of Network Disparities

Inequalities in informal network access and network returns can become entrenched as formal structures when organizations use them to create gateways in hiring, admissions, and career advancement. A common practice in many organizations is to encourage employees to refer prospective applicants for hire. Employee references are used as a screening mechanism to signal the quality of prospective applicants and their potential productivity. A representative survey asking metropolitan employers about their most recent hires revealed that network recruitment via referrals from current employees is the single most frequently used mode of hiring.[8] Many organizations incentivize referrals by offering cash and other bonuses to employees if their referrals are successfully hired by the company. Such organizational policies affect their employees' behavior in terms of the number of contacts they refer as prospective hires and who those people are, which together shifts the organization in a direction that could be more homogeneous or more diverse. Research shows that employees who refer individuals to jobs in their organization don't broadcast job opportunities broadly through their networks. Rather, they screen and withhold information from people who they think may put their own reputation at risk.[9]

Brian Rubineau and Roberto Fernandez, both management scientists, used mathematical models to test how the behavior of current employees in organizations and the referrals they make affect the demographics of new hires in organizations. When does the behavior of referrers make their workplace more homogeneous and when does it make it more diverse? Their models revealed that when one group of employees refers substantially more prospects from their personal networks than another group of employees, and if these prospects come from the same identity background as their referrers, then over time, the first group of employees will become the majority in the organization, making the workplace substantially more homogeneous than it was before.[10] Because people's networks tend to include people similar to them in social class, race, education, and professional and social affiliations, employees are more likely to refer people like themselves to their employer. On top of that, personal biases creep into employees' referrals when they make idiosyncratic judgments about which of their acquaintances to screen out or to refer.

So how might organizations mitigate these segregating effects? Rubineau and Fernandez's models suggest that organizations could amplify their internal communication toward employees from underrepresented groups, encouraging them to use the referral bonus

policy more actively and recommend people they know for advertised positions. Such a practice would increase the diversity of hires.
Moreover, because people hired through referrals are more likely
to stay, new hires referred by employees from underrepresented
groups would have a stable presence in the organization. Management could use these findings to modify their organizations' policies and practices related to referral hiring if they wanted to, but it
is not clear that they have.

Referrals played an important role in my son Alex's life. When
I asked him whether social networks had made a difference in his
college life and early career, his answer was swift. Two key moments
stood out in his mind where relationships and connections made a
big difference—getting admission into Bates College, an elite liberal arts college, and getting his first full-time job after college. Admission into Bates College was heavily influenced by Alex's relationship with his high school baseball coach, Joe Serfass, who knew the
Bates coach, Mike Leonard, from years before, when they had traveled the same college and professional baseball circuit in New England. Although Alex was a talented player, in his own words he "was
not overwhelming." When it came time to apply to college, though,
Alex wasn't particularly focused on an elite liberal arts education;
rather, he wanted a college where he would have an opportunity to
continue playing baseball. Coach Serfass pointed him to Bates College, where he might combine his love for the sport with an academic
environment that would challenge him. As a member of the New
England Small College Athletic Conference (NESCAC), Bates has
high academic standards and welcomes applicants who are scholar-
athletes. Coach Serfass vouched for Alex's "intangibles"—his work
ethic, mental toughness, leadership, and character—qualities that
aren't readily visible from the stands to a scout watching a prospect
play a couple of times. From Bates coach Leonard's perspective, acting on Serfass's recommendation was less risky than taking a tip

from a coach he didn't know. Leonard's job was to take his roster of baseball recruits to the Bates College admissions office grouped in three bands: A (academically outstanding), B (academically strong but on the cusp by Bates standards), and C (academically weaker). Alex was a B. Recruits in B and C needed various levels of athletic recommendations to be admitted by the college. Thanks to a mix of talent and a recommendation of a familiar high school coach, Coach Leonard vouched for Alex to the admissions office, which was the boost he needed to get into Bates. This process, under which colleges give admission preference to some applicants based on referrals independent of academic merit reflected in the written application, is common for student-athletes. It is also common for another group: wealthy college applicants to a school where family members are alumni and donors. In the wake of the 2023 Supreme Court decision that struck down race-conscious affirmative action in college admissions, colleges are coming under renewed pressure to put an end to this so-called legacy preference, which disproportionately benefits affluent and mostly white applicants. Preferential treatment for recruited athletes has been absent from the discussion so far but may not be far behind.[11]

Alex benefited a second time from his social network at another critical transition period of his life—when he applied for full-time jobs out of college. This time the connection wasn't a personal contact but an indirect one. The hiring manager at a large multinational company reviewing Alex's job application was a graduate of Colby College, another college in the same NESCAC network. He was also a former scholar-athlete. Looking at Alex's résumé, the hiring manager saw a younger version of himself. Each was a student-athlete from a liberal arts college in the U.S. Northeast; each knew how to be disciplined and juggle academics and athletics; each had been in an intellectually taxing environment. Even though Alex was only a year out of college and had only basic work experience, the hiring manager, influenced by their shared experience, took a chance and hired him.

Referrals and connections put a thumb on the scale to override performance-based merit. These connections are not evenly distributed. Some people have greater access than others to well-placed connectors who open doors. Small initial advantages and disadvantages that start with the accident of birth—a person's social class, race, and where they live—become bigger over time.[12] Intergroup inequality is magnified when more effective social networks help individuals from privileged backgrounds acquire useful skills and habits and further expand beneficial relationships.

Proximity and the Formation of Social Networks

Networks start with where we live—our neighborhoods, schools, colleges, and workplaces—and whom we encounter there. Networks based on the people we run into in our local built environments are supplemented by the people we seek out through hobbies, social clubs, religious organizations, volunteer activities, and so on. Because our physical and social environments tend to be segregated by class, race, gender, and religion, our initial comfort is with people similar to us on these dimensions who are in our local physical spaces. Later, we gravitate toward other people with similar characteristics because they too feel comfortable. This is how networks stay homogeneous over time even as they expand.

Take for instance, residential neighborhoods. Where we live is determined by where we work (assuming we are not working remotely full-time), the convenience of commuting, housing prices, housing stock, availability of schools, and other amenities of daily living. Sociological evidence abounds that the majority of residential neighborhoods are segregated by social class, race, ethnicity, and religion.[13] In one example, John Iceland and Paul Mateos compared where people live in the United States and Great Britain by race, ethnicity, and whether native-born or immigrant, using the 2000 and 2001 censuses of each country.[14] They found that Black people, both native-born and foreign-born, are more likely in the United States than in Great Britain to cluster in neighborhoods, segregated from other groups. In contrast, South Asians, both native-born and foreign-born, are more likely to be segregated from other groups in Great Britain. In each case, the group in each country that is most residentially segregated is also the group that is most disadvantaged: Black people in the United States and South Asians from the Indian subcontinent (particularly Muslim South Asians) in Great Britain. Where people live and who lives near them is the foundation of early relationships. This is how residential segregation leads to homogeneous social networks.

Beyond neighborhoods, the spatial design of cities and towns also shapes social networks and inequality. Three geographic features of urban landscapes are notable influencers of local human relationships, as Gergő Tóth and his colleagues found: the distance between residential neighborhoods to the town center, the spatial concentration of public amenities in town, and physical barriers dividing residential areas.[15] These researchers analyzed the physical geography of 474 towns in Hungary with roughly 2 million individuals living in them. They found that residents living in towns where neighborhoods were far from downtown, where physical barriers such as rivers and railroads divided the town, and where public amenities were spatially concentrated had more fragmented social networks. They were connected to people who lived physically close to them and less so with others who were on the other side of the tracks or the other side of the river, creating many small network bubbles (see Fig. 2). More fragmentation in town-level social networks was significantly associated with greater income inequality among town residents across a five-year period. Tóth and col-

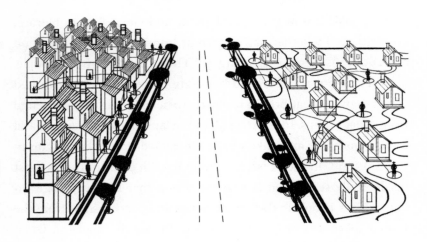

2. Human-created environments often segregate
people and interfere with social networks.

leagues interpreted their results to suggest that the town's physical landscape sorted and segregated human relationships. Once relationships were formed within neighborhood networks, people within each network may have been more likely to share their resources with neighbors than with others farther away. These relationships and exchanges amplified inequalities between economically rich networks and those that were less affluent. Tóth's findings are robust and strongly suggest that the design of these towns and cities indirectly increased income inequality, but these data are correlational and don't conclusively prove cause-and-effect.

On a smaller scale, physical proximity in college dorms also influences students' social networks and future job opportunities. Undergraduates enrolling at Dartmouth College, an elite institution in New Hampshire, are randomly assigned to roommates and hallmates in their first year. Economists David Marmaros and Bruce Sacerdote wondered whether students who live close together their freshman year simply by chance form relationships with each other as a result and end up in similar jobs four years later after they graduate. The researchers asked Dartmouth seniors where they had lived their first year of college, who their roommates and hallway peers were, and what their first jobs were straight out of college.[16] They found a strong correlation between students' own employment outcome and salary at graduation and the average job type and salary of fellow students with whom they were housed in their first year, simply by random assignment, not choice, which means that the results were not caused by students' self-selection of their roommates and hallmates. To make the results more concrete, imagine a scenario where 100 percent of a student's first-year hallmates entered high-paying jobs compared with a scenario where none of a student's hallmates entered high-paying jobs. Marmaros and Sacerdote's study implied that a student in the first scenario was 24 percent more likely to get a similar job compared with a student in the second scenario. Likewise, for students in the first scenario, a $1,000 increase in their first-year college hallmate's average salary was associated with a $267 increase in their own starting salary.

Lifestyle Similarities and Social Networks

In addition to social connections that emerge from sharing physical spaces, people also develop connections through shared hobbies and activities. Alex watched his college baseball teammates, especially those from wealthy families, reach out to the parents of other wealthy teammates to build professional connections. When he arrived at Bates, a private college, as a graduate of a public high school, Alex wasn't tuned into the culture of networking that is common in wealthy circles. But his college roommate was. Mike came from a wealthy family. He wanted to invest in private real estate after college and start his own business. From his early days in college, Mike identified baseball teammates whose fathers were in private real estate. He would chat them up, meet with them to get their advice, and ask them to introduce him to others in real estate circles. He learned this skill from older friends at his private high school and from his own dad. By the time Mike graduated from Bates, he had a job offer in private real estate, not because he had substantial real estate or related work experience on his résumé but because someone had vouched for him. His roommate's networking success helped Alex learn that the ability to make the right connections is as important to professional advancement as acquiring knowledge, skills, and work experience. He also learned that relationship-building is especially prized in wealthy circles.

Mike's networking illustrates the power of weak ties, which are links to distant acquaintances who move in different circles. By forming weak ties with new people through introductions from acquaintances who knew them, Mike was able to bridge to other networks that provided access to new information and resources. While strong ties link people to their relatives and friends whose social and professional niche is typically much like their own, weak ties are portals into new networks crucial to leapfrogging ahead.[17] Mike was able to leapfrog because he was taught how to network at an early age and because he had access to a wealthy network of baseball parents who were willing to introduce him to their business acquaintances.

The power of weak ties is evident from large-scale experiments conducted on LinkedIn, the world's largest professional network platform on the internet. Karthik Rajkumar, a computational social scientist at LinkedIn, Sinan Aral, a management scientist at Massachusetts Institute of Technology, and their colleagues used LinkedIn to test the extent to which weak ties increase people's job mobility.[18] Using LinkedIn's People You May Know algorithm, which recommends new connections to LinkedIn members, they randomly varied how often twenty million LinkedIn members were shown profiles of people to whom they were weakly connected (sharing only a few acquaintances) or strongly connected (sharing many acquaintances). Over the course of the study, two billion new ties and six hundred thousand new jobs were created. Rajkumar and his team discovered that when LinkedIn members were made aware of individuals with whom their connection was moderately weak, meaning they had roughly ten acquaintances in common, members' success in applying for and getting new jobs was significantly greater than when they were made aware of individuals to whom they were strongly connected, meaning that they had many mutual friends. Weak ties were especially beneficial in professions reliant on information technology and remote or hybrid work, whereas strong ties mattered more in professions that required greater in-person interaction.

Sometimes people get access to resource-rich networks through friendships that result from shared in-person activities with peers, even if their own background is economically modest. That's what happened to Elaina, my student, who was raised by a single mother. Elaina's mom is a schoolteacher and the assistant coach of Elaina's childhood soccer team. Doug became the head coach of Elaina's team when he moved into town. Like Elaina's mom, Doug was Jewish and white; they became friends. Doug recommended Elaina for a scholarship at Fayerweather Street School, a private K-8 school in Massachusetts. Her acceptance into this school with a scholarship became her entrée into resource-rich networks. The students at Fayerweather Street were mostly white and affluent and different from Elaina, who is biracial and middle-class. She also attended a summer camp for years, again free of cost, through another connection. Elaina credits Fayerweather Street School and the summer camp for teaching her social norms and etiquette that she used to navigate adolescent life and get access to new opportunities. As she said to me, these two environments "gave me opportunity to tap into my emotional intelligence and practice social skills in a very different way than public schools and town-run day camps allow." Elaina's private school and summer camp and Alex's elite liberal arts college opened the door to networks of peers, alumni, and parents who had valuable knowledge, resources, and a web of relationships. Many of them were strategically placed in professional and social roles and were willing to give informal advice. Through such networking relationships, both Elaina and Alex developed social skills and behaviors over time that enhanced their academic and professional opportunities. Wealthy kids are more likely to be taught these skills earlier in life than middle-class children like Elaina and Alex.

Elaina's and Alex's experiences echo those of students in the Dartmouth College study conducted by Marmaros and Sacerdote. Those researchers found that students' social networks were influenced not only by randomly selected dormmates and hallmates in their first year but also by the social organizations they joined in college. Students who chose to join fraternities and sororities and seek job advice from fellow members were more likely than nonmembers to obtain high-paying jobs in banking, finance, and trading after graduation. Men used their fraternities' help in job hunting significantly more than women used their sororities' help. White students used fraternity and sorority contacts more than students of color.

Learning the value and process of networking starts with access. Next, it requires the opportunity to observe people in action as they seek advice from individuals who have useful knowledge and resources by initiating new interactions. Learning happens through observing others, seeing their results, imitating their behavior, seeing one's own results, adjusting as necessary, and repeating the cycle. Without network access, people don't know what they don't know.

Conner Morgan is Alex's baseball buddy from high school. I've known him since he was thirteen or fourteen years old. Conner's parents wanted him to go to college. His parents started working straight out of high school, one as a bank teller, the other as a grocery store clerk. Nobody in Conner's extended family had a college degree. Because he enjoyed TV crime dramas, Conner thought forensic psychology would be a good major, so he searched online and found a university that offered a major in the field. He didn't think much about the quality of the university or whether his chosen major would position him for a future career. By his sophomore year, Conner couldn't see the path from forensic psychology to a career. Having racked up a lot of debt after two years on campus, he decided to return home, get a job, and finish his degree online. He began working as a door-to-door salesperson. Here he met the first person who gave him professional advice. Tim was the local director of the company where Conner worked. Tim took him to business mixers, and Conner watched him mingle with strangers. Conner started imitating this behavior without recognizing it as networking. A few years later, still searching for the right career, Conner reconnected with a high school friend's father, who had a financial planning business. Gary became the second person who taught Conner how to intentionally widen his circle of connections by joining local civic, social, and business organizations to grow relationships with prospective clients. Gary gave this set of activities a name—networking. Looking back, Conner realizes that he didn't know what he didn't know. He didn't understand that he should actively seek advice about college and careers, nor did he know from whom to get advice. Without access to a resourceful network and early informal guidance on how to reach out to get high-quality advice, he got lost in college. Young people from working-class families, like Conner, are particularly likely to experience such an academic misstep, while children from well-off families learn and employ networking skills early. Today Conner thinks of networking like athletic training: you see others engage in behaviors that you understand to be important, you try those behaviors yourself, and then you practice them repeatedly to achieve mastery.

From Individual Behavior to Structural Inequality

Taken together, network science and personal stories illustrate that social sorting starts with physical proximity and relationships that emerge in our local spaces. This initial sorting gets shuffled based on individuals' constrained choices of whether and where they go to college, where they work, what hobbies and other activities they pursue, what social or religious organizations they join, and how they balance social networking platforms with in-person interactions. Friendship networks of people who are working class, rural, and older tend to be more local, whereas friendship networks of people who are economically better off, urban, and younger are more geographically distributed and varied.[19] These myriad individual choices lead people who occupy the same social space to acquire shared lifestyles and tastes. They feel familiar to each other and comfortable in one another's company. Trust develops. In contrast, people across different social spaces feel less familiar and comfortable around one another, creating greater social distance and limiting trust. As networks become homogeneous because of physical segregation and differences in cultural lifestyle, people choose to share material resources, knowledge, information, and advice mostly with individuals within their network and less with others outside. Many individual decisions about whom to connect with, whom to help, and from whom to request help accumulate over time into webs of unequal social networks. Benefits amplify for people embedded within resource-rich social networks, increasing their advantage relative to others in resource-poor networks.[20]

To see how social networks are relevant to your life, reflect on the following:

- If you're someone who is comfortable networking with and seeking advice from people you may not know well, where, when, and how did you learn this skill? Did you learn it from a family member or trusted mentor?

- Think about where you live or work. Does the physical layout of your neighborhood or your workplace encourage different types of people to mix and become friends, or does it segregate people in bubbles and limit social mixing?

- In your work life or school life, do you learn about job or new opportunities through people you know? Have you gotten positions or opportunities because someone referred you or put in a good word for you? Were the people who referred you from a similar background as you in terms of their gender, race, religion, and social class or different from you? Do you see a pattern in who helps you?

- Have you ever put in a good word on behalf of someone looking for a job or opportunity? Was the person you referred from a similar background as you or different from you? If you've referred multiple people for opportunities over the years, do you notice a pattern in whom you recommend?

3

ANALYZING MYTHS

The Stories We Tell Ourselves

In childhood AE's speech was delayed. He struggled in primary school. At fifteen, he left school without a diploma. A year later, AE applied for admission to a technical school but didn't get in. He was advised to take more classes and try again. His second attempt was successful, but his performance in school continued to be just average. After receiving his degree, he applied to teach at several universities without any success. He ended up temping as a schoolteacher to make ends meet. Eventually, thanks to a friend, he landed a job at a patent office. He managed to juggle work and his own research, earning a PhD at age twenty-six. That year, he published four pioneering scientific papers that revolutionized physics. One of these articles became the foundation of quantum theory for which he received a Nobel Prize. AE is Albert Einstein.

If you observed Einstein's life as he was developing, you wouldn't have pegged him as brilliant. You would think he was just average. In the public telling and retelling of his story, Einstein's early struggles, failures, and seeming mediocrity got erased. His story became repackaged as the epitome of innate brilliance that emerged early in life. Learning and success, for brilliant individuals, is presumed

3. Cultural myths about talent and effort can make
inequality seem normal and deserved.

to be fast and effortless, and failure rare. If brilliant people struggle
or fail on occasion, it is attributed to external factors like bad luck
rather than a lack of personal talent. Prolonged effort, struggle, and
failure are tacitly assumed to signal a lack of talent.

Einstein's story illustrates the falsity of thinking of brilliance as
an inborn quality immune to failure. Yet the ubiquitous assumption
in many societies is that some individuals are born gifted. That's
why schools create programs for the gifted, try to identify lucky individuals born with innate brilliance, and nurture their development. Even later, in college and careers, some academic and professional fields and organizations value brilliant superstars presumed
to possess exceptional minds from the beginning while others take
the view that people grow into superstars with practice, discipline,
and mastery. Frequently repeated stories of inborn and effortless
brilliance, mythologized by trimming inconvenient details that
don't fit that narrative, are represented in Figure 3, by the two sil-
houettes on top of the mountain.

The Myth of Effortless Brilliance

Sarah-Jane Leslie and Andrei Cimpian, a philosopher and psychologist, wondered whether placing high value on brilliance signals "no trespassing" to newcomers who don't look like the field's current members. After all, when we think of brilliant geniuses, the image that pops into mind is mostly of men, not women, and even more specifically, white men. With their colleagues, these researchers contacted professors and graduate students in a wide range of academic fields across the United States and asked whether they thought exceptional talent was necessary to succeed in their own field.[1] Leslie and Cimpian matched people's survey responses with the actual percentage of PhD holders in each field by gender, race, and ethnicity, using publicly available data from the National Science Foundation, a federal research agency. As they suspected, the answers received from almost two thousand academics across thirty fields showed that fields that place greater emphasis on brilliance confer fewer doctorate degrees on women and African Americans. For example, departments of philosophy, music composition, mathematics, and physics tend to place a high premium on innate brilliance and graduate significantly fewer women and Black PhDs, whereas neuroscience, biochemistry, psychology, and education departments are less likely to define talent in terms of innate brilliance, and graduate many more women and African American PhDs. This pattern holds up across a range of fields in the humanities, social sciences, natural sciences, engineering, and computer science.

You might wonder, is field-specific brilliance a proxy for being a math whiz? The answer is no. Leslie and Cimpian looked at graduate student applicants' math test scores on the standardized Graduate Record Examination (GRE), which, until recently, was required by many U.S. universities for admission into PhD programs. Applicants' GRE scores were not associated with the proportion of women in the fields to which they were applying. Moreover, even after statistically adjusting for the effect of applicants' math test scores, people's survey responses endorsing the primacy of brilliance in their field remained a statistically significant predictor of fewer women in that field. You might be wondering, is brilliance more prominent in fields that demand long work hours, where the work is time-intensive, and there is less work-family balance? Anticipating that question, Leslie and Cimpian had also asked survey respondents how many hours per week they worked. They found that working longer or shorter hours did not explain gender gaps in doctorate degrees granted.

The subjective importance assigned to innate brilliance influences how students view their professors and the fields of study they choose to pursue in college. Daniel Storage, a social psychologist, teamed up with Leslie and Cimpian to analyze student evaluations of their professors on RateMyProfessors.com, a popular website where students write anonymous evaluations of their college professors.[2] They counted how often words like "brilliant" and "genius" appeared in more than 14 million evaluations of instructors compared with words like "excellent" and "amazing." While "excellent" and "amazing" were used equally often to describe male and female professors across fields, "brilliant" and "genius" were not. Fields in which students attributed "brilliance" and "genius" to their instructors overlapped neatly with the conferral of more bachelor's and doctorate degrees to men than women and more to white people than to African Americans.

Emphasizing brilliance and genius makes many women in these disciplines feel like imposters despite their accomplishments. Using a sample of four thousand academics from nine research-intensive American universities across the natural and social sciences, humanities, and medicine, Melis Muradoglu and her team found that the more a field prizes brilliance, the more women, especially Black,

Latina, and Indigenous women who are early-career faculty and graduate students, feel like imposters.[3] Feeling like an imposter was associated with lower feelings of belonging and less confidence in one's ability. Shaky confidence and fear of not belonging undermine talented people's persistence, putting them at risk of leaving their career path. Put differently, elevating the myth of brilliance in a field has the paradoxical effect of pushing out talented people, especially women of color.

This was Knatokie Ford's experience. As a child growing up in Akron, Ohio, in a blue-collar family, she loved science and math. Her parents encouraged her to strive for academic excellence. Seeing them struggle financially made her understand that education was the ticket to a better life for herself and her family.[4] Her curiosity about the natural world took her to Clark Atlanta University, a historically Black university, to pursue bachelor's and master's degrees in chemistry. College success made her eager to pursue a career in science, so she applied to the PhD program in biological and biomedical sciences at Harvard Medical School. To her delight she was accepted and eagerly moved to Massachusetts to attend Harvard. That's when things changed. The transition to Harvard was hard. Not only was she switching fields from chemistry to biology, but leaving a historically Black university in the South to enroll in a historically white Ivy League university in New England prompted severe culture shock. When she looked around, she rarely saw people who looked like her. She started to struggle in class. Before long she began to feel, "Maybe I'm not that smart after all; maybe Harvard made a mistake; what if someone finds out that I don't deserve to be here?" These imposter feelings shook the self-confidence that had previously grounded her as a child and a young woman. She began to retreat into a self-imposed shell. In class, where she was often the only Black student, she was paralyzed by the fear of saying something wrong and confirming what she thought everyone around her suspected—that as a woman and person of color she wasn't supposed to be good at science anyway. Knatokie spiraled into a deep depression. It was hard to go through the motions of everyday life and pretend everything was okay. After one semester she left Harvard and moved to Los Angeles to get as far away from science as possible.

She took a position as a substitute teacher in the Los Angeles Unified School District and was assigned to a middle school in the heart of South Central LA. Teaching adolescents in this school became a watershed moment. Knatokie realized that the insecurity she experienced in graduate school was the same emotion thirteen-year-old students in her seventh-grade class were experiencing. If feeling like an imposter had debilitated her as a graduate student despite all her early successes, how damaging were these feelings for a thirteen-year-old? After serving as a substitute teacher for more than a year, Knatokie felt ready to go back and finish her degree at Harvard. She wanted to prove to herself that she could do it and hoped that someday another young person would see her and think, "Hey, if she can do it, so can I." Returning to Harvard was even more difficult than enrolling the first time. The feelings of being an imposter were waiting for her at the front door. But this time her perspective had changed. She felt better equipped to reach out and ask for help. A key anchor who helped was the PhD mentor she chose, whose research lab was diverse, collaborative, and friendly, allowing her to grow as a scientist and as a human being. Small, incremental successes like winning a poster competition and publishing her first research article made her realize that she was thriving, not just surviving. Knatokie finished her PhD and went on to pursue a successful early career in science and technology policy on Capitol Hill in Washington, DC. But far too often that's not the case. Less than 40 percent of students who come to college interested in science and engineering graduate with degrees in these fields.[5]

As a substitute teacher, Knatokie had witnessed thirteen-year-olds in her class experience imposter-like feelings: uncertain confidence and a feeling that they were less smart than their peers. Clearly these feelings are learned from the local environment. Children are cultural sponges who pick up social signals from their environment very early. We know that by age seven, children in the United States learn the stereotype that math is for boys and reading is for girls.[6] Do they absorb the myth of brilliance too?

Lin Bian, a developmental psychologist, set out to investigate how early children learn the stereotype that brilliant people are male. She and her colleagues showed large numbers of five-, six-, and seven-year-old American children pictures of unfamiliar adults and kids and asked them to pick out the "really, really smart" person. Five-year-old boys and girls tended to choose individuals of their own sex. But by age six, girls were less likely to choose pictures of same-sex individuals as "really, really smart" people than boys were.[7] Children also selected fewer girls as teammates when playing an unfamiliar game described as something for "really, really smart" children.[8] Notice that the crystallization of the stereotype associating brilliance with maleness among children in the United States coincides with the age at which children start attending school fulltime. Age six is when elementary schooling becomes compulsory for children in most states within the United States.[9] Before age six, children are typically in kindergarten, often part-time, and there's more variability in formal education. Something in the cultural wallpaper of elementary school may be imprinting the brilliance-equals-male stereotype in children's minds.

To see whether and at what age brilliance stereotypes get internalized by girls and boys, Bian and her team introduced another group of five-, six-, and seven-year-olds to unfamiliar gamelike activities described as being "for children who are really, really smart." Then they asked these children how interested they were in playing these games. At age five, girls and boys were equally interested in these games. But by age six, girls were significantly less interested than boys, which is about the age at which brilliance-equals-male stereotypes are learned.[10] The wallpaper of elementary schools in the United States and its cultural socialization may be implicitly sending the message that intellectual brilliance is an inborn quality, and it is found in boys. As children develop, this message is likely to funnel away many capable girls from pursuits and professions that our society perceives as being primarily for brilliant people.

To the extent that brilliance stereotypes are learned early in life from the cultural wallpaper, we might expect this stereotype to vary around the world based on differences in national cultures. And indeed, it does. But you might be surprised to learn that the brilliance stereotype favoring men over women is *stronger* in countries that are affluent, capitalist democracies than in those that are less affluent and less capitalistic, across a mix of democracies and nondemocracies. Every three years, a global consortium called the Programme for International Student Assessment (PISA) goes around the world assessing fifteen-year-old adolescents' knowledge and skills in reading, mathematics, and science, and asks them questions about their self-confidence, future career aspirations, and attitudes toward competition. In 2018, about 500,000 fifteen-year-olds participated in the PISA study from thirty-seven nations of an international consortium committed to capitalist market economies and democracy. This consortium, called the Organisation for Economic Co-operation and Development or OECD, spans the globe, with representatives from North America (including the United States and Canada), Central and South America (Mexico and Chile), Europe (Germany and France), Asia-Pacific (Japan and Korea), and Oceania (Australia and New Zealand). The PISA study also included adolescents from thirty-nine non-OECD countries across the globe from Asia (China and Russia), South America (Brazil and Colombia), Africa (South Africa and Nigeria), and the Middle East (United Arab Emirates and Kuwait). Together, these OECD and non-OECD countries account for 80 percent of the world economy. In the 2018 PISA study, adolescents from these seventy-six countries were asked how much they agreed or disagreed that the following statement described their sentiments: "When I am failing, I am afraid that I might not have enough talent." This statement was not specific to any ability area. Agreement means that the respondent thinks that failure can't be overcome with effort; it requires talent, which is a fixed quality that you either have or don't have—it can't be changed through effort.

Delving into these data, Clotilde Napp, a mathematician, and Thomas Breda, an economist, looked at how beliefs about talent and failure vary across countries. They found that in OECD countries that are market-driven democracies, girls were significantly more likely than boys to attribute their failure to a lack of talent even when their objective test scores were equal to that of boys. This gender gap was significantly smaller in non-OECD countries. The wealthier the country (measured by gross domestic product) and the more policies it has on gender equality (measured by a composite of policies covering the labor market, education, health, and political representation), the more likely that a higher percentage of girls than boys believe that talent is fixed and innate. This is called the gender-equality paradox. For example, in the United States, Canada, United Kingdom, France, and Germany, girls are more likely to attribute their failure to a lack of talent than their peers in Brazil, Indonesia, Russia, and the United Arab Emirates, where the gender gaps in the survey are significantly smaller and sometimes absent.[11]

Other results are equally surprising. Interpreting failure as a lack of talent is believed more strongly by high-performing teenagers, especially girls, than by lower-performing teens. High-performing girls also express less self-confidence than high-performing boys.

Napp and Breda show that the confidence gap between girls and boys is explained by teenagers having internalized the belief that real talent is failure-free. In short, cultural messages about inborn brilliance and the interpretation that talent is effortless and free of struggle reinforce gender inequality. These messages are stronger in capitalist market-based economies that prize social mobility based on "natural" talent and competition.

Knatokie's experience at Harvard resonates with the conclusion from Napp and Breda's PISA study. Knatokie started to question her ability in science when she began struggling in graduate classes. She interpreted her struggles as a sign of inadequate talent. "Maybe I'm not that smart after all; maybe Harvard made a mistake; what if someone finds out that I don't deserve to be here?" In some countries there is a widely accepted narrative that experiencing struggle and difficulty in performance means that the person isn't sufficiently talented and won't succeed. This story line is in the cultural wallpaper and gets learned by its inhabitants from an early age. In Figure 3, it is represented by the struggling climber near the bottom of the hill.

But difficulty may also be interpreted to mean something else. In their cross-cultural research, Casey O'Donnell, Daphna Oyserman, and their colleagues compared how people interpret difficulty in the United States and in China and India. They found that Americans are more likely to associate difficulty with impossibility rather than with importance. When asked to write about what difficulty means to them, Americans used words like "can't," "futile," "helpless," "hopeless," and "impossible" more frequently than words like "crucial," "essential," "imperative," "important," and "valuable." In contrast, when adults in China were asked the same question, they interpreted difficulty as indicative of importance and impossibility equally often. In other words, things that are difficult are important and sometimes they may also be impossible. Adults in India were somewhat more likely to interpret difficulty as an indicator of importance than of impossibility.[12]

Taken together, these strands of research show that the conflation of talent as free of failure and difficulty is absent in some countries. In these cultures, effort is seen as a necessary component of talent, and difficulty signals both importance and impossibility. In contrast, in countries that are often affluent and market-driven, talent is assumed to be easy and effortless and difficulty signals impossibility. If an often-repeated cultural trope sends the message that talent is natural, and difficulty equals impossibility, it isn't surprising that parents, educators, and coaches in that culture would encourage young people to focus on achievement areas that come easily to them. In the United States, this translates into formal and informal practices oriented toward *discovering* natural talent at the expense of *developing* talent. As the cultural wallpaper gets imprinted in people's minds, adults sort children by presumed talent, and encourage them to self-sort as well, having taught them that talent is natural and easy. This sets the stage for gender and racial sorting by field and profession. Think about how students are tracked from an early age in academics, athletics, and music. Think of all the formal and informal mechanisms through which adults pluck out the presumed talented few, giving them more time, effort, and coaching, in an effort to convert the "discovery" into reality.

Einstein's story illustrates that talent grows over time and coexists with struggle and failure. Effort is one factor that helps overcome struggle by growing talent. But it's not the only factor. The conversion of talent to success also requires a mix of fortuitous connections, timing, and luck. Einstein struggled with exams and failed several times. But he was helped by a wealthy family and friends who intervened at key moments. Einstein's personal letters lay bare his financial and personal struggles, conflicts with professors and other scientists, and his difficulty obtaining an academic job, until in 1901, his classmate's father intervened to get Einstein a job at the patent office in Bern, Switzerland. Einstein's career was helped as well by his first wife, also a physicist, whose intellectual collaboration was hidden from public view until much later.[13] Mileva Marić was born in Serbia at a time when there were strong prohibitions against women studying science. In 1896, twenty-year-old Marić met Albert Einstein, a seventeen-year-old German, when both entered the Polytechnic Institute in Zurich to study physics. They studied together, shared a passion for physics and music, and fell in love. Letters and testimony suggested that they collaborated closely from the time they met in 1896 through their marriage to their separation, but her name doesn't appear in any of his published articles. Scholars have been arguing for decades about how much credit for Einstein's contributions to physics should be shared with Marić. This debate aside, the way Einstein's public story is told and retold elevates his personal brilliance as the sole cause of his success and pushes into the background the contribution of his wife, Mileva Marić, personal connections that got him a job, and parental financial support that provided a safety net. That type of storytelling hides the factors that made Einstein's career possible, absent which his life might have turned out very differently.

The Myth of Meritocracy Ignores Luck

"Talent is equally distributed, but opportunity and luck are not." That's what Ansh Motiani, an Indian American high school student, learned when he traveled to India to teach English and math to a small group of Indian children. Motiani arrived at an apartment complex in Vadodara, a midsized city in western India, in a bright white sedan, with the confidence of someone from an affluent country. He was met by seventeen bright-eyed students, one of whom he remembers most clearly. Deep, a seven-year-old boy, would quickly become the leader of the class. He was not the oldest or the smartest, but he had a special something. Deep was vocal, asked questions, helped others, and was an active participant in class. He had the desire to learn and succeed. He was bilingual, fluent in Gujarati, the local language, and in Hindi, one of the national languages of India. If the world was meritocratic, and the equation of Talent + Hard Work = Success was true, Motiani could imagine Deep growing up to become a CEO of a company one day. But talent is not enough for success. What's missing from the equation is luck. The lucky or unlucky circumstances of one's social class at birth and the opportunities that class brings often result in disparate destinies for similarly talented and driven individuals. Looking at Deep reminded Motiani of Sundar Pichai, the CEO of Google, who is also talented, and works very hard, but there is a key difference. Pichai grew up in an upper-middle-class family in India. He went to one of the finest technical universities in India, later landing in two elite graduate schools in the United States. Where Pichai was lucky to have had the opportunity to grow his talent because he was born into an affluent family, Deep was unlucky because he was born into a poor family, a misfortune that will probably limit his future success. Poverty is likely to force him out of school at a young age to provide for his family financially, a prospect that is likely to affect the trajectory of his entire life. Given an upper-middle-class upbringing, where could Deep's life take him in India or any other part of the world? What if his life was like Motiani's, whose parents immigrated to the United States? Motiani was born in Boston and educated at a private high school. While he likes to think of himself as accomplished, he recognizes that he is no better than Deep. Something clicked during that trip. Motiani understood the role of luck in his life, and his realization taught him humility and gratitude.[14]

On his last day, the students Motiani taught gave him a gift. In Hindi they told him they wanted to give him something before he left. They couldn't buy him anything, so they made him a paper watch, which is pinned to the wall of Motiani's bedroom in his upper-middle-class Boston home. The watch reminds him that any success he achieves in life started with being born in the right place at the right time. He was lucky.

A string of books and studies shows that people underestimate the role of luck in success.[15] To quantify the relative importance of luck and talent in success, physicists Alessandro Pluchino and Andrea Rapisarda teamed up with the economist Alessio Biondo to create a mathematical model that simulated the careers of a large number of fictional individuals across a working life of forty years.[16] Fictional individuals in the simulation were assigned various degrees of talent in the form of personal attributes—intelligence, skill, motivation, and creativity—that allowed them to take advantage of opportunity. Each of these fictional individuals began the simulation with ten units of success. Every six months, each encountered a number of lucky and unlucky events simply by chance. Whenever a person experienced an unlucky event, their success units were halved, and whenever they experienced a lucky event, their success was doubled proportional to their talent. What did the researchers find after simulating a forty-year period? Although individuals with more talent had a higher chance of success by taking advantage of lucky opportunities, talent by itself was not enough. The most talented individuals were rarely the most successful. Individuals with average talent who encountered more lucky events were far more successful than others with greater talent who encountered more unlucky events simply by chance. In the end, the most successful individuals in the simulation were those who were slightly above average in talent but with a lot of luck.

Ironically, the luckiest among us are especially unlikely to appreciate our good fortune. Wealthy people overwhelmingly attribute their success to personal effort and hard work rather than luck or other factors out of their control—born on third base, as the saying goes, they go through life thinking they hit a triple. The Pew Research Center asked Americans in a national survey a series of questions about success—to what extent is success in life largely determined by hard work? Or is it largely determined by forces outside our control? The researchers found that people who are affluent are significantly more likely to say that success is mostly determined by hard work than those with modest incomes. Only 2 percent of affluent Americans believe that success is largely shaped by luck and forces outside their control, whereas 50 percent of low-income Americans believe it to be so.[17] The frequently repeated myth that the sky is the limit if you work hard is captured in Figure 3 by the person who is halfway up the mountain en route to the top believing that their ability and effort will carry them to the top, oblivious to the luck of good weather and an even terrain.

The Myth of Neoliberalism

In telling stories of success, we celebrate individual merit and hard work, which together defines deservingness in countries where the cultural wallpaper presents neoliberalism as the best path to a good life. Neoliberalism is the dominant macroeconomic ideology in the United States. It has been around since the 1970s and rippled across the globe with varying degrees of adoption. It is a set of political and economic practices based on the premise that human well-being is best promoted by freeing individuals' "natural" entrepreneurial tendencies. In a neoliberal political and economic system, rights to property and other societal resources are privatized, economic markets and trade are unconstrained, government spending on social safety nets is sharply reduced, and so is government regulation of business.[18] The neoliberal project assumes that market forces will solve social and economic problems and is suspicious of government efforts to provide for the welfare of its citizens and regulate business. This ideology originated in the early twentieth century as a probusiness challenge to economic policies and legal regulations of economic markets and corporate activities in North American and Western European countries put in place after World War II. Neoliberal policies and practices became widespread in the 1980s embraced by U.K. prime minister Margaret Thatcher and U.S. president Ronald Reagan.[19]

The invisible influence of systemic neoliberal policies and practices on individual minds and behaviors reminds me of one of my favorite movies, *The Matrix,* a 1999 science fiction action film. It depicts a dystopian future in which intelligent machines have enslaved humans, harvesting their bodies as an energy source while keeping their minds pacified inside a shared simulated reality, called the Matrix, modeled on American society in 1999. People's minds are unknowingly trapped inside the Matrix, living an imaginary life they believe to be real. A few people uncover the truth, band together to free themselves from the Matrix, and start a rebellion. Early in the film, Neo, the protagonist, who is obliviously living a humdrum existence within the Matrix, is given a choice between two pills. Taking the red pill will reveal the truth about the Matrix, whereas the blue pill will return Neo to his former simulated life as a computer programmer. Neo takes the red pill and starts to see the Matrix in which his mind is trapped.

The neoliberal system that surrounds us is like the Matrix. It quietly shapes our worldview and beliefs about fairness, justice, and merit. Neoliberal values make it natural to view individuals as autonomous agents who are unconstrained by their social and material circumstances. If we believe individuals are free agents, then it's logical to interpret their successes and failures as the result of their own free choices. And, by extension, it's fair to allocate societal benefits and burdens in accordance with individuals' performance.

By framing performance-based rewards as the best and natural way to define fairness, proponents of neoliberalism suggest that people "get what they deserve and deserve what they get."[20]

Adoption of neoliberal policies in a nation-state is linked to the attitudes of people in that nation. Social psychologists Shahrzad Goudarzi, Vivienne Badaan, and Eric Knowles analyzed data on macroeconomic policies in more than 160 countries across twenty-four years (1995–2019) and measured the strength of association between each country's political economy and the understanding of fairness and justice expressed by people in these countries.[21] They found that the more a country adopted neoliberal economic and political policies at the national level, the more its citizens saw income inequality as fair, viewing it as an incentive for people to try harder. In their analysis, the data for each country's economic policies came from the Fraser Institute, a conservative think tank, which evaluates how much countries' economic policies fit with neoliberal principles. This think tank records each country's national policies related to government consumption, income and payroll tax, hiring and firing regulation, centralized collective bargaining, regulation of work hours, and transfers and subsidies. Higher scores on these metrics indicate higher levels of neoliberalism in that country. Goudarzi and colleagues then drew data from an international World Values Survey to measure how citizens of the same countries, during the same period, judged the fairness of different types of income distribution. Did people think incomes should be made more equal or did they think that large income differences act as incentives for people to try harder? After bringing together both sources of data, Goudarzi's analysis revealed that once a country adopted neoliberal economic policies, within four years the ideology inherent in these policies trickled down to individual citizens' worldview such that they were less likely to advocate for equality and more inclined to prefer proportional rewards for achievement as fair.

Neoliberal attitudes are strongly associated with the psychological acceptance of social hierarchies as natural and legitimate, found Flavio Azevedo, John Jost, and their colleagues. They conducted a series of surveys in the United States and the United Kingdom with more than ten thousand adults. Azevedo found that American and British citizens who endorse neoliberal attitudes were significantly more likely to accept as fair and legitimate hierarchical social systems in which people at the top have significantly more money and power than those at the bottom.[22] Based on these findings, they conclude that ordinary citizens who endorse procapitalist neoliberal economic beliefs are more tolerant of social and economic inequality.

If people interpret wealth and poverty as fair, legitimate, and appropriate, how does it affect the way they see their fellow citizens who are struggling financially? Goudarzi and her colleagues recruited a large group of people and measured the degree to which they think the American economic system is fair or unfair in providing individuals with equal opportunity and resulting in outcomes that are deserved.[23] The participants in their study held beliefs ranging from uncritical acceptance of the American economic system as fair and legitimate to harsh criticism of the unequal rewards under that system. Goudarzi showed them a video interview with a homeless person who spoke about their daily routines and struggles and another interview on a mundane topic with another individual. Reactions to the neutral video were the same regardless of people's beliefs about the economic system, but responses to the video of the homeless person were markedly different. People who believed the economic system is fair expressed less empathy and sadness for the homeless person and showed fewer physiological signs of distress as they watched the video, as measured by their heart rates, facial expressions, and skin conductance, than those who believed that the economic system is unfair. Because system justifiers interpret patterns of wealth and poverty as fair, legitimate, and appropriate, they were less distressed by homelessness and poverty.

Ultimately, neoliberal values encourage us to think of ourselves and others as free agents, self-made individuals, whose unconstrained choices, merit, and hard work determine how far we go. By accepting as a given the primacy of individual freedom and choice, neoliberalism promotes resentment when public resources are distributed based on need. Internalization of neoliberal values comes with faith in competition, rather than cooperation, as the best strategy for creating a good society.[24] Winners are elevated as the best and losers seen as subpar. Because individuals are viewed as free from their social and material wallpaper, neoliberalism underestimates unequal opportunity. It is oblivious to the reality that formal and informal privileges color some individuals brightly, making them stand out, while constraints color others in dull shades, making them fade into the wallpaper. When neoliberals do recognize inequality of opportunity, the solutions they advocate are typically individualistic—student scholarships, for example, and similar individualized resources for those who need help "getting in the door." While the intention is good, individual solutions don't always work. Let me give you an example.

My husband and I traveled to Kerala, India, on vacation. Although I was born in India, Kerala, a state in the southern tip of India, jutting out into the Arabian Sea, was new to me. Among all Indian states, Kerala has the highest literacy rate for both women and men.[25] To help us navigate across cities, towns, and villages, we sought out a travel agency that provided us with a car service. Our driver, Arsalan, was fantastic. He took care of our travel itinerary and hotels and organized side trips. We learned that Arsalan, who was twenty-four, had dropped out of college to support his family. His father, who had previously been the family breadwinner, had been injured on the job. The resulting disability forced him to retire. As the oldest adult child, Arsalan assumed the responsibility of supporting the family. Given the absence in India of disability income, college loan forgiveness, and provisions for working and attending college simultaneously, Arsalan was left with debt and the imperative to work full-time. I stewed on Arsalan's situation for days, wondering how we might help him. Creating a path for him to finish college and get his degree would open doors to social mobility. I ran the numbers. Given the exchange rate, my husband and I could imagine paying his college tuition to help him finish his final year of college. Eagerly we pitched our idea to him; we could sponsor his college completion. As we discussed our proposal, we were hit with the realization that it was not enough. Having the money to finish school would not free Arsalan of his family responsibilities. He needed a solution that embraced his family circumstances, a scholarship that supported his family's material needs in addition to paying for his college tuition. That was more than what we could do, so our idea stalled. I learned an important lesson that day. Individualized solutions often fail to create equal opportunity because individuals can't be divorced from their family and community circumstances. Individuals are not free agents who make free choices; we are social animals embedded in families and communities, and our constrained choices reflect those realities.

Persisting against all odds to get ahead as an individual in an unequal system comes with a heavy price. For low-income people, success exacts a toll on the body and the mind. Let's return to the United States, where people love a good rags-to-riches story. Despite widening income and wealth inequality and stagnant wages, many Americans still believe the American Dream—if people work hard and stay out of trouble, they can make it big. When children from low-income families do well in high school, graduate, avoid the pitfalls of drugs and early pregnancy, go on to college and middle-class careers, their stories are seen by some as "proof" that the American Dream is still true. But is it?

Gene Brody, a developmental psychologist, and his colleagues at the University of Georgia spent decades following a group of 489 African American teenagers in rural Georgia.[26] Most came from poor working families with an average annual family income of $12,000 in 2010. About half lived below the poverty line. Within this sample, Brody found a subgroup of resilient eleven-year-olds who, despite economic and social obstacles, were, according to reports from their teachers, diligent, focused, patient, academically successful, and socially skilled. Brody followed this group until they were nineteen years old, focusing on their mental and physical health. Would these resilient young people's success also improve their health? You might be surprised to learn that Brody found the exact opposite. On the surface these low-income African American teenagers were successful by all conventional markers—doing well in school, staying out of trouble, making friends, and developing a positive sense of self. Underneath, their physical health was deteriorating. Compared with low-income peers who did not attend college, the high achievers in the study were more likely to become overweight, even obese, to develop high blood pressure, and to produce more stress hormones, all of which put them at risk for diabetes, metabolic disease, and hypertension later in life.

Most participants in Brody's studies were the first in their families to attend college. They felt tremendous pressure to succeed to make their parents' sacrifices worthwhile. In college, many felt socially isolated and disconnected from peers from different backgrounds and encountered varying forms of racism and discrimination. They responded by doubling down on character strengths that had served them well—dogged persistence, long-term goal setting, navigating setbacks, and resisting temptation. Sherman James, a sociologist, calls this high-effort coping style "John Henryism." The name comes from the legend of a nineteenth-century Black railroad worker who was said to have outperformed a steam-powered drill in a contest, only to drop dead of exhaustion. In his early research on John Henryism, James found that lower-income African American men who express these traits were at greater risk for hypertension as they aged.[27]

To probe deeper and investigate how and why positive personality traits like dogged persistence, effort, and self-control—all part of John Henryism—affect low-income Black youth, Brody teamed up with psychologists Gregory Miller, Tianyi Yu, and Edith Chen, to follow a new group of 292 African American teenagers from age seventeen to twenty, as they transitioned into adulthood. Every year, the researchers visited these teenagers and their families to record household income, the teenagers' education level, their self-control, depressive symptoms, substance use, aggressive behavior, and other mental health concerns. When the youths turned twenty-two, the research team returned once again to collect blood samples in order to measure epigenetic aging.[28]

Epigenetics is the study of how external factors such as our lifestyle and social environment change the way our genes work. While we're all born with a fixed set of genes, how well this internal "machinery" performs depends on external factors. These include individuals' behaviors such as diet, sleep, exercise, and substance use, as well as environmental stressors surrounding them such as crowding, noise, poverty, trauma, and discrimination. All these factors can change how our genes function, affecting natural cycles of cellular deterioration, death, and renewal. Epigenetic change marks biological time. Although chronological age marks how many years we've lived since birth, biological age marks the age of our cells, tissues, and organs based on our physiological biochemistry. Epigenetic markers in the human body tell us the biological age of a person and how it compares with their chronological age.

So, what did Miller, Brody, and their team find when they looked at the effect of high-effort self-control on the lives of these Black youth? Among Black youth from economically comfortable families, better self-control in adolescence predicted favorable psychological outcomes and slower rates of biological aging. But for Black youth from poor families the results revealed a surprise: better self-control had opposite effects on their psychology compared with their biology. More self-control in adolescence predicted positive psychological outcomes—less depression, less substance use, less aggressive behavior, and fewer mental health concerns—but also negative physical health outcomes: faster biological aging and more cardiometabolic risks. As African American youth from poor families strive for favorable life outcomes while navigating systemic barriers and obligations such as underresourced schools, family responsibilities, and discrimination, that balancing act requires intensive self-control, which takes a toll on their physical health.[29]

In other words, individualistic strategies to get ahead through hard work and self-control, free from surrounding material conditions—the wallpaper—may work for people whose lives are not economically precarious. But for others facing societal adversity and economic barriers, this individualistic strategy comes with a heavy price.

From Individual Behavior to Structural Inequality

Collectively, the stories and research in this chapter reveal multiple ways in which our individual behavior feeds into structural inequality.

- If you are a parent, teacher, or coach, have you advocated for gifted programs and other related practices within your child's school and afterschool activities to pluck out a few lucky kids presumed to be born with innate brilliance to give them special enrichment that others don't receive? Do you think that your child belongs in this special group?

- If you are a college admissions officer, a professor, or a hiring manager, have you searched through applicants' files to identify, admit, or hire "brilliant superstars" presumed to have exceptional minds? Did they get special consideration and extra resources to attract them to your organization? Did the extra advantages make them do well down the road? Have you wondered what happened to other candidates who had strong potential and motivation but didn't receive the special designation of being brilliant? Could they have done equally well if given a chance?

- If you are a student, trainee, or young professional who doesn't see many people like yourself in your field, school, or place of work, and if you've sometimes felt like an imposter—did those thoughts arise in moments when the work was difficult and when you were struggling? Did you assume that if you were genuinely talented the work should be easy and effortless? Did it make you consider leaving your field, or have you perhaps already made the switch?

- When the work you're doing is difficult, what does the experience of difficulty mean to you? Does it signal you that you should try harder and then you will improve? Or does it signal that the work is impossible, and you should cut your losses and switch to something else? When dominant cultural narratives frame difficulty as impossibility, it undermines individuals' confidence, reduces effort, and increases the likelihood that they will give up and leave. This is more likely to happen for individuals who don't see people like themselves in the work environment, leading to self-sorting by profession, reinforcing underrepresentation, and baking in social and economic stratification within organizations and across professions.

- When you think of your success relative to others', what do you attribute it to—talent, hard work, something else? What's the role of luck? Were barriers in your path removed by others? Did you get special resources that paved your way?

- When you think of the necessary ingredients for people to get ahead in life, what do you think is the role of talent, hard work, luck, and the external terrain (barriers, obstacles)? If the road is rocky or external barriers loom large, should public resources be freely given to level the playing field? Our personal beliefs about these issues feed into our opinions about public policies at the local, state, and federal levels. If we assume that all success is the result of individual talent plus hard work, and luck or external barriers play no role, we become reluctant to support public funding for policies providing social safety nets such as universal health care, paid family leave, free childcare, unemployment benefits, and disability benefits, because we interpret these as handouts for the undeserving. Individuals from economically stressed families who strive to live by neoliberal rules while navigating systemic barriers pay a heavy price, sacrificing their physical health and life for the American Dream.

4

INCOMPATIBLE PATTERNS

Consequences of Cultural Mismatch

Have you ever walked into a new environment and quickly figured out how to behave? Psychologists call this cultural match. Cultural match makes things easy. When the social norms of a place are aligned with the way we grew up, things click in place. But when the norms of a new place are misaligned with how we grew up, there is increased risk of missed opportunity, falling behind, alienation, and expanding inequality.

Laura and Johnny, friends of mine, were reminiscing about parenting. Laura was raised in a middle-class, college-educated family. She envisioned parenting as managing her children's education, advocating on their behalf with teachers, and playing an active role in the PTA. Johnny, her husband, was raised by parents who were poor and hadn't finished high school. Johnny saw schoolteachers as the experts responsible for his children's education. He deferred to their decisions and was uncomfortable challenging them. Laura's style matched the school's expectations of involved parents informed by middle-class American norms of confident self-advocacy, whereas Johnny's reticence differed from the norm. Johnny didn't consider pressing the teacher to place his child in honors algebra instead of beginning algebra. But his wife did, insisting to the teacher that

4. People unfamiliar with a system stumble and miss
opportunities while others who know it well race ahead.

their son was prepared for the work. Her actions at a critical period
in middle school put their son on an upward trajectory in math that
would pay off later. Absent her advocacy, he might have gotten stuck
in the lower-level math track, which would have limited his options
in high school. Cultural match allows us to identify hidden opportunities in an organization's wallpaper and take advantage of them.
Cultural mismatch makes it difficult for us to recognize opportunities and capitalize on them. The maze in Figure 4 represents social norms within institutions. People who are culturally matched
to this maze and know their way through it get ahead quickly, while
those who are mismatched and don't know the way get stuck.

Cultural Mismatch Stifles Educational Mobility

This is not just a story of Laura and Johnny. A twenty-year lon-
gitudinal study by sociologist Annette Lareau shows that the so-

cial norms of schools, universities, and other institutions are more aligned with the childrearing practices of middle-class families than those of working-class and poor families, which place students in the latter group at a disadvantage that compounds over time.[1] Thanks to a better cultural match, middle-class parents acquire informal knowledge about how to navigate institutional bureaucracies, advocate for their children, and pass on these skills to them. In contrast, poor and working-class parents, who don't know the inner workings of mainstream institutional bureaucracies, are less able to advocate for their children and teach them these skills.

Lareau began her study with eighty-eight ten-year-old children and their families—an equal number of middle-class, working-class, and poor families. She conducted interviews, observed them in school, and followed some families for twenty years, interviewing the youth at age twenty and again at age thirty. She noticed three types of cultural knowledge gaps that prevented poor and working-class students from climbing the socioeconomic ladder. First, while middle-class families knew the informal "rules of the game" at school and college (what classes are crucial in middle and high school; what grades are necessary to get into college; how to drop a class in time; and how to secure a professional job) working-class and poor families often didn't have this informal knowledge. Second, middle-class parents and children felt more entitled to ask for help from teachers, coaches, and mentors, while working-class and poor youth felt shy and uncomfortable doing so. Third, when faced with institutional barriers, middle-class young adults drew on their knowledge of the inner workings of institutions to get accommodations and exceptions, whereas working-class and poor young adults felt frustrated by institutional bureaucracies and often failed to obtain available advantages. By age thirty, middle-class youth in Lareau's study were more likely to have higher-quality, secure jobs than youth from working-class and poor homes. The stories of two participants in Lareau's study illustrate how gaps in cultural knowledge held back one person while the other forged ahead.

Tara Carroll, a young Black girl, grew up in a low-rise housing project. Her urban elementary school was well regarded, but a large proportion of its students lived in poverty. When Tara's mother attended the fourth-grade parent-teacher conference, Lareau accompanied her. The teacher, Ms. Stanton, said she liked Tara, and that Tara was doing well in school. Yet she never explained why Tara had received a D in math, simply assuring Tara's mom that she shouldn't worry about the low math grade. The school didn't share details of Tara's educational progress with her mother. As someone who hadn't finished high school, Tara's mother relied on teachers and school officials to know what was best for her child's education. She didn't feel comfortable intervening. After graduating from elementary school, Tara was surprised not to be accepted at the two most competitive high schools in her district. She and her mother didn't know that getting a C or D in math would eliminate her from consideration. The school district didn't publicize this information, relying instead on informal information shared through parent networks. Neither Tara nor her mom was privy to such networks.

Tara was ambitious. She wanted to go to college and become a nurse. Her mom encouraged her but left the details of educational matters to high school personnel, just as she had done when Tara was in fourth grade. Because the school had few guidance counselors, Tara got limited guidance in selecting a college. She applied to eight colleges and universities but was rejected everywhere, an experience that hurt her deeply. Neither Tara nor her mother was familiar with the process of aligning applicants' strengths and weaknesses with college criteria to identify colleges that are good fits. They were unaware of the critical role of SAT scores in college acceptance. Tara had applied to colleges with median scores 200 to

300 points above her own score. Tara ended up enrolling at a community college, where she struggled with the pace of her biology class but felt uncomfortable seeking help from the instructor. She didn't know that academic policies allowed her to withdraw from a class without penalty within a window of time. Instead, Tara stopped going to the class, ending up with an F on her transcript. Tara's mom wasn't aware of her college problems. Although she was proud of her daughter's pursuit of college, she couldn't help Tara navigate this unfamiliar environment. Tara Carroll spent seven years earning an associate's degree from the community college, graduating with a GPA of 3.08 and $12,000 of debt.

She then attended a nursing program. Because of a string of struggles at home and a car accident, she missed several classes. Unaware of how to request academic accommodations by petitioning for an incomplete or a leave of absence, Tara continued attending classes intermittently and failed two courses, resulting in her dismissal from the program. She was devastated and wanted to appeal the decision but waited for more than a month before acting. Her appeal was denied. Had she submitted her appeal earlier, the outcome might have been better. Many students face bumps in the road, and most universities have formal and informal procedures to address such difficulties. Faculty members have discretion in academic matters but want to know about student difficulties as soon as they occur to make accommodations. Tara didn't know her school's policies or her teachers' expectations. She didn't ask for help, and no one at her school reached out to offer assistance.

At age thirty, Tara enrolled in another nursing program working toward a registered nursing degree. When Lareau interviewed her, she was in her first year of this program and felt "more disciplined" in her studies. If she passed the state licensing exam, the degree would open the door to a professional position. Many of the setbacks in Tara's journey had been due to a mismatch created by her limited knowledge of the workings of educational institutions and the institutional expectations of active self-advocacy. While Tara had tremendous grit and determination, she didn't understand that she could ask for help and access a range of formal and informal accommodations and resources. These norms and resources were the wallpaper familar to her middle- and upper-middle-class peers.

Compare Tara's journey with that of Stacey Marshall, a middle-class Black woman, almost exactly Tara's age. When Stacey was ten, her mother had detailed information about how schools operated. Although her mom had a demanding job and commuted ninety minutes roundtrip daily, she worked hard to "stay on top" of her two daughters' lives. She knew about the gifted program at Stacey's school, the entrance criteria, the availability of private tutoring, and various extracurricular programs. Her mother's knowledge came from a social network of other moms. Ms. Marshall was assertive in her interactions with school professionals. When Stacey barely missed the cutoff for entrance into the school's gifted program, Ms. Marshall paid to have her daughter tested privately. When Stacey's score remained two points shy of the cutoff, Ms. Marshall lobbied school officials. Stacey was admitted into the program.

Ten years later, Stacey completed her freshman year of college at the University of Maryland. Her mother remained active in her daughter's life, even as she tried to wean Stacey from overdependence. Stacey wanted to become a pediatrician, but in her first year at college she earned a series of C grades in her premed courses. Drawing on her own knowledge of educational institutions, Ms. Marshall advised her daughter to drop calculus ("You don't want your GPA to get too low") and get help from her academic adviser. "I really stressed with her that she needed to establish communication with [advisers]," said Stacey's mom. "You need to call Sarah . . . set up an appointment and go to talk to her . . . about your major. And see what advice she can give to you. That is what she is being paid for."

Ms. Marshall trained her daughter to be proactive in seeking help from university professionals. She saw help-seeking as a valuable life skill that Stacey needed to learn. It worked. Despite the struggles of her first year, by sophomore year Stacey saw the wallpaper—she began to understand the unspoken cultural expectations in college. She began to see that medical schools would not accept her with C grades. She put aside her dream of becoming a pediatrician. Drawn to the humanities, she majored in Africana studies, established connections with professors, and gained academic traction. She won a sports award and after graduation was invited to play basketball in Europe. She chose, instead, to go to graduate school in Africana studies at the Ohio State University, where she met her husband. Stacey's cultural and professional knowledge expanded. Of course, not everything was perfect. After receiving her doctorate Stacey had heavy student loans, as did her husband. Although their combined income was almost $100,000, their combined debt was around $90,000. Their home had lost value. They were financially underwater. But Stacey was proactive in negotiating better loan terms and staying abreast of the interest rates, terms, and the duration of each loan.

By age thirty, Stacey had internalized the lessons her mother taught her. She had extensive social networks of friends, relatives, and colleagues. She knew how to network, which helped her land her first job. Many factors contributed to Stacey's success. Yes, she was talented and worked hard. But she also benefited greatly from a parent who was knowledgeable about higher education and provided frequent hands-on guidance through school and college. Stacey was only vaguely aware of her mother's help in navigating institutions. Because her mom's advice and nudges were ever-present, they were an invisible part of Stacey's wallpaper.

As a professor who has taught at several universities, I have observed that students at elite colleges and universities are significantly more likely to assertively self-advocate than students at public universities. At the University of Massachusetts Amherst, a large public research university where I'm on the faculty now, I've seen students from middle- and upper-middle-class families be coached by their college-educated parents to come to my office hours to seek academic and career advice, investigate research assistantship opportunities, or negotiate a better grade on an exam or an extension on an assignment. These parents teach their college-aged child to notice that the wallpaper of university life is patterned with implicit expectations about assertiveness, negotiating rules, and seeking accommodations when barriers arise. From conversations with my working-class students, I know that most of them wouldn't dream of coming to me for an extension on a late assignment or to negotiate an increase in a grade. I have learned to reach out to them to understand why an assignment was late, why an exam grade was low, or how to interpret an absence from class. I've also learned to not attribute an absence or a missing assignment to a lack of caring or disrespect.

Colleges and universities reproduce social-class inequality because they are organized around middle- and upper-class expectations of independence and assertiveness.[2] When they come to college, American students are expected to separate from their parents, find their individuality, develop their unique voice, and follow their passion, thereby realizing their individual potential to influence the world. Young people from middle- and upper-class families learn independence and self-determination from a young age. Their parents pay careful attention to identifying and cultivating their children's personal preferences, opinions, and interests. The ample resources of middle- and upper-middle-class parents allow children the freedom to choose, control, and develop a sense of self-importance and entitlement.[3] For young people from these families, university culture matches the culture at home, making the transition to college relatively smooth. In contrast, young people from poor and working-class families learn the culture of interdependence from a young age. Because of economic adversity and the lack of a safety net, poor and working-class parents teach their children to be responsive to their family and community's needs, follow the rules, and recognize their place in the social hierarchy. These parents tell their children that "it's not just about you" and "you can't always get what you want."[4] When young people from working-class families come to a college or university, there is friction between the dominant culture of independence and self-determination and the interdependence learned at home, which often makes the college transition rocky. This is the essence of cultural mismatch theory proposed by Nicole Stephens, Stephanie Fryberg, and a team of social psychologists. Individual success, they argue, is contingent on people experiencing a match rather than a mismatch between their own family and community norms and the norms baked into a given institution.[5]

Stephens and her colleagues asked 261 university leaders from seventy-five leading universities and colleges in the United States about the culture of higher education in American society. The survey provided a list of cultural norms, half emphasizing independence (learn to solve problems on your own) and the other half emphasizing interdependence (learn to be a team player). Campus leaders were asked to pick the five most important skills that their academic institution expected students to develop in college. Campus leaders overwhelmingly selected independence-oriented skills—learning to express oneself, to become a leader, to solve problems on one's own, and to work independently. Only two interdependence norms were near the top of the list—learning to work with others and to do collaborative research. Other interdependence-oriented skills such as learning to listen to others, becoming a team player, and adjusting to others' expectations were rarely selected.

Stephens and her team then turned to 1,424 college students, some from working-class families whose parents didn't have college degrees and others from middle- and upper-middle-class families whose parents had college degrees. They asked these students to share their reasons for pursuing college. Working-class students gave reasons that reflected interdependence—I want to help my family, I want to contribute to my community—more often than reasons that reflected independence—I want to work independently, I want to develop my professional interests. Middle- and upper-middle-class students' responses were the opposite: the reasons they gave favored independence over interdependence. Moreover, students who emphasized independence-oriented motivations fit more easily within their university because of value alignment, which resulted in better academic performance for middle- and upper-middle-class students than for working-class students in a follow-up two years later.

Extending this work, Taylor Phillips and her team found that working-class students whose reasons for coming to college were more interdependence-oriented felt less comfortable in college and thought their personal values didn't fit institutional values. Discomfort and subjective lack of fit made them feel small compared to their peers—feelings that were associated with lower grade-point averages years later at college graduation.[6] Mismatch in cultural values in college increased negative emotions and stress, especially in situations involving performance evaluation, putting working-class students at greater risk of dropping out of college.[7]

This was the experience of Al Simon, my husband. Al's parents worked in a woolen mill in Somersville, Connecticut. Neither parent had finished high school because they had to work to support their families. Both sides of Al's family were poor and had immigrated to the United States in search of work. His father's family came from Syria and his mother's family from Quebec, Canada. In the all-white working-poor community where he grew up, money was always tight, home was millworker rental housing heated by a kerosene stove during cold New England winters, and the bathroom was an outhouse. His father died suddenly when Al was a baby. No one in his immediate family had gone to college. The only reason Al even thought of college is that in his public high school he was on the "bright" track and had received the second-highest SAT score in his graduating class. Some of his classmates were from middle- and upper-middle-class families. Because they were applying to college, Al did too, ending up with a hefty scholarship and an offer to attend Boston University. Al had no clue how to navigate college. Like Tara in the earlier story, he didn't know the expectations of academic life, how to go about selecting courses, or where to get help. He chose an Arabic class his first year to get in touch with his ethnic heritage and floundered with the unfamiliar language. He chose a political science class, which turned out to be more about science than about the politics that interested him. Al didn't see his professors as approachable and felt awkward interacting with them. In his working-poor community, he had been taught to be deferential and know his place, not to demand more. Al felt untethered in the independence-oriented university culture, where assertive search for one's path, proactive help-seeking, and relationship building were unspoken norms. He struggled through his freshman year, not seeking help from faculty or staff, who in turn offered none. Stress and shame accumulated, and he dropped out at the end of his freshman year. Forty years later, after a dual career in business and local politics, Al could finally see the wallpaper of mismatched expectations. He now understood that his younger self was stuck in a deferential mindset and assumed he had to solve problems alone. The cultural chasm between the mindset and behaviors he had learned at home and those expected in college had been too big. Once he could see the wallpaper and understand that his struggle was not a personal failure and he was not alone, he went back and finished college forty-one years later.

Consistent with Al's experience, Janet Chang and her colleagues' research on working-class college students found that self-reliance, resilience, and emotional toughness were life skills that poor and working-class people brought to college. These skills, often called hard independence, are different from university expectations that prioritize soft independence—being expressive, seeking help, and pursuing one's personal interests.[8] Through interviews with seventy-one working-class students, both white people and people of color, Chang and her team learned that when faced with academic, financial, and psychological problems in college, working-class students try to cope by hard independence, toughing it out alone. They are less likely to seek social support from college personnel, friends, and family because of concerns about burdening others, being judged, or making matters worse. Some are concerned that self-disclosure of problems in college might result in losing face and disrupt harmonious relationships at home. The mismatch between university expectations and the figure-it-out-alone approach these students practice means that most working-class students suffer alone without receiving the help they need. Some drop out as a result.

Cultural Mismatch Blocks Professional Mobility

Cultural mismatch is not limited to students' experiences at college. It shapes career opportunities. The wallpaper of mismatched expectations gets in the way of working-class job candidates' success in professional interviews with prospective employers. Daron Sharps and Cameron Anderson, business school professors, invited 158 soon-to-graduate students, half working class and half middle or upper-middle class, to do a mock job interview while being video-recorded.[9] A panel of experienced hiring managers watched the recorded interviews and made hiring recommendations. Trained observers coded interviewees' verbal and nonverbal behaviors. Did they speak fluently and confidently, or did they stumble and sound uncertain? Did they appear calm and relaxed in their body language and facial expression or come off as nervous and anxious? Did they make good eye contact? A separate group of 1,505 observers watched the videos and gave their impressions of interviewees' competence, socioemotional skills, and fit within the company to which they were applying.

Before the interviews, Sharps and Anderson had measured interviewees' intelligence and socioemotional skills using well-validated psychological instruments. They found working-class and upper-middle-class interviewees were equally intelligent, and in fact, working-class interviewees showed better socioemotional skills than their upper-middle-class peers. But observers watching the videos falsely believed that working-class interviewees were less intelligent and had fewer socioemotional skills. Why? Because observers mistook confidence for intelligence and social skills. Because upper-middle-class interviewees appeared more confident in speech and self-presentation than their working-class peers, observers inferred more intelligence and social skills. Hiring managers made the same mistake. They falsely interpreted confidence to mean the person was smarter, had more social skills, and was a better fit for the workplace, all of which biased their final hiring decisions. Failure to appear confident undermines working-class job candidates' chances of being hired.

Converging evidence for the same conclusion comes from Phoebe Chua's research at the University of California Irvine.[10] She interviewed fifty hiring managers at ten prominent technology companies to learn how they evaluated applicants during interviews. She compared their responses to that of applicants, some of whom were from working-class families, others from upper-middle-class families. She learned that hiring managers focused their evaluations of applicants on two dimensions: technical skills and behavioral skills. The interviewers' expectations about desirable behavioral skills gave upper-middle-class applicants a clear advantage over working-class peers. Managers expected interviewees to treat the interviewer as an equal and be comfortable initiating an equal exchange of ideas. They expected interviewees to confidently steer the conversation to explore different aspects of the job they were applying for. They didn't want interviewees to be narrowly focused on technical skills, but rather to broadly integrate insights from various disciplines into their work. They liked applicants who were comfortable voicing differences in opinion about a better way to approach a project instead of deferring to the interviewer.

These behavioral expectations fit the upbringing of the thirty-three upper-middle-class applicants whom Chua interviewed. These applicants reported feeling comfortable fostering a casual and fun atmosphere during interviews, often using humor to lighten the mood. Many mentioned that their parents taught them to view everyone as equals. For example, Frank, an upper-middle-class job applicant, described his mother's parenting style to Chua and how that had influenced his perspectives: "My parents don't require intense respect. My mom's a doctor, but she's very casual. She injects into your mind the idea that you're on par with anybody. You shouldn't let anybody treat you as lesser just because you're younger or have less experiences. You're capable of doing anything you want. I think that was really important [in shaping my views]." In keeping with the belief that they were equals with the interviewer, upper-middle-class applicants approached the technical problem-solving part of the interview like a collaboration, treating the interviewer as a problem-solving partner without fear of revealing gaps in their technical skills. Their collaborative interaction style fit the hiring managers' cultural expectations of potential employees who would easily collaborate as equals.

Rather than joking casually with interviewers, the thirty working-class applicants Chua interviewed reported being respectful, polite, and formal during interviews. They were acutely aware of the power dynamics between them and the interviewer, whom they saw as an authority figure. They had been raised to show respect to authority figures.[11] Many working-class applicants felt uncomfortable asking for help during the technical problem-solving part of the interview, concerned that help-seeking would reveal holes in their technical acumen. As Sophia, a working-class applicant, responded, "My parents, and especially my mom, raised me to be very independent so that wherever I go, I can overcome any obstacles that arise. So, when in the interview process, I wouldn't [ask for help] right away. That's not the best thing to do because you might present yourself as someone who is going to need a lot of help. And I think it can be disrespectful of their time if you're not even trying." This stands in sharp contrast to upper-middle-class applicants who felt totally comfortable asking for help and didn't doubt the interviewer's positive view of their ability.

Upper-middle-class applicants, having learned from an early age the behavioral skills and interaction style that matched the expectations of hiring managers, had an easier time landing jobs. Working-class applicants struggled to navigate the hiring process. They spent substantially more time applying for these positions and felt more stressed out trying to meet hiring expectations.

Culture Shifts Stymie Social Mobility

Another type of cultural mismatch happens when people move between tight and loose cultures. Tight cultures have strong social norms, clear rules, and sanctions for violations, whereas loose cultures have weaker social norms and are permissive of violations, says Michele Gelfand, a social psychologist. Cultural tightness develops in cultures that experience such external pressures and crises as economic scarcity, crowding, pain, natural disaster, and invasions. The absence of such pressures—economic abundance, spaciousness, environmental stability, and border security—leads to looser cultures where human differences are tolerated and even encouraged.[12] Tight cultures insist on rule followers, whereas loose cultures are tolerant of, even intrigued by, rule breakers.

Phoebe Chua's interviews with job applicants searching for tech jobs provide striking evidence of rule following among working-class job applicants and rule bending among upper-middle-class applicants.[13] Working-class applicants assumed that hiring happens through companies' official hiring process. So they followed formal recruitment channels to identify jobs: they went to career fairs, searched for online resources, and applied through official online portals. They avoided reaching out to distant contacts lest they unwittingly break some rule and come across as presumptuous and entitled. But upper-middle-class applicants skirted official rules. Instead of starting with formal online applications, they reached out to people in their networks, including friends of friends, and wrote cold emails to forge connections with people at companies of interest to them. They set up casual informational meetings to share their work experiences and learn about job opportunities. These exploratory chats happened outside of the official hiring process and gave upper-middle-class applicants an inside look at the company, introduced them to available positions, and allowed them to screen out positions they were not interested in. They also saw informational interviews as the way to secure referrals that would get them noticed by prospective hiring managers, increasing their chances of getting callback interviews. They considered formal applications without referrals a waste of time because of the high volume of submissions. An interviewee named James explained, "It's important to reach out to chat and get a referral. It's a way to cut through the noise and get an interview. It's pretty standard, so I don't think I'm asking a huge favor."

In the professional job search landscape, rule bending through informational coffee chats and referrals is an unspoken cultural norm that's part of the wallpaper. Students from upper-middle-class families are taught by their parents to employ this strategy. When asked where she learned this application tactic, Julie credited her mother: "[My mom] is a hiring manager and I learned it from her. She ingrained in me the importance of personal connections. She'll say things like: 'Get coffee with people at companies you're interested in. Not in a "get me a job" way, but just asking what their company is doing, so you know if it's a good fit for you and what kinds of people they're hiring.'" Working-class applicants who don't know these tacit norms follow the official rules. Their applications are likely to get buried and never get on hiring managers' radar.

The consequence of moving from a tight to a loose culture can be dramatic depending on the person's age at the time of the move. What happens to a child whose family moves from a neighborhood where poverty is common to one where it is rare? Communities characterized by poverty have tight cultures. Economic scarcity, crowding, and crime nudge people in these communities to develop strong social norms of acceptable behavior and clear sanctions for norm violation. Communities that are safer and economically comfortable have looser cultures, allowing greater individuality, rule bending, and norm violation.[14] Moving from the tight culture of a poverty-dominated community to the looser culture of one relatively free of poverty is particularly rocky for adolescents who have been socialized to navigate strict social norms and sanctions and then have to learn to embrace permissible rule bending and norm violations.

Evidence for that rockiness comes from an experiment conducted by the U.S. Department of Housing and Urban Development called Moving to Opportunity. Between 1994 and 1998, a large number of families in public subsidized housing, 4,604 in total, received different types of housing vouchers that were distributed by lottery. One-third of these families received vouchers that moved them to economically well-off neighborhoods. Another one-third received vouchers that moved them to different public housing with no constraints about neighborhood poverty. And the final one-third continued to live in their existing public housing. Economist Raj Chetty and his team followed the children from these families over time to test whether and how their long-term outcomes were affected by the randomly assigned change in their living circumstances.[15] Chetty discovered that for children who were eight years old on average when their families moved from poor to well-off neighborhoods, the move significantly improved their college attendance, earnings in adulthood, and the likelihood of settling in better neighborhoods as adults compared with the other two groups. But for children who were fifteen years old on average when their families made the same move, the effects were negative on all metrics. Chetty and colleagues think that the move disrupted these teenagers' social networks, especially for those who moved far away from the housing project where they started. I think there is more. Moving from a tight community to a loose community—from an environment, in other words, with clear norms that function as guardrails to one where norms and rules are more elastic—was probably jarring for teenagers in a phase of life where exploration and boundary testing are common.[16] The cultural knowledge they had absorbed from their family and peers in the previous neighborhoods and schools didn't work in this new environment. Most likely, no one pointed out the new wallpaper with its looser rules and fewer strong sanctions for rule bending. It is possible that these older teenagers, failing to grasp the tacit local expectations, deviated too far, and got in trouble. Younger children who made this move earlier in development probably had the opportunity, through early-life interactions in the new community with peers, as well as direct instructions from teachers and other adults, to get used to the new wallpaper and adapt to it.

Elisa Vega-Burns had to learn new cultural norms when she moved from her working-class roots in Brockton, Massachusetts, to Tufts University, where she received a degree in electrical engineering. She then had to learn another set of norms in her first job at Raytheon Corporation. There were "angels along the way" who helped her get there. As an engineer at Raytheon, Elisa was under the impression that she needed to "work hard, keep [her] head down, and [avoid] the social shit." The result? She didn't get promoted. Talking to her manager, she learned that keeping her head down gave the impression that she wasn't interested in building relationships and becoming a team leader. She learned that she needed to initiate relationships with her colleagues by socializing with them, and to develop an understanding of what they needed. For a new recruit with little power, building relationships with people with more power and influence was the way to learn, gain a sense of control, and advance in her career. After that talk with her manager, Elisa felt as if somebody had "peeled off the blinders," and she could finally see the wallpaper.

Mismatched Motives Create Friction

When people are in positions of power, they feel independent, self-sufficient, and free to focus on their own goals. In contrast, people in roles of less power are dependent on the powerful, less able to pursue their own goals, and finely attuned to their relationships with others to reduce uncertainty and increase a sense of control. Differences in power create a cultural mismatch in what information individuals attend to, how much they tune into each other's needs, and how accurate they are in understanding others. Power asymmetry creates a misalignment of motivations between people, which increases the odds of misunderstanding.

When people are placed in high or low power roles, even randomly, it changes their motivations and behavior, found Ana Guinote, a social psychologist at the University College of London. In roles of high power, individuals focus on task-oriented goals (what needs to get done now?), whereas in roles of low power, they focus on people-oriented goals (how is everyone feeling now?). Power reduces people's responsiveness to the needs of others. Guinote and her colleagues placed research volunteers in contrasting power roles by the flip of a coin and discreetly observed their decision-making behavior in groups.[17] They found that people with little power were more communal and socially engaged. They smiled more and were more friendly and approachable in their decision-making team. Their actions were more supportive and empathic than those with more power. People placed in the role of high power took charge of the decision-making situation and appeared more knowledgeable and competent than others in the less powerful role, although the objective quality of their decisions was no better. Power holders are less likely to pay attention to their subordinates when their organizational context is product-centered rather than people-centered. In product-centered organizations, power holders are less able to discern the unique needs and characteristics of their subordinates, and less likely to showcase stories about employees in the company's report.[18]

Power often leads to stereotyping. Because people who have social power pay less attention to subordinates and seek less information about them, they are more likely to develop inaccurate impressions of subordinates and rely on stereotypes. In contrast, those with less social power seek more information about others to enhance a sense of control and prediction, thus forming more accurate impressions.[19] Ana Guinote and Adele Phillips investigated this phenomenon in the workplace. They asked seventy-eight managers and subordinates in England to evaluate people who had applied for a job to be a teacher or a disc jockey. Some were native-born English applicants of Anglo descent while others were Afro-Caribbean applicants who were children of immigrants. Guinote and Phillips found that evaluators in subordinate roles spent more time reviewing information about job candidates than did evaluators in managerial roles. For their final hiring recommendation, managers evaluated Afro-Caribbean candidates as more suitable for a job as a DJ than as a teacher and white candidates as more suitable for a job as a teacher than as a DJ, suggesting that their evaluations were tainted by racial stereotypes. Subordinates' evaluations and hiring recommendations were not influenced by racial stereotypes.[20]

Power also affects people's perceptions of justice. People in positions of power feel entitled to resources and slighted when they don't get them. Takuya Sawaoka, Brent Hughes, and Nalini Ambady found that people who were temporarily made to feel powerful were faster than others made to feel less powerful to notice if they received fewer resources, to call it out as unfair, and to take action against unfairness when it affected them personally. But they were slower to notice when they received more resources than others and less likely to call it out as unfair than people placed in less powerful roles.[21] In other words, people in powerful positions care more about fair resource allocation for themselves whereas those in positions of less power care more about a fair process, in having a voice in how things are run regardless of the outcome. Cong Liu, Liu-Qin Yang, and Margaret Nauta surveyed more than three hundred employees across several organizations and found that when people in roles of little power felt that decision-making processes at work were unfair, they experienced more depression, anxiety, and conflict with their supervisors, especially if they expected their workplace to be less hierarchical.[22]

From Individual Behavior to Structural Inequality

The science and stories in this chapter point to at least three ways in which individual actions resulting from cultural match or mismatch reproduce structural inequality. First, cultural match makes it easier for middle- and upper-middle-class people to navigate college successfully and receive advanced degrees, which boosts their economic security throughout their lives. In contrast, cultural mismatch increases the likelihood that many more working-class people will drop out of college, often with debt, permanently jeopardizing their economic security and negatively affecting their health. In both cases the end result is to exacerbate class disparities in education, income, and health.[23]

Second, cultural match may also shape the expectations of individuals making admissions decisions at colleges and universities. In evaluating applicants, they may be implicitly looking for evidence of a cultural match between applicants' persona and institutional norms. Individual admission decisions accumulate to feed into income-based gaps in college access, which are large and growing. In top-tier colleges and universities in the United States, almost three-quarters of the entering class of students have family incomes in the top 25 percent of the wealth distribution.[24]

Third, hiring decisions in white-collar jobs are also shaped by cultural match. As we have seen, hiring managers in some types of jobs prefer candidates who are comfortable enacting upper-middle-class cultural norms and mistakenly infer that their confidence means more intelligence and social skills compared with others who appear less confident. Such individual-level hiring decisions accumulate over time to reinforce the class-based segregation of people into different types of jobs, creating structural inequalities within organizations.

A few takeaways bear repeating. Although individual grit and effort to get ahead are important, they are often eclipsed by whether people know the unspoken rules to help them navigate societal institutions that are stepping-stones to social mobility—schools, universities, and workplaces. Many of these American institutions operate based on upper-middle-class social norms. People who navigate them successfully are likely to have been coached by family members, mentors, and others to notice the normative wallpaper and play by its unspoken rules. Here are five tacit rules they are advised to put into action in mainstream American contexts:

- Present yourself with confidence; it leads others to form a favorable impression of you.

- Advocate for yourself. Seek help proactively when you need it; this is key to success.

- Know that most rules have exceptions; request exceptions for yourself when useful.

- Seek out information about organizations and roles you want to pursue through informal conversations with people who are knowledgeable, even if you don't know them well.

- Understand that stepping from a role of little power into one with more power can affect an individual's motivation, behavior, and sense of fairness. Seek out and consider the perspectives of people with and without power to build better relationships with them.

People who see the wallpaper and act accordingly make initial advantages accumulate over time and follow an upward trajectory. Their cultural advantages accrue like compound interest in their bank account. People who don't see the wallpaper stumble repeatedly, allowing initial disadvantages to compound over time as well. Their cultural disadvantages accumulate like fees on an overdrawn bank account.

PART II

HOW TO
CHANGE THE
WALLPAPER

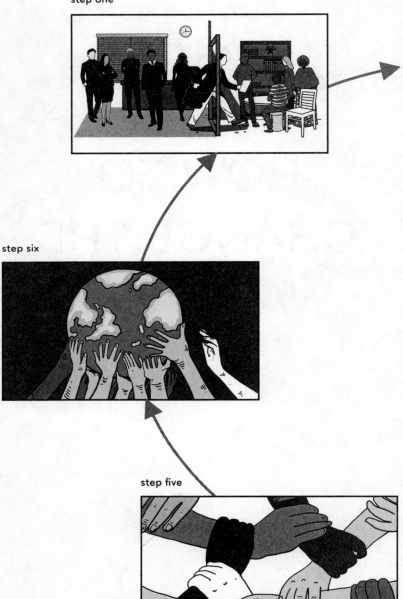

step one

step six

step five

step two

step three

step four

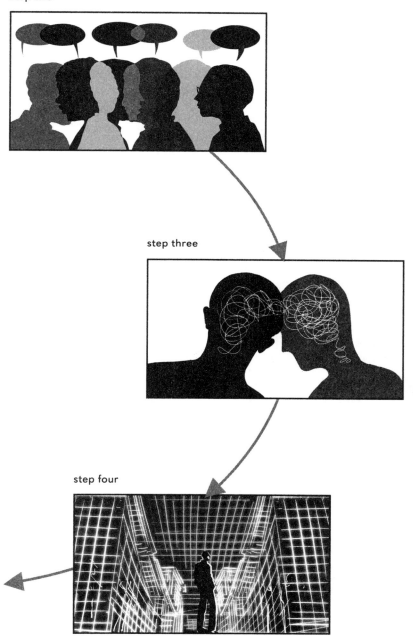

5

SEEING IS BELIEVING

How People and Places Promote Belonging

Come to the corner of 14th Street and V Avenue in Washington, DC, and you will find yourself at Busboys and Poets, a restaurant, bar, performance space, and bookstore. As you enter, arresting art catches your eyes. A big mural takes you on a journey through the civil rights movement. Women suffragists and peace activists are the focal point of the room. At the top of the mural are words from a Langston Hughes poem: "Let America be America again. Let it be the dream it used to be." A message aspiring toward true democracy. Iconic portraits greet you from other walls: King, Malcolm X, Gandhi. The menu appeals to a broad palate—catfish, shrimp and grits, pasta of various sorts, hummus, quinoa bowl, blackened salmon. Tucked inside the restaurant is a bookshop showcasing books on social movements and struggles. Busboys and Poets is a community space where racial and cultural connections are intentionally elevated. A place where people come together for conversation that blends performing art and ideas to inspire social change. It feeds the body, mind, and soul.[1]

Busboys and Poets is the inspiration of Anas (Andy) Shallal, an Iraqi American whose family immigrated from Baghdad to the United States in 1966. Growing up outside DC as an eleven-year-old,

5. Enter environments that encourage social mixing among diverse people.

Shallal remembers being a kid who didn't fit in school because he was neither Black nor white.[2] As an entrepreneur, he wanted to create a multiracial restaurant that brought people together. He chose U Street, the Black Broadway of DC, where, at the height of segregation, Duke Ellington, Ella Fitzgerald, Cab Calloway, and others played to packed houses. Destroyed in the 1968 riots, U Street life was now slowly reemerging. Shallal hoped to spark a new vision of U Street with a restaurant named after Langston Hughes, American poet and a leader of the Harlem Renaissance. Hughes was a busboy at Wardman Park Hotel before he caught a break by slipping his poems to a restaurant guest, a prominent literary critic.

The physical design and esthetics of Busboys signals that it is a place for people of all races, incomes, and identities to come together, eat comfort food, and talk. As you sit at a table and look around, you see people who are multiracial, old and young, locals and visitors, working class and professional class. Clearly Busboys has hit the sweet spot. Figure 5 illustrates the difference between the vibe of a multiracial and multigenerational space compared with one where people are more homogeneous. Imagine entering the room on the left side of this illustration compared with the one on the right side. Can you feel the difference?

No space is neutral. Its location, architecture, and interior design always communicate some message, even if it is unspoken. Location conveys history. Architecture and interior design signal whom the place is for and what activities it encourages and discourages. This, in turn, affects who comes in the door, and whether they interact with people they don't know while inside. At a place like Busboys, the location and esthetics attract a multiracial crowd. Communal tables, the bar, artwork, and events invite conversation among strangers. Humans are social animals. We are attuned to environments that say, "You belong." We notice when the ambiance of a place acknowledges our needs. We like seeing our values reflected in others' words and actions.

Interior Designs That Welcome Everyone

I became aware of how the design of restaurants can include or exclude people when I started spending time with a colleague who was in a wheelchair. Like many workplaces, ours has a culture of gathering in local pubs for happy hour and occasional dinners. Before our colleague joined our university, my coworkers and I would choose pubs and restaurants close to work with fairly good, moderately priced food and drink. Physical accessibility was not on our radar. When our group expanded, we started noticing the physical constraints of restaurants. Where are we going this Friday after work? Could we go to the pub on Main Street, our frequent haunt? No, that wouldn't work because it's on the second floor and there's no elevator. What about the little bistro? Nope, the tables are too close. There's no way to navigate a wheelchair around those tables. What about the local brewery? Oops, only high tops and booths that are unfriendly to wheelchairs. Most of our usual go-to places didn't work, except one. Johnny's Tavern was built with inclusive design in mind. We wheel into the restaurant easily through the wide entrance. The lack of steps means that our colleague doesn't encounter obstacles from the get-go. As the host walks us to our table, our friend wheels his chair in between widely spaced tables without having to worry about bumping into other guests' chairs and disrupting their meal. We are seated at a table of normal height. I know from being around my colleague that going to public places always requires advance planning. Nothing is simple. Extra phone calls to ask about wheelchair accessibility, types of seating, and stairs. Even one step can be an insurmountable obstacle. He doesn't like situations where public attention is focused on him, where he feels different. The best restaurants for him are ones where the physical layout accommodates his needs without requiring extra work or a flurry of attention. Where he is like any other guest. Where he feels comfortable and welcome.

Restaurants are not the only places where spatial design tells us who's welcome. Imagine walking into a workspace where you see vibrant nature posters on the wall, puzzles, a bookshelf with a variety of books, and stacks of water bottles in the corner. Would you want to work in that room? What if the workspace had *Star Wars* posters on the wall, science fiction books on the bookshelf, videogames, and a stack of soda cans in the corner? Sapna Cheryan, a social psychologist at the University of Washington, and her colleagues wondered whether the décor of a workspace would affect women's interest in computer science education and tech careers. They discovered that the esthetics of workspaces conveyed clues about its culture, values, and norms. A room at a university with science fiction paraphernalia and videogames signaled a masculine geeky culture, whereas a room with nature posters and puzzles signaled that all genders are welcome. Women were more interested in computer science classes and majors if they were in a room with nature posters than one with *Star Wars* posters. They felt they belonged. These women were totally unaware that the room's ambiance guided their inferences about the local culture and its people, and nudged their choices.[3]

Employees at real workplaces are similarly affected by the spatial design of their office and the ambiance it creates. Drift is a startup that prides itself in promoting real-time, personalized conversations between buyers and sellers so that they can build trust and accelerate business. The company has won many awards for the best leadership team, best company culture, best company for diversity, the list goes on.[4] When a new person joins Drift, they notice that the boss doesn't have a fancy private office. As one employee puts it, "There are no offices for execs at Drift. So, David Cancel, known as DC, sits with the team at a desk just like anyone else. He's super approachable, incredibly transparent, and is always interested in what you are working on." The intentional layout of an office with company leaders working side by side with employees creates an ambiance of equality and opportunity to form authentic relationships.

The physical design and esthetics of a place make up its wallpaper. When it signals inclusivity, it attracts more diverse people because they feel welcome. If this is a workplace, its employees feel more satisfied and want to stay, reducing turnover. If this is a college or university, it's able to attract, support, and ensure all students succeed, even in fields where they are usually underrepresented. As the wallpaper pulls more diverse people into the organization, it changes the perspective of coworkers and organizational leaders, and transforms the local culture. What are the esthetics and physical design of your organization? What's the ambiance like and who does it welcome or leave out?

When people who are strangers interact across racial and ethnic lines, they may initially enter these cross-race interactions with concerns about prejudice. In contemporary American society, many white people are concerned about appearing prejudiced, whereas many racial minorities are concerned about being targets of prejudice.[5] These competing concerns bring mismatched motivations: white people want to be liked by their interaction partners, whereas people of color want to be respected.[6] The clash of motivations increases anxiety and disrupts the quality of interaction between them.[7] What if these interracial interactions were not short, one-shot interactions between strangers, but instead more frequent and longer? What if people worked together in a community organization, or were on a sports team together for a while, or were assigned to be college roommates? A growing number of field experiments in real-world settings show that when local situations are intentionally designed to create opportunities for frequent, longer interactions between strangers, it increases trust and empathy, reduces bias, and results in the formation of real relationships that benefit all involved.[8] Moreover, longer interactions have beneficial impacts even when they take place in the shadows of violent intergroup conflict.[9]

Neighborhoods That Spark Cross-Group Mingling

Let's rewind to the 1950s. It's a time of racial segregation in the United States. Imagine you stumble on old photographs of two housing projects. One looks like a checkerboard. Black and white families live in separate buildings intermixed within the same housing complex. Another looks like a racial island. White families live in houses closely clustered together and physically separated from other houses in which Black families live. Residents at both places were asked their opinion on public housing—should they remain segregated or be integrated? When social psychologists Marie Jahoda and Patricia Salter West asked residents this question in 1951, they learned that white residents in the checkerboard complex who

saw their Black neighbors regularly were less supportive of continu-
ing segregation. Living side by side normalized everyday interracial interaction and made it possible for them to imagine integrated
housing. But white residents in the racial island who rarely saw their
Black neighbors couldn't imagine anything other than segregated
housing. When spatial design promotes proximity, it normalizes interracial mingling, and makes residents more supportive of public
policies for racial justice.[10]

"The houses are too close!" I said to my husband as we walked
through a neighborhood in search of a new house. We were moving
from one state to another so that I could be closer to work. When we
came upon this neighborhood, a new housing development, we noticed it was different. The houses were close together with very few
fences separating them. The front stoop of each house was close to
the sidewalk. Single-family homes were woven in with condos, affordable housing, and an assisted living home—all within the same
neighborhood. Despite my initial reservation, buying a home in this
community ended up being the best decision. As my husband and
I sit on our porch with our morning coffee, our proximity to the
sidewalk sparks hellos to passersby, quick conversations about the
weather, and exclamations over a cute passing dog. When I take my
regular morning walk around the neighborhood, I wave at an el-
derly woman making the rounds on her walker and another rest-
ing on a bench with a crossword puzzle. Because our sidewalk life
encourages casual conversations, I've come to know residents in
the affordable housing near us. Lowering physical boundaries low-
ers psychological walls that separate us. The intentional spatial design of our neighborhood creates openings for conversation with
neighbors across age, race, class, and other social divides. The sum
of many such small moments has created camaraderie and trust.
Some of these chance sidewalk conversations have sparked deeper
unexpected friendships.

Political scientists Eric Oliver and Janelle Wong also noticed that urban design affects human relationships. They looked at the racial composition of neighborhoods in three major American cities—Atlanta, Boston, and Los Angeles—and its relation to everyday interracial interactions.[11] In racially diverse neighborhoods compared to homogeneous ones, Black, Latino, and white residents felt their relationships with other racial groups were less antagonistic. They felt less concerned about immigration and harbored fewer negative stereotypes about groups different from their own than their counterparts in racially homogeneous neighborhoods. You might wonder, is this because people who were less biased to begin with opted to live in integrated communities? That question had occurred to Oliver and Wong. So they measured how comfortable people felt (or not) living in a residentially integrated neighborhood by giving them five pictures each showing a neighborhood with houses whose residents varied in race. These pictures ranged from neighborhoods where all households had residents who were racially similar to research participants to other pictures with a few or no households whose residents were of the same race as participants. They were asked to prioritize these neighborhoods from the most to the least desirable. From their choices, Oliver and Wong captured the racial composition of respondents' ideal neighborhood. They found no matter which type of neighborhood racial composition respondents preferred in their ideal world, if they happened to currently live in a racially diverse neighborhood, they harbored fewer stereotypes and felt less threatened by racial and ethnic groups different from theirs. Chances are this is because living on the same street or close by sparks frequent interactions among neighbors of different backgrounds. They are also likely to meet through local civic activities—volunteering in schools and food banks and participating in local clubs. All these interactions accumulate over time to weaken social divides and increase interracial familiarity and comfort.

An important observation from Oliver and Wong's work is that the most important type of residential diversity is at the neighborhood level because this is where people experience everyday meaningful interactions with others that accumulate over time into something substantial. A diverse neighborhood wallpaper increases acceptance and the feeling that we're all in it together. In contrast, living in a racially diverse city or county doesn't necessarily mean that people interact with others from different racial and ethnic backgrounds because residential segregation in cities and counties keeps people separated in different parts of town.

Neighborhood social spots, if designed well, are particularly good at encouraging casual conversation with strangers from different walks of life. For barbecue lovers, Brad's Bar-B-Que in Oxford, Alabama, is heaven. Eighty-year-old Eleanor Baker felt that her visit here in April 2019 was especially divine. She is a widow and lives alone. Her family lives out of town. Eleanor was by herself at Brad's Bar-B-Que. Three young men were at the next table. Jamario Howard looked over and saw Eleanor. He hates seeing people eating alone. So he walked over and said, "I saw you sitting here alone. Do you mind having some company?" "Go right ahead," she said. They started talking. Soon Jamario invited Eleanor to join their table for dinner with his friends. These twenty-somethings felt a connection with her. As one of the young men said, "When you make that sort of connection with someone, it's hard to let it go like that." That chance encounter was the beginning of an unexpected friendship.[12]

The intergenerational and interracial friendship sparked at Brad's Bar-B-Que fits with Aneta Piekut and Gill Valentine's research. They are cultural geographers in the United Kingdom. Piekut and Valentine find that social gathering spots like casual restaurants, cafés, pubs, and community centers attract people from varying ethnic and religious walks of life and foster friendly interactions. These positive interactions, in turn, encourage people to

6. Repeated interactions increase familiarity and goodwill.

reach out and form amiable relations with other neighbors from religious and ethnic backgrounds different from theirs, leading to casual conversation as illustrated in Figure 6.[13]

Seeing, Believing, and Becoming

Each year, thousands of college students across the country enroll in required mathematics classes. For students wanting to pursue careers in science, technology, or engineering, a strong foundation in math is essential. Obviously it makes a big difference to students whether their professors are good at teaching math, but some years ago I wondered: does the professor's identity group matter to students as well? To answer this question, my graduate students and I conducted a study in an introductory calculus class at my university. Because of high enrollment, this class was divided into smaller sections with identical content and exams but taught by different professors. We recruited students from many sections, some taught by women and others taught by men, all selected because they had equally positive teaching evaluations from prior years. We followed students' progress through the semester, all the while measuring their interest in math, behavior in class, and aspirations to pursue math-intensive careers.[14]

Although all students, women and men alike, said they liked math when we asked them directly via surveys, when we measured their attitudes unobtrusively, their implicit preference revealed something different. Women students showed a stronger implicit preference for math if they happened to be in a calculus class taught by a female professor rather than in one taught by a male professor. Similarly, they related to math more, felt more confident, and participated more actively in math class if their professor was female than if he was male. In contrast, male students' confidence, relation to math, and class participation was the same across sections taught by female and male professors—they were unaffected by the professor's gender. Did these findings emerge because women professors were better teachers? No. Remember we had intentionally preselected instructors with similar teaching skills. And all sections had identical content, lectures, and exams. Our results suggest that women students were inspired by a role model from their own identity group in a classroom and academic major where most students and professors are men; there are relatively fewer women in math. These women students' interest and motivation in calculus class show that increasing gender diversity at the top among visible experts pulls in diverse talent at the bottom among novices.

Some Role Models Backfire

Take a look at this biography:

> Very few people can match Oprah Winfrey's remarkable fame and everlasting mark on the face of television history.

She demonstrated an inborn talent at a very young age.
Winfrey was still in high school when she began her broadcasting career at a Nashville radio station. Then, at the age
of nineteen, she became the youngest person to anchor the
news at a TV station in Nashville. Winfrey excelled rapidly
and established herself as one of the most important figures
in popular culture. In 1996, she launched the *Oprah Winfrey
Show,* which made her one of the most popular TV hosts in
the United States. Today, Oprah Winfrey is one of a few bil-
lionaires in the world.

Does this story light the fire in your belly and make you want to be
like Oprah? In our research, Shaki Asgari, Jane Stout, and I discovered that, when readers encounter a narrative about Oprah Winfrey
as a brilliant superstar, this description backfires when they try to
apply her story to themselves.[15]

What if you read this version of Oprah's story instead?

Few people would have predicted that Oprah Winfrey's trying childhood and adolescence held the promise of a successful future. Moving in with her father as a teenager en-
abled Oprah to finish high school and to go on to receive
a college degree in communication and drama. Her first
job after graduating from college was at a small radio and
television broadcasting company in Nashville. A few years
later, after gaining more experience, she became the host
of a TV talk show in Baltimore. After several years of hard
work, she was able to host her own morning show at a Chicago TV station. In 1996, she launched the *Oprah Winfrey
Show,* which made her one of the most popular TV hosts in

the United States. Oprah Winfrey's success came from hard work, small successes, keeping an open mind, and sticking to her plans.

This is more inspiring, isn't it? Why? Because this second version is more relatable. Oprah had an average beginning, struggled, achieved some small successes, kept going, and then grew into greater success over time. Our research reveals that the first version of Oprah's story—the brilliant, unique superstar—makes readers feel her success is out of reach. Although they admire her, her impressive accomplishments don't inspire them to aim as high because they seem out of reach. In our studies, we gave young women short biographies of successful professional women leaders. For some readers we emphasized the women leaders' brilliance and uniqueness. For other readers we emphasized the same leaders' ordinary beginnings, small successes, and struggles. We found that young women felt more inspired by leaders whose stories amplified life's potholes as well as its successes, and they also felt more similar to them. Feelings of similarity caused these women to implicitly imagine themselves as leaders. They felt they belonged in the group of future leaders. Brilliant superstars didn't inspire such imagination. So if you're an organizational leader trying to inspire your team, or a parent trying to inspire your children, be careful how you describe the journey of the role models you've selected: the same person can be inspirational or intimidating depending on how you tell their stories.

Sometimes it's more effectual to see a role model who is just a few steps ahead of us in life. When a person is new to an environment and hasn't yet found a like-minded community, just one authentic relationship with a peer mentor from a similar background can be enough to get started. Lisa grew up in a small working-class town in Massachusetts. She attended a vocational high school before going to college to become an engineer. Coming from a community where most people didn't go to college—and as the first person in her family to do so—Lisa experienced college as a culture shock. She was in the honors college surrounded by peers from middle- and upper-middle-class families. Her classmates' parents were college graduates who were guiding their children through the college transition. They came from high schools with better educational resources than Lisa's, as well as advanced placement classes that provided college credit and accelerated their progress through the engineering program. Coming from a vocational high school and a working-class background, Lisa didn't have such privileges.

But she had a Sherpa—a student peer mentor, Kelly, who was a senior in electrical engineering. "Girl, you need to get a laptop. An iPad won't cut it in engineering." This was early practical advice from Kelly. Sometimes Kelly's counsel was about the nuts-and-bolts. Sometimes it was emotional support. Sometimes it was about making connections. Kelly was the student president of the Society of Women Engineers and brought Lisa to a SWE event, introducing her to other students. Would Lisa have gone to the event alone? Probably not. It would have been too intimidating. Lisa remembers carpooling with fellow students to a SWE conference. She met other engineers, all women, heard their engineering presentations, demonstrations, and discussions about balancing work and family. That was eye-opening. From Kelly's experiences Lisa learned about the range of possible internships she could apply for. It was cool to see a senior woman who had achieved what Kelly had. "If she can do it, then I can do it."

Lisa was a research participant in my eight-year field experiment on peer mentorship. Our study was motivated by two questions—is there a special benefit for students like Lisa to have a relationship with a female peer mentor in a profession where there are few women? Or are male and female peer mentors equally effective?

Whatever the impacts, how long do the benefits last? My research team—Tara Dennehy, Deborah Wu, and Kelsey Thiem—and I recruited Lisa and hundreds of other new undergraduate students, all women, who had expressed interest in engineering the summer before they started college. We also recruited and trained a group of soon-to-graduate engineering students, both women and men, who had volunteered to be peer mentors and had been recommended by faculty and staff. Then, by lottery, we assigned some new students female peer mentors, others male peer mentors, and yet others no mentors. Mentors and mentees met a few times during the mentees' first year in college, after which the mentors graduated and the mentoring relationship ended. Mentor-mentee pairs had wide latitude in how they used their time together. Each mentor was told that their primary goal was to be their mentee's friend, to be attentive to her needs, and to tailor their conversations, advice, and activities to what the mentee needed. We followed mentees from the moment they entered college through graduation and beyond.[16]

We discovered that women who were assigned a female peer mentor for one year remained steadfast in their sense of belonging in engineering, maintaining confidence and motivation to persist in engineering through their entire college life and pursue graduate degrees beyond college, whereas women assigned a male peer mentor, or no mentor, steadily declined in their feelings of belonging, confidence, motivation, and interest in pursuing graduate degrees in engineering. Having female mentors preserved mentees' emotional well-being, whereas women with male mentors or no mentors declined in emotional well-being, becoming vulnerable to emotional exhaustion and burnout across their years in college. On objective metrics, having female peer mentors increased women's success in securing engineering internships by 21 percent compared with having no mentors and by 17 percent compared with having male mentors. It increased their graduation rate with degrees in engineering and allied fields by 11 percent compared with having no mentor and by 14 percent compared with having a male mentor.[17] In short, a low-cost, light-touch mentorship experience in a critical transition period in life yielded dividends through the college years and one year after graduation, long after mentorship had ended.

I reached out to Lisa eight years after she participated in my study to see what she was up to and share with her the long-term results of our study in which she had participated. When I told her how a one-year mentoring relationship with a woman in engineering positively impacted all mentees' lives through college graduation and beyond, long after mentorship had ended, Lisa wasn't surprised. She commented, "My relationship with Kelly allowed me to see what success looked like, what the future holds, and made me feel confident about the future."

Our research makes clear that young people who are underrepresented in a local setting often feel isolated. Connecting them with people who share an element of their identity can alleviate that isolation. This may be a brief interaction with a successful professional like David Cancel, the CEO of Drift, who makes a point of hanging out in the same workspace as his employees. Or an opportunity to form an authentic relationship with an admired peer. Or an invitation to join a peer group on a shared journey. By creating such opportunities consistently, the local culture provides a haven for people to develop a sense of belonging, confidence, and professional identity. Timing matters. These experiences of community and connection are especially important when people enter a new environment where they feel uncertain about their standing—students starting high school or college, for example, or new employees joining an organization. During transition periods, the local culture can nudge their transformation from seeing to believing to becoming.

Seeing people who look like us matters far more than mission

statements. Drift's employees give the company high marks because its emphasis on diversity and inclusion isn't limited to words.
It's reflected in actions. And it starts with who's at the top. The co-
founders of Drift are two Latino men, David Cancel and Elias Torres, who view the diversity of ideas as the key to innovation. David
and Elias are also candid when the company falls short in hiring
more women and people of color. Drift employees feel heard and respected. As one person remarked, "The leadership team prioritizes
feedback and genuinely cares about every role in the company. Love
Drift leaders!"[18]

Organizations draw attention to their values in many ways. The
two most common strategies are statements about diversity, equity,
and inclusion, and the representation of diverse people within the
organization. Diversity statements have become a common practice in organizations. We see them everywhere—websites, organizational brochures, and job ads. But do they work? In 2008, Valerie
Purdie-Vaughns and her colleagues found that more than diversity
statements, what job seekers from minority groups trusted was seeing diverse employees in the workplace. Pictures showing a diverse
group of employees in an organization's informational materials increased prospective job seekers' trust in the company. If the diversity of a group of people in an organization was prominent, diversity
statements became less important.[19] The greater importance of actual numbers of diverse employees, relative to promises of diversity,
has only increased in the decade since the previous study. In 2020,
social psychologists Leigh Wilton, Cheryl Kaiser, and their colleagues found that when organizations claim a positive and diverse
climate but don't show robust numbers of diverse employees, African American and Hispanic respondents view this message as diversity dishonesty. On the positive side, however, showing evidence
of diverse employees in a workplace reduces perceptions of diversity dishonesty and increases respondents' feelings of belonging in

the organization. The message is "show me the numbers"; claiming commitment to diversity without numeric representation is interpreted as lip service.[20] New recruits see symbolic signals of diversity as disingenuous, lose trust, and are eventually likely to leave.

Seeing diverse people matters not just when people are looking for jobs. It also matters when we're the customer, looking for services from a business. Imagine you're a lesbian, gay, or transgender person looking for a new doctor. You've narrowed your list to three options, and now you're looking at the websites and brochures of each healthcare provider's office. One has a mission statement highlighting diversity, equity, and inclusion as core values; another has pictures of diverse clients; and a third has neither. Which one would you choose? When social psychologists Rebecca Cipollina and Diana Sanchez did this study, they found that lesbian, gay, and trans people most trusted a medical provider whose materials showed a diverse clientele. That's where they felt they would receive high-quality treatment. Here too, seeing a diversity statement made no difference.[21]

Creating the Conditions for Structural Change

How might you apply these solutions about people and places to your life, in ways that promote social justice? Here are four suggestions.

- First, if you are a hiring manager looking to recruit diverse talent, understand that seeing a homogeneous team is likely to turn off prospective job seekers from underrepresented identities. You may also have difficulty retaining diverse talent. If you intend to recruit and retain diverse talent, new people need to see people like themselves in the organization. This creates a chicken-and-egg problem. One solution is cluster hiring. Recruit a cohort of new employees from underrepresented groups who are in different organizational units, but who all joined the organization at the same time as a cohort and are all of the same rank. Create opportunities for this group of diverse employees to connect and get to know one another, form relationships, and be mutual mentors to one another, strengthening their sense of belonging within the cohort and also in the organization.

- Second, notice the spatial design of your workplace if you work in a physical location rather than remotely. Are the offices of people in leadership roles on the same floor as the offices of people in less powerful roles? When workspaces are physically close, people are more likely to have real conversations, not just transactional interactions. If you want an inclusive culture at work and you have leadership clout, consider placing your office near your associates and support staff to spark casual hallway conversations across rank and role, allowing genuine relationships to form across social divides, as shown in Figures 5 and 6. You will learn firsthand what your employees care about. Break down silos by creating a communal lounge where people across role hierarchies gather informally as equals. Inclusive spatial design allows people in diverse roles with differing degrees of power to have frequent exchanges, both casual and meaningful, some of which may evolve into friendships. As the wallpaper pulls different types of people into the organization and engenders real relationships, it shifts the perspective of coworkers and organizational leaders, transforms the local culture, and reduces turnover.

- Third, if you are a parent, teacher, or professor motivating your children or students to believe that yes, they can, or a leader wanting to inspire employees who don't see themselves reflected in the organization, choose role models for them with care. Highlight the struggles of successful individuals and "near peers" to make them relatable; don't present them as superstars whose achievements seem unattainable. Relatable role models matter especially for young people who don't see others like them in influential roles in their local environment.

- Finally, notice the physical layout of your neighborhood and your house, condo, or apartment within it. Does it allow meaningful interactions with neighbors from different backgrounds? If you're looking to move in the future, pay attention to the design of the neighborhoods you're considering. Are they designed to encourage mixing? Many cities and towns are redesigning urban spaces to be more compact, walkable, and dotted with public plazas and parks where people can mingle. Some are intentionally mixing single-family homes, apartments, and affordable housing in the same neighborhood to encourage social mixing.[22] This type of human-scaled urban design is different from sprawling, low-density residential areas popularized in the 1950s, when foot traffic was unusual and spontaneous interactions among strangers rare.[23] The neighborhood my husband and I chose to move to uses human-scaled urban design. Living here has shaped our relationships in the community and our opinions about neighborhood issues. Frequent casual conversations with neighbors across age, race, class, and other social divides have shaped my opinion that all residents should have a voice in our residential association. Community decisions should not be made by property owners alone, excluding low-income renters in affordable housing. Sidewalk conversations among a few people expanded to a larger organized group that mobilized to act collectively to change the rules. (I tell this story in Chapter 7.) Look for opportunities in your neighborhood, workplace, or gathering spot to have conversations with people from different backgrounds. Perhaps there's a café like Busboys and Poets somewhere near you. You might learn something new, something of concern that compels you to join forces with others to act for a common cause.

6

TAP INTO EMOTIONS

Use the Power of Storytelling

Tony is thirteen years old and just got out of ninety-nine days in juvenile hall. Until recently, he was facing years of incarceration. Today, Tony is participating in a ceremony organized by a local nongovernmental organization (NGO) that brings together people facing criminal charges, their families, and communities to become change agents. When a family is successful in bringing their loved one home by beating the charges or receiving a reduced sentence, the group hosts a ceremony to honor them. As Tony erases his name from a board in the room, his mother thanks the community who walked with her and her son through their darkest days. Tony's mom plans to keep attending the meetings and assisting other families who find themselves in the position she once did.[1]

This is participatory defense—a process created by community organizer Raj Jayadev and his organization Silicon Valley De-Bug, in San Jose, California. They bring the ethos of community organizing to empower low-income people facing the criminal justice system. At its core is a group of people who gather each week: people facing criminal charges, along with their families and supporters. They share stories about the family member or friend facing criminal charges and learn concrete skills to advocate for their loved one in court. Jayadev asks families to create visual stories of their loved one—the accused—and share them with the judge. While incarceration dehumanizes defendants, personal stories told by their families humanize them. Some families create collages of photographs. Others make short videos. All show their loved one in daily life, playing with their children, cooking a meal for the family, and hugging their mom. When the judge sees these stories, suddenly an abstract and dry case file morphs into a real human who arouses empathy. The results of this visual storytelling have been remarkable. Jayadev has seen charges dismissed, sentences significantly reduced, and acquittals won at trial. This is the power of storytelling.[2]

I've experienced the impact of storytelling more than once. One story that stands out is that of Jen, a college student, in one of the first classes I taught in my career. Jen was an engineering student in my psychology class. I was surprised and curious to hear her story. She was leaving engineering and switching to a psychology major. Why? Was she struggling with difficult classes? Did she feel her foundation in math and science from high school was not adequate? The answers were no and no. In fact, she was doing well in engineering. Jen had been recruited from high school as an engineering prospect. Initially, Jen's classes were filled with the familiar faces of other women students. But as she advanced through the coursework, there were fewer and fewer women in her engineering classes. One day in a large class she looked around and realized she was the only woman in the class. Jen felt weirded out and began to question whether she belonged there. She started to wonder whether she cared enough about engineering. Her quest to understand what she was feeling and why brought her to my class. Jen's experience resonated with me. I heard her isolation, uncertainty, and self-doubt. I understood why she was leaving engineering. Before hearing her story, I had assumed that the source of her departure was spurred by inadequate high school preparation for a difficult major, or perhaps

simply by a loss of interest. But the real reason was isolation and uncertainty about belonging. Losing interest was not the cause. It was
the effect. Jen's story nudged the direction of my own research to
search for why people leave academic and career paths even when
they are doing well. Stories are like patterns on wallpaper. At one
level the patterns are about individuals' experiences, emotions, relationships, obstacles, and efforts to resolve them. By building re-
latability and narrative tension, the arresting patterns draw you
in. When you zoom out, there is a bigger pattern—themes and lessons—that subsume the narrative details of individual characters. I
wondered—can we design a storytelling wallpaper whose expansive
pattern incorporates a broad variety of individual characters, making talented people of different sorts feel at home in the room and
want to stay?

What Stories Do to the Mind and Brain

When we hear personal stories from real people and read or watch
stories of imaginary people, they transport us into someone else's
world. We, as listeners and readers, infer the mental states and experiences of the characters. We imagine what they might be wanting,
thinking, and feeling. And we step into their shoes. Mental simulation helps us experience the thoughts and emotions of the characters and virtually experience events in the stories that may be far
from our own reality.[3] In other words, simulation gives us insight
into the reasons for someone's actions. Psychologists call this developing a "theory of mind."[4] More than nonfiction topics like science
and economics, say, stories feel personal because readers and listeners are reminded of their own experiences.[5] Stories activate in the
listener's mind self-knowledge, not just general knowledge, which
gets woven into the narrative and creates the feeling of being trans-

ported. Perhaps Jen's story reminded me of a time when I had felt out of place, and that's why her story stayed with me.

Jen's story affected me in a way that was more emotional than if I had read scientific articles on the same subject. Human brains are pattern-seeking machines that feed off stories. Neuroscientist Clare Grall and her colleagues at Dartmouth College found that personal narratives engage the brains of listeners differently than nonnarrative messages. Hearing personal stories synchronizes the brain activity of multiple listeners, especially in the frontal lobe, responsible for higher-order thinking and planning, and the parietal lobe, which processes sensory information and integrates information from multiple modalities in the body.[6]

Synchrony in the brain activity of multiple listeners becomes even stronger when they encounter emotional stories, according to a fascinating study by Dr. Lauri Nummenmaa, a professor at the University of Turku in Finland.[7] Imagine you're watching a movie. Instead of sitting on your couch, you're lying inside a magnetic resonance imaging (MRI) machine. This version of the machine—called a functional MRI—measures small changes in blood flow in your brain associated with your brain activity. Nummenmaa and his colleagues showed one group of people, who were lying inside an fMRI machine, a movie whose plot made them feel positive emotions. Another group saw a different movie that made them feel negative emotions. And a third group saw an emotionally neutral movie. Later, they asked these same people to watch the movie a second time and say how good or bad and how aroused or calm they felt as they watched each scene. When stories made movie watchers feel bad, their brain activity became synchronized in regions involved in emotion processing and understanding other people's intentions and actions. But when stories made movie watchers feel amped-up and aroused, attention networks in their brains started acting in a coordinated way. By synchronizing brain activity across many people, these results show that emotional stories create a common understanding of characters and events among viewers.

Stories Arouse Empathy and Reduce Bias

By imagining the experience of characters in a plot, we start to care about them and identify with them. We adopt the character's viewpoints, participate in their experiences, and feel their emotions. The boundary between ourselves and the character dissolves, and we become immersed in them for a moment in time. This is exactly what happens when we read good fiction. Reading fictional stories improves readers' ability to understand, interpret, and respond to social information. Frequent readers of fiction score higher on empathy and are better able to understand others' mental states than readers of nonfiction and nonreaders.[8] Reading fiction is also correlated with having a strong social network in one's real life and feeling less lonely. Of course, correlation is not causation. Support for the causal benefits of reading fiction comes from experiments that delve deeper into cause and effect. In multiple experiments, some people were randomly assigned to read fiction while others were assigned to read nonfiction or nothing at all. The results of these experiments converged on a common conclusion: exposure to fiction increased readers' ability to accurately understand what other people are thinking and feeling, which in psychological jargon is called mentalizing. And it also increased their ability to enter others' emotional experience, which is called empathizing.[9]

Mentalizing, empathy, and identification are how stories reduce prejudice toward people who feel foreign to viewers. Imagine that an average American television watcher is channel surfing and stumbles on a sitcom telling the story of a community of Arab Muslims living in a small American town. The viewer sees them falling in love, arguing with parents, and navigating school and work. The characters are relatable, likable, flawed, just like everyone else. Watching a few episodes, the viewer chuckles, nods, and gets involved with the story and the characters, who are easy to identify with. Although this viewer knows very little about Muslims, has no Muslim friends, acquaintances, or neighbors, and had thought of Muslims as foreign to their own experience, they understand these characters.

This is exactly what Sohad Murrar, a social psychologist, and her colleagues predicted would happen. They invited a group of midwesterners to watch multiple episodes of a television sitcom. By luck of draw, some people were shown a program called *Little Mosque on the Prairie,* a story about a multigenerational community of Muslims with various beliefs, lifestyles, and occupations, living in a small Canadian town. The story showed their relationships with one another and with non-Muslim characters. It was personal, relatable, and humorous. Other people saw the sitcom *Friends,* a story about the group of young adult friends—all white and non-Muslim—who share apartments in the same building. For whichever show they watched, Murrar asked viewers how much they got absorbed in the show, how much they identified with the characters, and at the end she asked about their attitudes toward various social groups, including toward Muslims. She found that viewers who were randomly assigned to watch *Little Mosque on the Prairie* expressed more favorable attitudes toward Muslims than others assigned to watch *Friends.* These positive attitudes endured a month and a half later when viewers were contacted again. Viewers' favorable attitudes toward Muslims as a group were associated with a stronger sense of identification with Muslim characters in the sitcom.[10] These types of stories that educate viewers about a social issue wrapped up in an absorbing plot are called entertainment-education and are accessible across multiple media—TV, web series, podcasts, film, and radio.[11] At one level entertainment-education tells stories of particular protagonists, their relationships, experiences, and dilemmas. At another level they convey broader lessons about an issue without being explicit—this is the wallpaper. Muslim people are like you; you could easily be one of these characters; they could be your friends.

Stories are powerful even when they are conveyed in a compact form. My colleague Luis Rivera and I created brief paragraphs with the life stories of highly regarded and famous individuals who identify as gay or lesbian and paired them with their pictures. In each story, we described the admired person's accomplishments and contribution to society and mentioned their sexual orientation in passing. We then recruited a community sample of people from a small city and showed half of them these short life stories and showed the others, our control group, stories of nature. We found that when straight people read stories of admired lesbians and gay men, they showed 17 percent less antigay bias compared with the control group, on a test measuring their spontaneous implicit attitudes toward gay people. And they were 7 percent more willing to vote for state and local policies to protect gays and lesbians from employment and housing discrimination, and to support marriage equality at a time when same-sex marriage was illegal, compared with the control group. Research participants who didn't know any gay or lesbian people personally experienced the biggest benefits from reading these stories. They showed 34 percent less implicit antigay bias and were 30 percent more willing to vote for policies to protect gay and lesbian civil rights after reading the brief biographical stories.[12] Because the human brain processes media stories similarly to the way it processes real-life experiences, people often react to real and fictional media characters in ways that are similar to face-to-face interactions. For individuals who don't know any gays or lesbians personally, media exposure to gay people expands their social network virtually, beyond what they have access to in real life. This gives them empathic insight into the lives of people different from them.

Few of us have had personal interactions with people who are undocumented migrants—our lives couldn't be more different from theirs. Our knowledge comes from the media, where undocumented migrants are often portrayed as gang members seeking to spread crime in the United States or as unaccompanied minors who are pawns in the hands of smugglers and traffickers.[13] Both narratives exaggerate reality when compared with statistics tracked by the U.S. Department of Homeland Security (DHS). When migrants are assumed to have criminal intent, we don't feel much empathy for them, and we are more likely to support antimigrant policies. This is where personal stories become useful—they can be a powerful corrective.

I stumbled upon a video on CNN of an emotional reunion between a mother and her eight-year-old daughter. Angelica Rebeca Gonzalez-Garcia had fled her home in Guatemala with her daughter because of severe abuse and domestic violence, seeking asylum in the United States. She had been separated from her daughter at the Arizona border and had not seen her in fifty-five days. In the CNN video, this thirty-one-year-old mother was finally reunited with her daughter. Gonzalez-Garcia wrapped her arms around her daughter and wept. Her face was awash with love, remorse, shame, and fear. "Forgive me for leaving you alone. Forgive me," she kept repeating in Spanish. "You know that I love you, right? You know that I missed you. . . . I'll never leave you alone again, never. Forgive me, my darling, . . . forgive me."[14]

Social psychologists Samantha Moore-Berg, Boaz Hameiri, and Emile Bruneau used this video to explore whether watching this mother-and-daughter story would induce empathy toward undocumented migrants in American viewers and shape their opinions about national immigration policy. They recruited a sample of 958 American adults (65 percent Democrats, 35 percent Republicans) and, by a flip of a coin, randomly assigned them into four groups. Members of one group watched the video and were asked to guess what proportion of undocumented migrants who cross the border are gang members or pawns of smugglers. A second group watched the video, was asked the same questions, and then shown DHS statistics from the U.S. government to illustrate the discrepancy between their guess and reality. The third group saw only the DHS statistics. The final group saw nothing at all. All participants were then asked how they felt about parents and children separated at the border, their emotions about illegal or undocumented migrants in general, whether they saw this group as primitive or barbaric, and their opinions about a series of anti-migrant federal policies. The results were clear: providing Americans with a video narrative depicting the suffering of migrants when accompanied by corrective information worked the best compared with all other groups. Together, these two components humanized the plight of undocumented migrants, induced empathy, neutralized the impact of misinformation, and increased opposition to antimigrant policy. While the video alone without the corrective statistical information increased empathy, it did not change policy opinions. And merely providing correct immigration statistics did nothing. In sum, to move people's opinions about immigration policy, you need personal stories that evoke empathy plus accurate information.[15]

What in our brains creates feelings of empathy? Economist and neuroscientist Paul Zak and his colleagues discovered that empathy emerges from the synthesis of a neurochemical called oxytocin. Some call it the love hormone. It signals that it's safe to approach others and increases sensitivity toward others. Zak and his team wondered whether watching stories would activate the oxytocin system and motivate people to help others. So they conducted a study.

Ben is dying, says his father to the camera. Ben is two years old and doesn't know that a brain tumor will kill him in a few months. We see him play in the background. Ben's father says it's hard to be joyful around Ben, knowing what's coming. Will Dad have the in-

7. Hearing others' stories broadens perspectives
and promotes empathy across social divides.

ner strength to stay in the present moment during the last weeks
of Ben's life without grief overtaking him? We learn that Ben's dad
finds a way to be at peace right up to his son's last breath. As viewers we intuitively understand that someday we too may face challenges that will demand deep inner strength. People watched Ben's
story on video and Zak measured their oxytocin levels with blood
draws before and after the story to see whether watching the story
changed oxytocin levels in viewers' bodies. He found that Ben's
story caused more oxytocin synthesis in viewers. And the amount of
oxytocin released was associated with how willing they were to help
others by donating money to a charity associated with Ben's story.[16]

In later studies Zak dug deeper to uncover what features of
these stories motivate cooperation. He found that effective stories
sustain viewers' attention by building tension. A compelling story
starts with something surprising. It builds tension as the protagonists encounter difficulties, and work to figure out ways to overcome
them, which pushes the story to a climax. When a story is successful in creating tension, it sustains viewers' attention. They begin to

step into the protagonist's shoes, resonate with their emotions, and begin to care. When the crisis is resolved and the story ends, viewers often continue to mentally simulate their feelings and behaviors.[17] This experience of absorbing someone's emotions and gaining empathic insight into their experience is illustrated in Figure 7.

Stories Packaged with Entertainment Increase Social Acceptance

When we are invested in a story, we are more open to persuasive messages embedded in it. Entertainment-education reduces our sense that we are being "sold" something, which makes us more receptive to messages in the plot.[18] The more subtly a story conveys its message, without hitting the audience over the head, the more accepting receivers are of its influence. In fact, stories may be more persuasive for those who hold strong attitudes that go against an issue conveyed by the story if the viewpoint is implied subtly rather than stated explicitly. An issue introduced as a side plot rather than as part of the central storyline, for example, stays at the periphery of the viewers' minds like wallpaper, rather than at the center of attention. Viewers with countervailing opinions may also be persuaded because the cognitive and emotional demands of a story leave them with less motivation and fewer mental resources to criticize and argue against the issue they disagree with. This makes entertainment-education an effective tool with which to invite people to become more accepting of difference and to change their behavior.

Sometimes stories don't change people's beliefs, but instead guide their behavior by changing their understanding of the social norms in the community. When the bloody civil war in Rwanda ended, social psychologist Elizabeth Levy Paluck, in collaboration with Radio La Benevolencija Humanitarian Tools Foundation, a Dutch NGO, conducted a daring study to test the power of storytelling against the background of intergroup violence.[19] They filled the airwaves with two radio soap operas. Some regions heard a radio story about two fictional Rwandan communities between which relations crumbled, leading to violence, death, and trauma. The fictional storyline paralleled the history of Rwanda leading up to the 1994 genocide. But unlike the real genocide, in the soap opera, some characters banded together across community lines, spoke out against powerful leaders who advocated violence, and supported an interethnic romance. Other parts of Rwanda heard a radio soap opera on a topic unrelated to intergroup conflict. Listeners of the soap opera about conflict and reconciliation were more likely to change their understanding of community norms than those who heard the other soap opera. They became more willing to dissent, talk about sensitive topics, accept interethnic marriages, and cooperate with the other side, even though their overall beliefs hadn't changed. Put differently, sometimes storytelling, while not necessarily changing people's private beliefs, can shift their response to the wallpaper of community norms, leading to changes in their behavior.

Although stories that are broadly shared in society are often produced by large media corporations, the rise of new digital media has created an opening for grassroots storytellers from marginalized communities to tell their own stories authentically. As an example, Hispanic teenagers in East Los Angeles created an English language telenovela with characters drawn from their own community.[20] What's different about this digital medium is that it is distributed as a free web series accessible over mobile phones, putting it within reach of low-income youth. It's also unique in that the story in the web series hops across platforms to a website and other social media. Viewers are encouraged to explore the website for resources on issues raised in each episode, including legal aid counseling, domestic violence, and health. Fans interact in real time with the show's characters using website features. And their comments and suggestions inform the direction the story takes in the future, making them both consumers and producers. By weaving the fictional story across multiple internet-based media platforms, and by making it free, series like this can appeal to younger tech savvy audiences across social-class divides.

How Stories Create Social Glue

Storytelling within a community functions as social glue. Communication researchers Yong-Chan Kim at the University of Alabama and Sandra Ball-Rokeach at the University of Southern California discovered that people's connection to a storytelling network in their neighborhood is the best predictor of their sense of belonging, their involvement in civic participation, and the belief that their neighbors are willing to band together to solve collective problems. The stories within the network create a shared reality, strengthen emotional bonds, and motivate collective action. Being enmeshed in a storytelling network is even more important in ethnically diverse neighborhoods and other communities where people move a lot.[21]

We have seen a perfect example of such a network in Silicon Valley De-Bug, Raj Jayadev's storytelling, community-coordinating, advocacy organization. Their goal is to debug the criminal justice system. By bringing together people to share emotional stories about their family member facing criminal charges, De-Bug strengthens the bond between the storytellers and listeners, increases empathy, and invites listeners to band together on behalf of the storyteller's family. A collective show of support in the courtroom on behalf of the person facing criminal charges is a critical piece of Jayadev's strategy. Another critical piece is spreading these stories to a broader public through the organization's bilingual magazine, website, video, music, and art. De-Bug rolls out its storytelling wallpaper that comprises digital and in-person channels across San Jose and Santa Clara County to create a shared reality about criminal justice issues in the public's mind and force greater transparency, accountability, and fairness.[22]

Hearing a story directly from a person, rather than in writing or visual media, has a unique power because it constructs a shared world between humans: the speaker and listener. Neuroscientist Uri Hasson at Princeton University and his colleagues were curious to learn what goes on in listeners' brains when they hear spoken stories. How do listeners' brain responses relate to the storytellers' brains? Do the two brains dance together? It all starts with a speaker who is asked to remember a story and describe it to the listener. In turn, the listener must understand the words and construct the events in her mind, even though she did not experience them herself. Using fMRI and a verbal communication task, Hasson and his colleagues traced movie watchers' neural patterns as they watched parts of a movie and later described its scenes to listeners who had not seen the film. They also recorded listeners' neural activity as they mentally constructed the events, comparing these data with speakers' neural patterns taken from when they had watched the movie. Hasson and his team found that responses in the listener's brain became aligned with responses in the speaker's brain. The greater the neural alignment between the two brains, the better the communication, as measured with story comprehension tests administered later. Brain regions that process sound, language, and higher-order reasoning all produced coordinated neural activity in listeners who heard the same story.[23] This goes to show that human brains are well-tuned pattern-seeking machines that feed off stories. Stories are processed in specific brain regions that get synced up between storytellers and listeners, helping to transmit the memory from one to the other.

When two people speak the same language, we expect communication to be relatively smooth. So we may not be surprised to learn that there's neural alignment between the speaker's and listener's brains. But what happens when a story is told in one language and translated into another? Does something get lost in translation? Or do listeners pick up the same meaning? To answer these questions, Dr. Christopher Honey, a neuroscientist at the University of British Columbia, and his colleagues recorded people's brain activity as they listened to a story while lying inside an fMRI machine. One group of native Russian speakers heard a story being told in Russian. Another group of native English speakers who spoke no Russian heard an English translation of the same story. When Honey and his team compared the brain activity of the two groups, they found similar brain responses despite differences in the linguistic structures of the two languages. The similarity in listeners' responses extended from brain regions just outside early auditory areas that process sound, all the way through the frontal cerebral cortex responsible for higher-order abstract reasoning. These results suggest that storytelling breaks language barriers.[24] Messages in a story told by one person in one language embedded in their own culture, when translated into another language, can create a shared reality with a listener from a very different culture. Well-translated stories function as shared wallpaper across cultural and geographic divides, allowing perspective-taking, insight into others' experience, empathy, and greater understanding.

Stories Illuminate Systemic Inequalities

In addition to creating a shared understanding between individuals, stories provide a window into complex social inequalities and their causes. Race, class, and gender inequalities related to health, education, and the impacts of climate change are caused by institutional policies and practices that shape and in turn are shaped by cultural norms and assumptions. Relying only on data and abstract language to explain these problems risks losing much of the audience. These system-level explanations are best conveyed through stories about the lives of people whose experiences illustrate the various systems at play. This is especially important when engaging people who think that problems are mostly the result of bad personal choices. For example, the perception that poverty is caused by poor choices by individuals rather than systemic failures.

I had a visceral understanding of the systemic causes of poverty while watching the Netflix series *Maid*—based on the best-selling book of the same title. The story opens with Maddy, a young woman, creeping out of her home with her toddler in the middle of the night to escape her husband, who suffers from alcoholism and is prone to violence. Maddy has no safe place to go. Her mother has a mental illness, and her relationship with her dad is tenuous since her parents' divorce. There is no room in the shelter. After sleeping in her car for a while, Maddy ends up at social services. As I watched, I was surprised to learn about the gaping holes in social services. I learned that in some jurisdictions domestic violence is defined so narrowly that resources aren't available to a person who hasn't been physically assaulted by their partner. A partner who punches a wall, throws things, and threatens you might not make you eligible for protection. I learned that low-income housing isn't always available to a domestic violence survivor who doesn't have a job. I learned social services might not help survivors find childcare, which would free them up to work for pay while leaving their kids in a safe place. In short, public resources for low-income housing, work, and childcare are sometimes like mismatched jigsaw puzzle pieces that don't fit the lives of real people in crisis. I found myself trying to identify the missing piece that would complete Maddy's jigsaw puzzle and create interlocking supports to fit her life. I understood that Maddy's inability to get out of this situation was not because she lacked personal responsibility. It was because the publicly funded

8. Hearing others' stories provides insight into systemic
barriers and increases skepticism about cultural myths reifying
personal choice or fate as the cause of inequality.

social safety system that was supposed to help her had restrictions that didn't fit her circumstances. Maddy's story told through *Maid* revealed systemic barriers that create and perpetuate poverty that I had not known about before. Like wallpaper, these systemic barriers are typically in the background and don't attract much attention. I had not gone looking for this wallpaper before. But because I stumbled onto this show while on my couch one evening, I got it. Like the character in Figure 8, I gained insight into barriers I hadn't known about, and people stuck behind them.

Even when stories are set in a fantasy world, they can drive our behavior to advocate for structural change in the real world. The Marvel film *Black Panther* paints a vivid picture of community empowerment and cultural celebration in an all-Black society, protected by superheroes. Watching the nation of Wakanda being attacked in *Black Panther* resonates with viewers who feel that the Black community is under attack in the real world. This is exactly the message that Movement for Black Lives leaders Kayla Reed, Jessica Byrd, and Rukia Lumumba were looking for. When *Black Panther* attracted record-setting audiences, they saw an opportunity to parlay that success on behalf of their organization's goal to build Black political power in the United States. The film's community empowerment theme inspired #WakandaTheVote: as moviegoers left the theater, they were greeted by organizers who connected the dots between *Black Panther*'s Wakanda and the real world. "We need someone to defend our communities against attack," said Reed, a St. Louis–based organizer. "We can all be superheroes and we can all be change agents in our communities." As a result of organizing around the *Black Panther* story, thousands of people registered to vote in the United States in 2018.[25] The story of *Black Panther* became the spark that activated collective action.

Creating the Conditions for Structural Change

How might you apply these storytelling solutions in your life? Here are four suggestions.

- Use personal stories to advocate in your community for a local issue related to social justice. Such an opportunity presented itself in my life in December 2016, right after the U.S. presidential election, when anti-Muslim and anti-immigrant rhetoric was on the rise nationwide. Some friends and neighbors and I organized a group of town residents to talk to our local elected leaders on the town council. We used personal stories to urge our councilors to designate the town a sanctuary city. We were worried about the culture of hostility seeping into our town, targeting Muslims and immigrant residents. One person who spoke was a young Muslim woman. She told her story of growing up in our town and loving it. But now the climate had changed. The anti-immigrant hostility swirling around made her afraid for her safety and the safety of her family. She worried that her hijab and her husband's kufi might make them targets. She worried that her children and friends at the local mosque might be targeted. Her story laid bare her daily experiences of vulnerability. I think that personal story touched a nerve. A couple months later, the town council unanimously passed a resolution affirming that our town welcomed people of all religions and national origins. And they resolved that town officials and institutions would not assist or enforce federal initiatives that target, surveil, or diminish the freedom of residents based on religion or immigration or citizenship status.

- If you are in a role where you introduce speakers to large groups, here is a second action you might try. I have noticed that speakers at professional events are often introduced in ways that elevate them to the status of superstars. At university events, we often list the speaker's awards and accomplishments in introducing them. While this honors the speaker, I started wondering whether such glowing introductions might alienate some students in the audience, especially those who feel like small and insignificant novices in their profession. This was informed by comments from students who mentioned they couldn't imagine achieving these speakers' accomplishments. I realized that introducing speakers as "superstars" might paradoxically undercut the motivation of some young people who are listening by making these accomplishments seem unreachable. So I flipped the script. Now when I invite accomplished professionals to give talks to students, I introduce them differently. One speaker gave a talk describing how he used his science to help policymakers in the U.S. Senate. In introducing him before his presentation, I told the story of his journey: his humble beginnings in the Bronx, his educational path, his interest in connecting science with social good, culminating over time in a policy fellowship at the U.S. Capitol. Later that week, several students said they were excited by the speaker and looked for opportunities to engage with him one-on-one. They sought his advice on how to relate their educational training to social issues they cared about. I could see these students were creating a map connecting their present selves to their future possible selves and careers.

- Third, think about creating an informal group of people to watch and discuss movies and shows telling stories of people and communities you don't know much about. Think of *Little Mosque on the Prairie* or *Maid*. Perhaps the show you choose could focus on a social issue you want to learn about. As a group, talk about what you learned. How did you feel? What surprised you? Did you learn about social or systemic obstacles or wallpaper that you hadn't known about before? Is there some action you could take as a group?

- Finally, consider creating a dialogue group in your community that people can join to share stories about their lives. The exchange of personal stories helps people in a group develop a better understanding and appreciation of how lived experiences shaped their own and others' values, priorities, and perspectives, particularly when participants come from different backgrounds. Dialogue is a form of conversation intended to increase mutual understanding, appreciation, and respect. It may be used as a process of getting to know one's neighbors or coworkers and can also be used to facilitate a collaboration or decision-making process. Dialogue groups have some key components: storytelling, discovery, inquiry, civility, and empathy. The group agrees on a set of shared norms that guide their process: respect, active listening, no interruptions, a set amount of time for every speaker, and limiting questions to those seeking clarification from the speaker, not ones that engage in counterargument. When used to facilitate collaboration or collective action, dialogues help participants consider different viewpoints, weigh competing options, examine unfamiliar information, understand complex issues, and reflect on their own beliefs, opinions, values, or biases. Organizing Engagement is a useful website with guidance about how to create effective dialogue groups.[26] If there is some issue in your local community related to inequality, use a dialogue circle to exchange stories, learn more, and create social glue among people who have opted in. The relationship bonds created and strengthened through story sharing may become a foundation for organizing and acting collectively in the future.

7

NETWORK FOR SOCIAL JUSTICE

Your Action Changes Others' Action

My husband and I moved to a mixed neighborhood. This community was intentionally created to bring together homeowners, condo owners, renters in affordable housing, and older people in an assisted living facility. Living close together sparks conversation with neighbors from all backgrounds. I've come to know residents in the affordable housing down the street, homeowners around us, and older people in assisted living at the corner. Given the spirit of this mixed neighborhood, I was surprised to learn that our residential association rules don't give renters any voice in neighborhood decisions even though they comprise a healthy percentage of neighborhood residents. Only property owners have voting rights. Renters are represented by a commercial entity that owns the affordable housing. This governance structure goes against the values of our neighborhood. When two neighbors realized this, they gathered a few of us to discuss their concern about whose voice is excluded from decision-making. After a few such conversations, we created and distributed flyers to invite more neighbors into the conversation. We also personally reached out to people we knew. As the group grew, our numbers attracted more people to join. Before long, our group of concerned citizens included almost 50 percent of all residents in the neighborhood. We pushed collectively during homeowners' association meetings to change the voting rules to give some voice in decision-making to our low-income neighbors. We didn't win this fight. But we did accomplish two ancillary goals. Our coalition-building and coordinated action created and tightened bonds among a group of residents who are willing to mobilize again when the opportunity arises. It also changed many residents' perception of the commercial company in our midst. While previously most of us saw them as a purely benign actor motivated by the altruistic desire to expand affordable housing in an expensive town, now many residents understand that this company is driven by a strong economic interest to deliver profits to their investors with little desire to share power with their renters. This experience taught me a couple of things. It is the company of my neighbors, our conversations, relationships, and organizing, that translated my observation—noticing something unfair—into action. Absent that, noticing that something was unfair may have remained just that—an observation. The translation from noticing to action is easier in a group than as isolated individuals. This experience also reminded me that some changes require repeated collective actions over time—for old and sticky wallpaper, a single event may not be enough to tear it down.

My experience in community action in our neighborhood is consistent with the science of social networks. People get more traction spreading their ideas and getting others to act when they talk to those they know rather than to strangers. Even in the world of social media, where everyone is connected to hundreds of others online, ideas spread faster through connections that have a foundation in real face-to-face relationships. A study conducted with 61 million Facebook users by Robert Bond, a political scientist at the University of California San Diego, showed that people's Facebook messages during the 2010 elections influenced their friends' political expression, information seeking, and voting behavior. The impact was much stronger between real friends who had real in-person rela-tionships than among people connected only through social media.[1] In short, strong ties are instrumental for spreading both online and real-world action in human social networks. If you become aware of inequality or unfairness in your neighborhood or at work, think about the role you might play. How might you spread the word to people you know?

Although we are most influential with people we know com-pared with strangers, there's an exception. Our ideas influence oth-ers who are physically near us even if we don't know them person-ally. The power of physical proximity on persuasion is clear from a study by Cassandra Handan-Nader, a political scientist, and her col-leagues, who examined the impact of a neighbor-to-neighbor grass-roots campaign to get out the vote in a Virginia election. Unpaid volunteers each contacted three registered voters who lived close to them and who were unlikely to vote based on their past voting his-tory. Another group of equally unlikely voters who also lived close to the volunteers weren't contacted. When Handan-Nader compared the behavior of both groups on election day, she found that more people voted if they had been visited by volunteers who lived close to them compared with others who didn't get such a visit. The closer the volunteer lived to the voter, the greater their likelihood of show-ing up at the polls on election day, even though volunteers and vot-ers didn't know each other. Living close together makes it easier to connect with someone new.[2] Perhaps volunteers who were neigh-bors of potential voters gained an edge by having knowledge of local issues important to the voters they visited.

Our Behavior Is Contagious Three Times Removed

Patrick Chettri is a community development facilitator in an ur-ban slum in Kolkata (formerly Calcutta), India. Kolkata was my childhood home, and I'm intimately familiar with the city. Patrick works for World Vision, an international NGO. I met him through a friend. Patrick's territory is Mazdurpara, a slum of thirty-five hundred people living in densely packed makeshift shacks perched on top of a defunct landfill. Mazdurpara is a one-kilometer-long area bounded by an open sewage canal on either side. Its residents are migrant laborers who arrive in Kolkata from adjacent states and villages to look for work. The challenges here are enormous and multilayered. When Patrick started his job, the grinding poverty and illiteracy were accompanied by a flourishing heroin trade. The local mafia used slum dwellers to peddle heroin, which cascaded into other problems—robbery, human trafficking, rape, domestic violence. Patrick's job description was wide open, and he was thrown in with little training. He spent the first six months shell-shocked. To get a clearer sense of the community, Patrick started joining local teenagers for pickup soccer games every morning. This is where he learned about the residents, built trust over time, formed relationships, began to understand the cast of characters, and recognize the trouble spots. Patrick noticed Pappu, a seventeen-year-old, who was popular with teenagers and adults. As they became friendly, Pappu became a liaison to spread Patrick's messages to the broader community. Then there was a group of women volunteers—Sayra, Noor Jahan, Bulbuli, and Shabana—who spent a lot of time inside people's homes, drinking tea and listening to women in each family talk about their problems. These volunteers kept Patrick in the loop about happenings within the social network of womenfolk. Patrick's goal was to engage local children and teenagers in sports, street theater, and education in order to keep them away from drugs and foster a culture of cooperation instead of competition over scarce resources. Over time, the word of the activities of Patrick and his teenage volunteers spread from the soccer group and the children participating in Patrick's enrichment programs to their friends and to friends of friends. Five years later, by the end of Patrick's tenure as a field worker, heroin peddling had receded in Mazdurpara. With it, so had violent crime. And the local mafia that had controlled this slum had lost much of its power in the community.

Research on social networks shows that, like new ideas and behaviors that spread from teenager to teenager in Mazdurpara, our behavior is contagious three times removed, even if we don't know the people we're spreading to. In other words, my words and actions influence not only the person I interact with but also, via that person's words and actions, a second person, and, via the second person's words and actions, a third. Political scientist James Fowler at the University of California San Diego teamed up with sociologist Nicholas Christakis at Harvard University and discovered that cooperative behavior spreads from person to person even when people don't know who they are cooperating with and contact between the two is fleeting. Fowler and Christakis put people in groups of four and gave each person some money. Everyone had a choice to contribute some portion of their money toward a group project or keep all of it for themselves. Individuals had a choice about how generous or stingy to be. Any contribution to the group was equally divided among all four members. In the next round of the game, the same individuals were placed in a different group of four, where they again had a choice to contribute some money to a new group project or keep it all to themselves. In each subsequent round, the process was repeated. Fowler and Christakis found that individuals' behavior in any given round was influenced by other people's prior generosity who were three degrees removed from them and with whom they had no contact. The influence of generosity persisted for multiple exchanges. Each contribution a person made to the larger group in the first round of the game was tripled over the course of the experiment by others who were directly or indirectly influenced to contribute more as a consequence of the previous person's actions. In short, generous behavior spreads in social networks even when people don't know one another and reciprocity is not possible.[3]

It gets better, as David Rand at MIT and his colleagues discovered: because human interactions are dynamic, generosity and cooperation are amplified in social networks. People update their networks strategically by strengthening ties with generous cooperators and breaking ties with individuals who are uncooperative.[4] This creates additional incentives to cooperate and extends the spread of positive norms and actions in social networks.

In the Mazdurpara slum, despite its social and economic constraints, when incentives were right, residents often chose to strengthen relationships with generous cooperators and distance themselves from others who were uncooperative. Iqbal, a teenager at Mazdurpara, was initially in Patrick's youth network but drifted away as he got deeper into heroin peddling. But he maintained a loose connection with Patrick. When Iqbal got roughed up by local mafia members who thought he was stealing from them, he reached out to Patrick for help. Patrick connected him to a local ward councilor and put in a good word, which helped Iqbal strengthen cooperative connections within his community, find a job, and break the toxic connections to the local mafia.

The Power of Central Roles in a Network

Collective action in local spaces often starts with a few people in the center of a social network who are connected to many others. In the Mazdurpara slum, Patrick identified ten teenagers who were heavily involved in youth activities and curious about the new guy in the neighborhood. They were early adopters of the new ideas Patrick was spreading—the importance of education, teamwork, generosity, and the ambition to be better. He persuaded them to partic-

NETWORK FOR SOCIAL JUSTICE

ipate in World Vision's training and take over the leadership of the children's club. These teen leaders encouraged other youth to get involved in team sports and street theater, pulled them into collaborative cookouts, and persuaded them to go to school. Collectively, they redirected young people's attention away from substance use and drug peddling by providing a new sense of direction. As word about the children's club spread, it attracted more youth in the slum to join.

Many thousand miles away in my neighborhood in Northampton, Massachusetts, it was one couple who noticed that renters didn't have a voice in local governance. They were the ones who reached out to a few of their friends and acquaintances to take the pulse of local opinion. In both examples, a few individuals emerged as central players in their local neighborhood: the couple in my neighborhood and the ten teenagers in Mazdurpara. These individuals had special influence because of their ties to many others and because people liked and respected them. Their relationships gave them frequent opportunities to spread information, persuade others, and encourage them to act. In our neighborhood, my husband and I were easily convinced of the unfairness of ignoring the voices of low-income neighborhood residents. We were among the early adopters.

Network science shows that during initial activity around a new idea, a cluster of influencers who occupy central roles and early adopters reinforce one another's behavior and, with some coordination, can successfully spread the idea and generate action. People become early adopters of an idea or action when they learn about it from individuals with whom they have strong ties and who occupy central roles in the network. Others on the sidelines slowly become persuaded when a large number of people with whom they have weaker ties start adopting the idea. Endorsement of an idea or action by a critical mass of people gives it greater legitimacy.[5]

Those who occupy central roles in a network have special power to change their local culture in several ways. By what they say and do, these individuals shift social norms. In a series of studies Raina Brands, a management scientist, and Aneeta Rattan, a social psychologist at the London School of Business, learned that women to whom coworkers come for advice occupy central roles in the workplace, even though these roles might be informal. These central influencers are more likely to confront instances of gender bias at work than others who occupy peripheral roles. People around them see the women in central roles as more confident and expect them to stand up against sexism. By taking advantage of their central position and speaking up, these women become models for others and shift norms in the workplace.[6]

The same principle applies outside work. When Noor Jahan, who calls Mazdurpara home, started working for World Vision in 2001, many families around her had more than ten children. Family planning and birth control weren't part of the local culture. As Noor Jahan visited young women and their mothers-in-law in each household, she often spoke up about the benefits of family planning and birth control and offered to connect the women to a local health clinic. It took several years for her counsel to make a difference. Over time, as birth control became frequently discussed in women's circles, and as the women struggled to manage large families, the idea became normalized. Noor Jahan started to notice that mothers would tell their daughters, daughters-in-law, and other women friends about birth control. In ten years, the number of children per family dropped to four or five. Another ten years later, it's down to one or two children per family.

Advice from some types of people in central roles rubs off on advice-seekers particularly well based on the context. Herminia Ibarra and Steven Andrews at Harvard University found that employees' perceptions of their organization's culture are shaped by whom they get professional advice from, more than by who their friends are. People in an organization who are commonly sought out for work-related advice by their coworkers occupy central roles in the advice network. They have access to information, resources, and legitimacy. Advice from them shapes the opinions and experience of their coworkers who are advice-seekers. Connections with other people who may be popular as friends have less impact on employees' experiences of workplace quality. Put simply, when it comes to work, professional advice networks matter more than friendship networks.[7] People who occupy central roles in workplace networks may be informal advice-givers or they may be in formal managerial roles. In his research, Kai Lamertz, a management scientist, found that employees' beliefs about the fairness of their organization were connected to the opinions of informal advice-givers as well as to solid relationships with managers who opened access to upper levels of the organizational hierarchy.[8]

Role Centrality and Good Listening

Patrick's reputation in the Mazdurpara community was as someone who listened to everyone—whether it was a kid, an adult, a drug dealer, or a drunk. He was attentive and listened to anyone who wanted to speak with him. People in the community joked that, although he listened closely, he later did what he thought was right regardless of what the speaker wanted. Over time, the ability to listen made him become an important influencer in the slum. As we have seen, influential people in a network are centrally located and connected to lots of other people. But that doesn't mean they do all the talking. In fact, in networks where knowledge is distributed rather than concentrated, the most influential people are not the well-connected talkers, but rather the well-connected listeners who proactively seek out the opinions of others to whom they are connected. When reaching a consensus within a network, people tend to be swayed by the opinions of influential listeners.

Economist Luca Corazzini and his colleagues at the University of Padua in Italy conducted a fascinating study looking at who is persuasive within social networks in which each person has bits and pieces of information and nobody has all the information. They connected individual research volunteers to a few others in the network and varied the direction of communication among them. Some people were speakers who spread their opinion to their interaction partners. Other people were listeners who received opinions from their interaction partners. And yet others were speakers with some partners and listeners with others. After many rounds of communication, Corazzini found that how persuasive people became depended not only on how many others they spoke to but also on how many others they listened to. In fact, individuals' influence grew as the number of people they listened to increased.[9] In converging research, Dan Ames, a social psychologist at Columbia University, and his colleagues asked people to anonymously evaluate their coworkers' listening skills, speaking ability, and ability to persuade others. They found that regardless of people's communication skills, those who were evaluated as good listeners, who were able to get others to open up, share information, and listen to alternate points of view, were significantly more successful at persuading others, building coalitions, and getting tasks done.[10]

When Noor Jahan and Sayra, who work for World Vision, visit families in the slum, their goal is to listen. The women they visit are eager to have someone hear their concerns. Sometimes Sayra and Noor Jahan might ask follow-up questions and offer suggestions. But mostly they just listen. These listening sessions happen frequently and allow these volunteers to help women in these families get the resources they need to start a business, access medical care, or find a sympathetic ear when they have relationship problems. Listening also helps Noor Jahan and Sayra identify common needs emerging in the neighborhood and to organize all-community educational programs targeting those common issues. By prioritizing active listening, Sayra and Noor Jahan gained the respect of the women they visited and were able to nudge individuals toward behavior changes to improve children's education and women's health and to reduce child labor. Coalitions of these individuals formed and grew sufficient momentum to bring about community-level change around particular issues.

From Intergroup Contact to Collective Action

When people who don't know each other initially meet across group lines, especially when their groups are sharply different in power and status, the initial interaction often has an undercurrent of wariness and apprehension. You may have witnessed this or experienced it yourself during interactions involving people of different races, ethnicities, religions, castes, social classes, or gender identities. The person from the high-status group implicitly wants reassurance that the person from the lower-status group likes them and sees them as a good person, whereas the individual from the lower-status group wants to know that the higher-status person respects them and takes them seriously.[11] Frequent positive cross-group interactions involving the same people shifts this dynamic toward greater trust and empathy, reduces bias, and fosters real relationships, as we saw in Chapter 5.[12]

For members of high-status groups, trust, empathy, and relational bonds increase awareness of inequality and encourage solidarity, including support for and willingness to participate in social movements promoting greater equality. But for members of low-status groups positive interaction with high-status group members has a paradoxical effect. It is associated with less awareness of discrimination and structural problems, less support for social change, and less willingness to participate in collective action.[13] Consider this example from South Africa, where thirty years after the legal end of Apartheid, race-related inequalities persist. White South Africans continue to have significant socioeconomic advantages over other groups in the country, even though Black South Africans are in political power and are the numeric majority. When social psychologists Huseyin Cakal, Miles Hewstone, and Gerhard Schwär surveyed 1,464 Black and white South Africans at a racially mixed university, they found that for white students, the more positive interracial interactions and friendships they shared with Black peers the more willing they were to support university and government policies aimed to improve the lives of Black South Africans. But for Black South African students, the effect was opposite. The more positive interactions and friendships they had with white peers, the less disadvantaged they felt relative to white South Africans, and the less they supported university and government policies aimed at improving Black South Africans' lives, presumably because they thought these affirmative actions were no longer necessary.[14]

This paradox starts to make sense if you listen in on what people talk about when they interact with others across group lines. In such conversations, individuals from high-status groups typically avoid talking about power relations and mostly focus on cross-group similarities, which demobilizes their lower-status conversation partner by drawing attention away from structural inequalities. But when high-status individuals talk about their own group's privilege and power, acknowledge its illegitimacy, communicate their respect for the less-privileged group, and express their support for efforts to increase intergroup equality, it moves the conversation beyond warm and fuzzy feelings for each other as individuals, toward greater solidarity and the desire to act collectively for justice as illustrated in Figure 9. This theme emerges in many countries. It is

9. Greater insight motivates people to
rally together in support of local change.

evident in the United States and Europe, in studies investigating the
types of interracial, interethnic, and gay-straight conversations that
mobilize solidarity and support for collective action across group
lines. Similar findings emerge in South Africa when white South Africans have conversations with Black South Africans acknowledg-
ing the illegitimacy of their group's privilege and in Turkey when
ethnic Turks have similar conversations with Kurds who have less
power and status. In a nutshell, while interacting with people from
different groups over time is an important first step, to take that to
the next level and convert talking into meaningful action requires
having some hard conversations.[15]

Use Your Individual Behavior to Create
the Conditions for Structural Change

If you want to use your network to promote social justice, begin
with three steps.

- Notice what's going on in your local environment—notice people around you, how they relate to one another, the issues they are talking about, and how they approach them.

- Listen to a wide variety of people; especially those different from you—be curious; ask questions to deepen your understanding; listen more and speak less.

- Once you've identified key concerns, reach out and gather people to join a conversation and explore next steps.

As you notice and listen, focus on the 3Rs where inequity and injustice usually hide: Rules, Resources, and Recognition. What are the rules that guide how things get done in the work, social, or neighborhood organizations to which you belong? These may be formal rules or informal practices that become de facto rules. For example, at work, school, or in your local community, do rules or informal customs lead some people to have a seat at the decision-making table while others don't have a voice? Do rules or customs lead some people's interests or concerns to get prioritized while others' concerns rarely get discussed or resolved?

For resources, notice whether there is a pattern such that some people get tapped for special opportunities, a chance to serve on an important team, and leadership development, while others don't, creating everyday inequalities in resource distribution. Notice whether some people get precious time with the boss, an important visitor, or a client while others don't. At your child's school or university, ask whether some students get special attention and opportunities from teachers or coaches while others don't. Your understanding of these issues will probably require attention to the subtleties of your local culture and active listening to a broad array of people.

Pay attention to recognition, as well: Who gets elevated through awards and who doesn't? Whose work is publicly praised by leaders in your organization and whose is not? In your child's school, notice whether some students' accomplishments are elevated to the broader community through news and social media while others' accomplishments get less attention.

You can apply these takeaways to your workplace, volunteer organization, your child's school, or your neighborhood. If you're someone to whom people come for advice, even if informally, it means you occupy a central position in your network and have special power to change its local culture. So speak up on others' behalf if you notice something that's unfair. Some may share your concern even if they have not voiced it publicly. Others who have not thought about this issue before might start listening to your opinions. It may get them to notice something that had previously been part of the wallpaper and inform their future actions. This is an opportunity to create an alliance, act collectively, and build momentum for small-scale changes in your local environment, much like the actions of Sayra, Noor Jahan, and Patrick in Mazdurpara, and that of my neighbors in Northampton, Massachusetts, who noticed something unfair and decided to do something about it collectively.

8

TALENT IS MADE, NOT BORN

How to Transform Potential into Excellence

For doctors battling COVID-19 on the front lines, Kizzmekia Corbett is an inspiration. She led a team of researchers at the National Institutes of Health that developed one of the world's first COVID-19 vaccines. Corbett attributes her success to her undergraduate experience in the Meyerhoff Scholars Program at the University of Maryland Baltimore County. "Had I not been exposed to . . . the Meyerhoff Program . . . I'm not even so sure that I would be a scientist." The program "is a place where every single person was special and would be loved. The goal is not to fail you out, but to lift you up," Corbett says.[1]

Since its inception in 1989 the Meyerhoff Scholars Program has launched the careers of eleven hundred Black and Hispanic students. It welcomes students of all ethnicities and backgrounds who want to pursue science and engineering and who are also committed to issues of diversity, inclusion, and social justice. Between 1989 and 2018, 71 percent of almost fifteen hundred students in the program have been Black or Hispanic, 84 percent of whom graduated with science or engineering bachelor's degrees. And 76 percent of graduates went on to pursue graduate or professional degrees. Because of the Meyerhoff program, University of Maryland Baltimore

County is the number one originator of Black scientists who received joint MD and PhD degrees in the United States.[2]

Adrian Davey was sitting in the back of his church when he first heard of the program that would change his life. Davey, then a high school senior, was finishing high school strong. Tanya Davis, a fellow congregant at First Missionary Baptist Church, had some advice: "You should apply to the Meyerhoff program." Four years later, he was a leader on campus, mentoring younger students and conducting original research on air pollution sensors. He's also a poet and an aspiring young adult novelist.[3]

Strong Bonds, Norms, and the Consistent Application of Effort

The wisdom of the Meyerhoff program comes from the recognition that growing the next generation of scientists, engineers, and doctors who are Black and Hispanic requires more than scouting for the best and most brilliant superstars. We often mistakenly think that talent is a fixed property of individuals—we talk of finding "the best person." Looking for "the best" assumes that talent is an innate fixed quality waiting only to be discovered. The Meyerhoff program is built on a different philosophy: that talent is made, not born. While people may come with some inner raw potential, the direction that takes depends on the training environment. Potential will grow in a rich environment but wither in a harsh one. Meyerhoff cultivates that talent by immersion in an enriched environment with a high-quality training regimen.

The Meyerhoff program's curated environment has three critical ingredients. First, the program gives primacy to human relationships—young people are expected to look out for each other and are supported by close relationships with faculty and staff. Second, students are not just in the program for themselves; they are encouraged to pay it forward by mentoring younger students and through community service. Third, students are expected to apply consistent effort and practice to learn, refine, and master new skills. Consistency of effort is the gold standard. Being the best is not a priority. These three social norms—the wallpaper of the program—fulfill three core human needs: to belong, to feel competent, and to create a path that is personally meaningful. The Meyerhoff program has spread to several universities across the United States, with the ultimate aim of scaling nationally and growing a diverse generation of budding scientists and engineers.[4]

My colleagues and I experimented with creating a local culture to lift up working-class students who are first in their family to attend college, allowing them to flourish. Many working-class students feel a dissonance between their interdependent family-oriented culture at home and the typical American university culture, which emphasizes independence, self-directed learning, and pursuit of knowledge for its own sake. These students feel alone and different from classmates raised in college-educated families who know how to operate within the university system. Many working-class students struggle academically and are at high risk of dropping out without a college degree. What if we created a community-oriented living-learning environment in the first year of college just for these students? Would that ease their transition, allow them to find their feet, and close the achievement gap between working-class students and their economically privileged peers? To answer these questions, we conducted a study in which we invited low-income first-generation students who were about to start college to apply to join a living-learning community with peers from similar backgrounds. We called the program BioPioneers and targeted students with an interest in biological and health sciences. Among students who applied to this program, we used a random lottery system to accept half the applicants for the limited seats, then compared them with the other, equally qualified, half who were not admitted—our comparison group.

Randy Le was a student in the BioPioneers program. He moved from Texas to the University of Massachusetts in the fall of 2018. You might remember Randy from Chapter 1. As the child of low-income immigrants Randy grew up quickly. His parents are Vietnamese immigrants who came to the United States in 1995 and worked many jobs to give their children a better life—at a 7-Eleven, a grocery store, a nail salon, a florist. Randy and his sister were informal English translators for their parents and took care of paying bills and interacting with the English-speaking American society outside the family. As a result of his role in the family, Randy was used to being independent. When he enrolled at UMass, he was fine academically but struggled to adjust socially. By the middle of his first semester Randy was terribly homesick. He stopped caring about school and wondered whether he should transfer to a different college in Texas. One day in October, his first semester in college, two friends from the BioPioneers program showed up in his dorm. "What's up?" they said. Everything tumbled out from inside Randy—the homesickness, the apathy, the thoughts of leaving UMass and going back home. That was the first time he had opened himself up to others. "This is what it's like to depend on others," he later thought. "BioPioneers was probably the best decision I made," he said to me, reflecting back. Being around other low-income students made him feel normal. His closest friends in college came from the program. The biggest lesson he took away from BioPioneers is the mantra "you are not alone."

That feeling of safety while being vulnerable, of knowing that his friends cared for him and that he could trust them, gave Randy the courage to open up to his biology professor Randall Phillis and his adviser Linda Ziegenbein. Randy loved Professor Phillis's biology class. He marveled at his professor's passion for the subject and wanted to be like him. He later became a teaching assistant for Professor Phillis. Randy's initial goal in college had been to make his parents happy. But through his experience in BioPioneers and advice from friends and professors, he started considering, "How can I make both my parents and me happy?" A research presentation on health disparities caught his attention. A pamphlet in his adviser's office about an internship opportunity at the National Institutes of Health in Washington, DC, made a possible path more concrete. The intellectual exposure to biology his first year, together with the strong bonds he had developed with fellow BioPioneer students, his professor, and his adviser, helped keep him on the path through the horrible COVID-19 pandemic during his sophomore and junior years, when he applied to the NIH fellowship with support from his faculty adviser. The BioPioneers program helped Randy make connections. It exposed him to research conferences and medical research labs at the UMass medical school, and it helped him learn to write in a compelling way. When I spoke to Randy, he had just started a research fellowship at the NIH. And he was exploring the possibility of pursuing dual MD and PhD degrees in medicine and biochemistry.

Randy's experience is not an outlier. He is emblematic of most students in BioPioneers. We tracked the progress of all students in the BioPioneers program through their first year in college and one year after they had left the program. As a group, on average, BioPioneers students expressed significantly more sense of belonging in science, had more motivation and confidence in their academic ability, and were less anxious and self-doubting than students in the comparison group. Their biology grades were substantially higher, and they remained in science majors at a higher rate than the comparison group one year after they had completed the program. We also compared BioPioneers students to another group of honors students who mostly came from more affluent, college-educated families, who were participating in a separate living-learning program. We found that BioPioneers students persisted in science majors at the same rate as honors students. Their self-confidence in their science ability, their motivation to persist, and their feelings of belonging were the same as those of honors students. Essentially, participation in the BioPioneers residential program for one year closed the achievement gap between working-class students and their peers from economically advantaged backgrounds. In contrast, working-class students in the comparison group who, by lottery, didn't get to experience BioPioneers lagged behind the other two groups.[5]

The key to success was the structure of the living-learning community and its wallpaper of social norms that emphasized communal and collaborative learning with peers and caring relationships with professors and staff. Students took their first two biology classes together as a cohort. They also took a seminar together where they learned about biomedical research and met professors, including some who were, like the students, the first in their family to attend college. Participating students' roommates were also fellow students in the same program. Each student had a peer mentor who was also from a working-class family. These peer-to-peer relationships normalized the presence of working-class people in college. Bonds were strengthened through social events and camaraderie. By the end of the first year, participating students had acclimated to college life, found their support system, and were ready for the rigors ahead.

Our BioPioneers program and the Meyerhoff program are not isolated examples. A growing number of studies and systematic reviews show that programs that bring together groups of students who otherwise feel out of place in college create a culture of companionship and interdependent learning, and boost students' sense of belonging and self-confidence.[6] These feelings ground students in the local ecology and power their performance and persistence.

Other successful initiatives are summer bridge programs that occur before college entry; others take place in the first year of college.[7] They are effective when they create affinity groups of students from similar or overlapping identity groups—working-class backgrounds, Black, Hispanic, and Native American students—who often enter college with fewer material resources and fewer academic opportunities in high school.

The wisdom of these programs is the recognition that learning is not confined to traditional classrooms. It also happens informally in college dorms and cafeterias, as well as through extracurricular activities that grow a web of relationships, as illustrated by Randy Le's experience. Moreover, learning is not just about the subject matter of academic disciplines. It includes understanding the culture and expectations of an unfamiliar system, acquiring resources and developing adaptive habits to navigate it. Immersive cohort-based programs during the transition to college make explicit the unspoken rules of the game in college and familiarize students with campus resources they can utilize. Studies show that students are more likely to use campus resources if they hear from senior peers with whom they share a common social identity about the challenges those students faced and overcame by using those same resources.

Social psychologist Gerardo Ramirez and his colleagues followed a group of summer bridge program participants, most of whom were students of color, first-generation students, and/or low-income students. All participants received information about campus resources to assist their learning. But only half of them also heard from senior first-generation college students of color who shared personal stories about encountering and overcoming obstacles in college related to their racial identities and first-generation status with the help of campus resources. Stories from senior peers made those resources personally relevant to incoming students and created a mental map of how they might use the same assets in their own lives as they navigated the university system. Students in the resources-plus-stories group became more interested in using campus resources to support their college journey than did those who did not hear accounts from senior peers.[8] In another study by social psychologist Nicole Stephens and her team, using campus resources and forming relationships with faculty improved working-class students' end-of-year grades and closed the achievement gap between them and their peers from college-educated families.[9] An important goal of immersive programs for cohorts of incoming students from historically underserved backgrounds is to make it easier for them to approach and form strong relationships with faculty, who are important sources of social capital in university life, through both formal and informal interactions. Once formed, these high-value relationships open doors to new opportunities and assist students in overcoming barriers as they navigate college life.

When field experiments like BioPioneers demonstrate that cohort-based programs clearly and consistently enhance student success and well-being, social science researchers often share their results with college and university leaders. In the ideal scenario, campus leaders who are attuned to research-informed decision-making adopt these programs and implement them on their campus for all students from underserved groups. At the University of Massachusetts, the BioPioneers program has now expanded and spread to working-class students in other academic majors, given research evidence of its impact. Leaders who understand the benefits of data-informed decisions are quick to leverage programs and initiatives informed by social science research that converge with their organizational mission. But that doesn't always happen. There is often a gap in knowledge transfer and translation between social scientists who do this type of research and organizational leaders who are in positions to convert the lessons into policies, programs, and practice. Many organizational leaders don't look for research evidence to inform such decisions. Thankfully, some do.

Informal groups in the workplace have similar benefits for people who are underrepresented in their organization—women, people of color, lesbian, gay, and trans employees. Employee resource groups, as they are called, are voluntary employee-led networks where people come together with others who share their identity and have encountered similar challenges of exclusion. Colleagues provide social and professional support to one another through mentoring and information sharing, and by increasing the visibility of their group to senior leaders. Some employee resource groups focus mostly on empowering individuals to navigate and advance within the existing organizational system by increasing individual opportunity. Others aim to challenge the system. Yet others try to strike a balance between the two.[10] Using data from one large company with more than 100,000 employees across multiple states, Raymond Friedman, a management scientist, and his colleagues found that Black, Hispanic, and Asian employees who joined race-specific employee resource groups felt more included in their organization and more connected professionally and socially. Black managers expressed optimism about career advancement and were interested in staying in the organization. Similar findings were echoed across several studies.[11] Employee resource groups that are geared toward personal support and professional mobility are good for individuals but less effective in motivating structural changes in organizations. But powerful organizational transformation is possible when individuals coalesce within these groups and use their collective influence to push for structural change.

At Metropolitan Healthcare, a group of gay and lesbian employees gathered informally over dinner in 1985. Their dinner conversation sparked a monthly event with a slightly larger group of employees. By 1989 this group had grown to fifteen employees who had become visible within their organization as an informal gay and lesbian group. In 1993, the group sent two of its informal leaders to approach management and advocate for three pressing issues: expansion of the company's nondiscrimination statement to include sexual orientation; expansion of company-sponsored healthcare benefits to include domestic partners of gay and lesbian employees, who couldn't get legally married at the time in the United States; and improvement of the sometimes-hostile climate toward lesbian and gay workers. Two years later, the company's leaders expanded the organizational nondiscrimination statement. The workplace climate was slowly improving. Healthcare benefits for partners of LGBT employees proved to be a longer-term issue that eventually was resolved in 2004.

The story of Metropolitan Healthcare is a perfect example of how informal individual interactions grow into relationships, start conversations about shared concerns and inequalities, and create a grassroots alliance around these issues, leading people to act collectively and purposefully to push for structural change within their organization. For the first fifteen years or so, the LGBT group was informal, operating without official recognition. In 2000, its members asked for company recognition as an employee network, naming themselves LGBT and Allies Network, and including transgender people within their scope, with the idea that official recognition would advance their cause. Along the way, employees in this group reached out to straight coworkers, managers, and the employee union to inform, educate, and convert them into allies.[12] Similar activities were taking place at other large companies across the United States. Momentum accelerated in the early 2000s, when the adoption of domestic partner benefits at several large companies led to systemic change in the civil rights for gays and lesbians in the

10. Collective action empowers individuals, increasing their
willingness to act in solidarity with others now and in the future.

United States. Employees with same-sex partners finally began seeing policy changes and material benefits to address long-standing
inequalities.[13]

For people who face enduring societal barriers and inequality,
being in a workplace, school, or other organization that provides opportunities to connect with similar others strengthens belonging,
makes room to discover shared concerns, and creates a sense of collective agency to act together and advocate for the removal of barriers, as illustrated in Figure 10. Collective action is the critical step to
transform individual behavior into broader structural change.

Emphasize Social Good as the Purpose of Work

Individuals' potential and promise bloom into excellence more easily when the environment around them facilitates work that is personally meaningful and contributes to social good. Jessica Moseley's
story illustrates that well. Moseley is the adult child of deaf adults.

Both her parents are deaf, and American Sign Language is her first language. She considers the deaf community her family and the culture in which she feels most like herself. Moseley saw her parents struggle in their daily lives and in their small business to communicate with their hearing colleagues who didn't know sign language. Moseley became their interpreter at a young age. When her parents experienced personnel problems in 2008, they called her to help replace an employee. She ended up becoming that replacement. But before long, motivated by her desire to have an impact, with her mother she restructured the family business into a sign language–interpreting agency with sixty-two employees and $6.5 million in revenue. Today, Jessica Moseley is the CEO at TCS Interpreting, a provider of sign language–interpreting services nationwide. "Watching my parents succeed, after seeing the obstacles and challenges they constantly faced, was incredibly motivating," she said. "I wake up every day motivated to make a positive impact in our community."[14]

The desire to pursue personally meaningful work is a fundamental motivation that guides people's choices. When people can connect their work to a problem or concern that is relevant to their family or community, an issue they care about, it keeps them engaged and persistent. Economist Ina Ganguli, April Burrage, and I discovered that the motivation to prioritize social good in one's professional life drives women more than men. "What motivates you?" we asked a group of scientists, engineers, and technologists who had expressed interest in learning about entrepreneurship to convert their research outputs into commercial goods and services. Compared with men, women replied that solving social problems was their driving purpose more than profit. In another study we sent emails inviting more than nine thousand scientists, engineers, technologists, and their graduate students to participate in entrepreneurship training workshops that would teach them how to translate their scientific discoveries into business products and services. For half of the recipients, the subject line of the email invitation read, "Learn to Translate Your Research to Address a Societal Challenge" accompanied by an image of a green planet in a pair of hands. For the remaining recipients, the subject line read "Learn to Translate Your Research to Create a Breakthrough Product" accompanied by an image of a light bulb in a pair of hands. The content of the email was otherwise identical. We found that women were more interested in entrepreneurship training when it was framed as promoting social impact rather than commercial impact. Men were equally interested in entrepreneurship training regardless of how the email message was framed.[15] Along the same lines, economist Jorge Guzman and his colleagues at Columbia University found that women technology entrepreneurs were more responsive to recruiting messages that emphasized social impact rather than monetary profit, while men were more motivated by profit than social impact.[16]

Taking it one step further, organizations' motives influence who is attracted or repelled. When organizations emphasize a social justice motive as the primary reason for why diversity and inclusion matter to their mission, they attract more women, gays and lesbians, and African Americans as prospective employees. However, when they emphasize a profit motive, arguing that diversity is good for business and the bottom line, the same people are alienated. Imagine you are looking for a new job. You come across an organization that is looking to hire. As you check out its website, you come across the following statement.

Diversity and inclusion are part of our company's commitment to equality. Behind this focus is a simple but powerful idea: that diversity simply is the right thing to do. Our diversity and inclusion initiatives drive a sense of community

by advancing our values of respecting, supporting, and nur-
turing diverse talents. We also strive to create an environment in which our company can empower our diverse employees to grow and thrive as human beings whose ideas are
heard and appreciated.

Or imagine you see a different statement on the site:

Diversity and inclusion are part of our company's commitment to performance. Behind this focus is a simple but powerful idea: that diversity simply makes good business sense.
Our diversity and inclusion initiatives drive positive business results by advancing our reputation to attract, retain,
and engage diverse talents. We also strive to create an environment in which our company can leverage the unique
contributions of our diverse employees to develop innovative solutions for our diverse customer base.

Which of these messages makes you feel like you would belong in
this organization? Which one makes you feel valued? Would you be
interested in applying for a job here? These are the questions social psychologists Oriane Georgeac and Aneeta Rattan asked their
research participants, who were lesbian, gay, bisexual, transgender,
and queer professionals attending a large conference in their field.
Some conference attendees were shown a statement that emphasized a social justice–oriented reason for promoting diversity and
inclusion in an organization, while others were shown a statement
that emphasized the business case for valuing diversity in the same
organization. LGBTQ professionals who were randomly assigned
to read the organization's social justice statement anticipated feeling more connected to that institution and expressed more interest in applying for the advertised job than other LGBTQ people who

read the diversity-is-good-for-business statement. Another study revealed similar results: Black professionals and soon-to-graduate Black college seniors were attracted to organizations whose message emphasized a social justice motive as the reason for their commitment to diversity and inclusion rather than a profit motive. In other words, a focus on "the bottom line" made Black, gay, lesbian, and transgender people feel they were merely tools to help the business make money.[17] This makes sense—the "good for business" argument is great for shareholders and leaders at the top of organizations who profit from their commercial success, but it doesn't necessarily benefit rank-and-file employees.

Emphasizing social good is important to people early in life, when they are as young as thirteen and fourteen, we discovered. My research team and I spent five years observing the culture of 317 mathematics classrooms in ten middle schools across the country that touched the lives of almost three thousand students. We learned that when some teachers taught math, they talked about how this subject is used to solve social problems, while other teachers made no mention of the social relevance of math. As we followed students across the school year, we discovered that when teenagers understood the social relevance of math, they felt a stronger sense of belonging in math class, more confidence in their math ability, and more motivation. These psychological ingredients, in turn, nudged them to participate more actively in class, produced better end-of-year grades, and made math more important to students' sense of self. Amplifying the social relevance of math was particularly energizing for Black and Hispanic adolescents in predominantly white classes. Increased sense of belonging in math also boosted their math grades at the end of the school year—an effect that was not observed for white students. Greater belonging also predicted stronger math identification for Black and Hispanic adolescents compared with their white peers.[18]

An emphasis on social good inspired Jessica Moseley to start a company that offered sign language–interpreting services nationwide. Social good is also embedded in the ethos of community service of the Meyerhoff Scholars Program that Kizzmekia Corbett attended. And interest in social good is exactly what motivated Randy Le to pursue a career applying science to remedy health disparities. Randy is interested in genetics research—he wants to study genetic variations that increase the risk of certain diseases among some racial or ethnic groups and other genetic variations that provide resilience to diseases. The common thread is that when the local culture of classrooms, project teams, and organizations makes social good an important value that is connected to the work done there, it attracts diverse people, motivates them, enhances their performance, and keeps them engaged over the long haul.

Cultivating Collective Intelligence

The Wang School of Elite Sports in the heart of Oslo, Norway, has been training teenage student-athletes in twenty sports since 1984. The school trained many junior prospects, converting them into national senior athletes. Among the most successful is the flat-water kayak team. More than half of all paddlers in Norway's senior national team attended the Wang School. Norwegian paddlers have won medals at every Olympic Games from 1992 to 2008. Key to their success is a holistic approach to talent development that stresses the local ecology of the training culture, starting with collaborative relationships among athletes. As one coach remarked, "The relationship between prospects and elite athletes is immensely important. The athletes learn training culture, technique, everything. I call it osmosis because knowledge simply diffuses. The athletes don't know who taught them what, but they have learned the trade. I believe all Norwegian top paddlers are a product of a little help here and there rather than one coach or one program." One prospect added, "All sports have their role models. What is unique for our environment is that I actually meet these role models every day. I try to beat them in training and I listen to their advice." Another commented, "Just as I stretch to reach the elite paddlers, so too these young paddlers stretch to reach me. In a hard training session, I paddle the waves of the elite athletes, and in a slower session, the youngsters paddle my wave."[19]

Kristoffer Henriksen, a sports psychologist, and his colleagues identified key ingredients of the athletic culture at Wang School's kayak club in Norway. At the center are collaborative relationships between junior prospects, senior athletes, and coaches. The club has surprisingly limited financial resources but benefits from a world-class natural environment in a fjord that provides perfect conditions for flat-water racing. Key values, norms, and stories define its culture. The most salient value is being an inclusive community open to all motivated young paddlers. It's the norm for athletes at different skill levels to train together. Junior prospects ride the waves of more experienced paddlers. The respect and recognition associated with being a senior athlete at the top of the hierarchy motivates them to include younger athletes in their training. The club's core belief is that motivation, discipline, and autonomy are more important than innate potential. Completing hard training sessions and tests are the true markers of future excellence. Defining talent as persistent effort and discipline is conveyed through a frequently repeated story about a Norwegian Olympic champion's lack of natural aptitude for the sport. "In his early years he was certainly not among the best. But he managed to train hard, stay motivated and improve a little bit every day, and today he is among the best in the world," says a young prospect. Another core belief is that talent requires social skills so that athletes can collaborate effectively with others at diverse skill levels and create a productive community.

A very different local context—eighth grade classrooms—provides converging evidence for a similar idea. In our study of adolescent students, we found that some teachers emphasized collaborative learning in their classrooms, organizing students to work together in pairs or small groups, while other teachers emphasized individual learning, giving students tasks to work on independently. We found that when adolescents worked collaboratively with peers, they expressed more belonging in math class, which translated into more in-class participation and increased the importance of math to their sense of self. Increased belonging boosted students' math grades at the end of the school year—an effect that was stronger for Black and Hispanic students than for their white peers.

The Wang School's kayak club in Norway, the Meyerhoff program in Baltimore, and eighth grade collaboration-oriented algebra classes in my research all take a holistic approach to talent development. Research from other sports, including soccer, track and field, and sailing, also show the benefits of holistic talent development that cultivates a critical set of social norms in the training environment.[20] These norms not only elevate the importance of consistent effort to master hard skills, but also prioritize social skills, collaboration, strong bonds among students, teachers, and coaches, as well as mentorship of beginners. Together, these norms fulfill athletes' need to belong in the training environment, to reach for higher levels of competence, and to pursue a path that is personally meaningful. By living through this process, individuals' potential gets converted into excellence over time.

Strong bonds and collaboration not only help individuals, but they also magnify the effectiveness of teams. The collective intelligence of collaborative teams is more than the sum of intelligent individuals, finds Anita Woolley, a cognitive scientist, and her colleagues. A group's collective intelligence predicts its superior performance on complex tasks better than the aggregated intelligence of all its individual members. The secret sauce of collective intelligence comes from group members aligning their skills with their contribution, sharing responsibilities strategically, being perceptive of and responsive to each other's feelings, and communicating frequently and cooperatively, without a few voices dominating. The more women in a group, the greater the group's social perceptiveness, and the more its collective intelligence. Being tuned into one another's emotion—the essence of social perceptiveness—is one critical ingredient of collective intelligence.[21]

Social perceptiveness in groups allows people to feel psychologically safe taking interpersonal risks, speaking up, asking for help, and admitting mistakes with confidence that their team won't embarrass, reject, or punish them. This confidence comes from mutual respect and trust. Numerous studies show that when people in work teams feel psychologically safe, the team's learning and performance is of substantially higher quality than when psychological safety is low.[22] Although psychological safety matters to most people working in groups and teams, it is particularly important to individuals in environments where few others share their identity— such as racial and ethnic minority employees in predominantly white organizations.

This is consistent with Knatokie Ford's experience at Harvard. You'll recall that when she started her PhD at Harvard, Knatokie rarely saw students or professors like her. She was often the only Black student in class and felt paralyzed by the fear of saying something wrong and confirming what she thought everyone around her suspected—that as a woman and person of color she wasn't supposed to be good at science anyway. Her experience revealed a poignant lack of psychological safety. As we have seen, she left Harvard after her first year. When she returned after a long hiatus, one choice that made a big difference the second time around was the faculty mentor she chose, who had created a research team that was diverse, collaborative, and friendly. The atmosphere in that team gave Knatokie the psychological safety to thrive, to grow as a scientist and as a human being. This time she finished her PhD. Knatokie's experience the second time around is consistent with the results from an employee survey conducted at a midwestern company by Barjinder Singh, a management scientist. Singh found that employees' job performance was of higher quality when they felt psychologically safe expressing their opinions to their colleagues and felt that the workplace climate was fair. These associations were stronger for Black, Hispanic, Asian, and multiracial employees than for white employees.[23]

In another survey of more than one thousand women managers across multiple industries nationwide, Susan Ashford, a management scientist, and her colleagues learned that women who saw their organization as supportive, with norms that encouraged raising concerns, and who had trusting relationships with key decision makers, felt safe voicing concerns about gender inequity at work without worrying that others would reject their concerns. Women managers' comfort and willingness to speak up were shaped entirely by their local work environment and the norms and relationships within it, not by such features of the larger organization as its top-level leaders or upper organizational structure, nor by their own individual personalities.[24]

The implication is that psychological safety within a local environment where people live, work, and interact with colleagues is a vital ingredient that allows them to speak up, challenge the status quo, identify problems to organizational leaders, offer ideas for improvement, and nudge their organization to learn and change. When individuals speak up and others echo the same concern, the result is an amplified group voice that's more powerful in encouraging organizational change. Do the norms in your work team feel safe so that you and others can speak up about equity concerns? Do people coalesce to voice concerns together? If you are a leader of a project team, tune into the psychological safety within your team. Does your team have a culture of openness to learn about members' concerns and show a willingness to change?

Prioritize Growth Potential Instead of Perfection

The culture of elementary school classrooms created by teachers' actions informs ten-year-old children's understanding of intelligence, concluded psychologist Junlin Yu and his colleagues at the University of Helsinki in Finland. Yu's team asked twenty-two hundred ten-year-old students across multiple elementary schools in Finland about their beliefs about intelligence. Did they think intelligence is an innate and fixed quality that you either have or don't have and that can't be changed? Or can it grow with experience, effort, and practice? They also recruited these students' teachers, 358 of them, and asked them about their teaching plans and in-class practices. Connecting the instructors' teaching style with their students' views on intelligence, Yu and colleagues found that when teachers allow students to explore their own ideas, find answers through guided exploration, and work in small groups of mixed ability, their students subsequently interpret intelligence as an changeable quality that grows with experience and practice—often called "growth mindset." In contrast, when teachers don't allow much independent exploration and guided inquiry, favor individual work over collaboration, group students by perceived ability, and assign them different types of tasks, their students later come to believe that intelligence is a fixed property of individuals—often called "fixed mindset."[25]

On the other side of the ocean, in the United States, social psychologist David Yeager and his colleagues came to a similar conclusion from their nationally representative study of 9,167 adolescents in ninth grade classes taught by 223 teachers. When teachers had a growth mindset, adolescents in their classes showed substantial improvement in achievement over time, whereas when teachers had a fixed mindset, adolescents showed little change over time. When students started the year with a growth mindset, but their teachers did not share that belief, their achievement was suppressed. However, when students with a fixed mindset transferred to a different class where the teacher had a growth mindset, they showed large gains in achievement, even larger than their peers in the same class who started the year with a growth mindset.[26] What this means is that for young people's talent to develop, teachers must communicate the message that intelligence grows over time, they must reward students' effort, and they must give them opportunities to practice and improve, in ways consistent with that philosophy. A culture oriented toward learning and improvement advances equity and social justice because it is particularly helpful for students facing challenges and for other students in moderate and low-achieving schools with limited resources.[27]

As adolescents mature into adults and enter college, their professors' beliefs about intelligence and teaching practices also play a role in creating a welcoming environment or an alienating one. A study of 150 professors teaching more than fifteen thousand students, conducted by Elizabeth Canning and her social psychology colleagues at Indiana University, reveals that professors who believe intelligence grows with effort and practice create classroom cultures that shrink the racial achievement gap by twofold compared with professors who believe that intelligence is a fixed commodity that students either have or don't have. Students are more motivated to do their best work in classes taught by professors with a growth mindset. They think these instructors use teaching practices that emphasize learning and development, which results in better grades for all students, and especially for Black, Hispanic, and Native American students.[28] The message here is that professors have the power to create classroom norms that allow their students' talent to flourish if they treat intelligence as a capacity that grows with effort and practice. The norms they create—the wallpaper of the class—lifts up all students, especially Black and Brown students who have been historically marginalized in higher education.

If you pay attention, you will notice this normative wallpaper not only in ten-year-olds' elementary school classes and fifteen-year-olds' high school classes, but also in professional workplaces. The orientation toward learning and growth is a quality of teams and organizations, not just a quality of individuals. Some teams and organizations view talent as developmental. They reward improvement in employees' abilities and work process; they emphasize collaboration, mentoring, and coaching. Others view talent as fixed, essential qualities of people that can't be changed. These organizations place more emphasis on recruiting individuals they believe to be naturally talented while weeding out others believed to be less so.

It turns out that an organization's mission statement signals its collective mindset, found Dr. Elizabeth Canning and her colleagues in a series of studies.[29] They analyzed mission statements from Fortune 500 companies, grouping them by how much the language emphasized growth or fixed mindset. Some mission statements revealed a growth mindset with statements like "we offer opportunities for personal growth and professional development." Others leaned toward a fixed mindset, revealing the effort to recruit the best and the brightest with statements like "our success has resulted directly from the talent of our people; we are interested in attracting . . . talented people." Then Canning's team linked mission statements from real companies to job satisfaction ratings of employees within the same companies using data from Glassdoor.com, a website that collects anonymous employee evaluations of their companies. The researchers found that employees who worked in companies that had a growth mindset orientation were more satisfied with the culture within their company than those who worked in companies that had a fixed mindset orientation. A follow-up study found employees experienced the norms and practices within growth mindset companies as more collaborative, innovative, and ethical, which in turn predicted greater employee trust and commitment. In essence, growth mindset within organizations fosters an inclusive and creative culture.

Creating the Conditions for Structural Change

The path from individual action to culture change requires relationship-building, alliances, and collective action. The Bio-Pioneers program that I described earlier was the brainchild of one person at my university, Tracie Gibson, who found others who shared her passion, including me, and got endorsements and funding from a few campus leaders to pilot test the program for two years. The program yielded such clear measurable success and was so popular with students that it has transformed into a permanent program held up as a model of inclusive excellence and being emulated elsewhere in the university.

If you are a person from a historically marginalized group looking to promote social justice, look for opportunities to create or join a grassroots group with others who share your values, look for common issues of shared interest, and engage a few key allies who are leaders or informal influencers in the organization—just as gay, lesbian, and transgender employees did at Metropolitan Health.

If you are an educator, manager, or leader, introduce the following ingredients into your team, school, workplace, or any other organization to which you belong. Find colleagues who share your passion and work together to increase the impact of your actions.

Strengthen relational bonds and giving-back norms; foster social skills and a sense of personal meaning.

- Take the time to get to know and build relationships with people in your organization.

- Encourage mutual support, mentorship, and giving back.

- Encourage sensitivity to others' feelings, which allows people to feel safe taking interpersonal risks and builds respect and trust.

- Communicate frequently without a few voices dominating.

- Help people connect their work to an issue that's personally important to them to keep them motivated and engaged.

Encourage collaboration across skill levels and consistent practice; provide frequent feedback and leave room for autonomy.

- Bring together people of various skill levels to collaborate.

- Emphasize the consistent application of effort and practice, not innate talent.

- Characterize mistakes, struggles, and failure as essential steps to future excellence.

- Provide multiple learning opportunities and repeated feedback.

- Allow people the freedom to grow along multiple paths.

- Align group members' skills with their responsibilities.

EPILOGUE

How You Can Act

If you have arrived at this Epilogue, you now know a lot about the power of wallpaper. By sitting silently in the background, the environment of assumptions and cultural defaults, more than deep personal beliefs, shifts our behavior toward equity and justice or away from it in small cumulative ways. Now what? What do you do with this knowledge? If you are persuaded and motivated to act in ways that make a difference instead of feeling like you're spinning your wheels, I have some actions to suggest. Which of these are doable for you will depend on the specifics of your local culture and your role within it—how much formal power or informal influence you have. Some of the actions I propose below are for all of us regardless of role or power; other actions are for readers in leadership roles who have power to make decisions within organizations.

ACTIONS FOR EVERYONE

Choose Places to Spend Your Time with Social Justice in Mind

Spend some of your free time in gathering places that attract people who are diverse in multiple ways—race and ethnicity, social class, culture, age, beliefs, and ideology. The more we're exposed to differences, the deeper our understanding of, and comfort with, cultural variations, which, as research shows, increases our likelihood of reaching out in the future to interact with people who are different from us.

When possible, choose to live in neighborhoods that are diverse in race, class, culture, and age. Studies show mixed neighborhoods spark casual interactions between people from different groups, as we saw in Chapter 5. Sometimes these interactions lead over time to more mutual self-disclosure, understanding, empathy, friendships, and insight. They also create more opportunities to act together on local issues to address inequities.

If you have the financial means (and I recognize that many people don't), choose to live in neighborhoods built on principles of new urbanism. This is an urban planning approach that designs communities in ways that increase foot traffic and the likelihood of people running into each other on local sidewalks, in parks, and in other public spaces, creating opportunities for spontaneous conversations. In residential neighborhoods built on new urbanism principles, houses are closer together, few are separated by fences, front porches are more popular than back decks, garages are fewer to reduce car use and encourage more walking and cycling. Small parks dot these neighborhoods. It's even better if you can find a neighborhood like this designed for a mix of people—homeowners, renters in affordable housing, and people in assisted living. These design features foster interaction among neighbors while reducing negative environmental and traffic effects. Think of it as the opposite of suburban sprawl where people live far from one another, in houses surrounded by high fences, or in gated communities, all of which reduce social interaction and keep people out.

Open Yourself Up to Stories You Don't Usually Hear

Join a book club or movie club that emphasizes stories of people whose voices are often systematically excluded. As described in Chapter 6, stories provide a window into the causes and consequences of complex social inequalities, through the lives of people whose experiences illustrate various systemic barriers. Reading or listening to stories in a group creates a forum to discuss and process the material, hear other people's perspectives, and most important consider, as a group, how you might convert what you learn into action in a coordinated way. Reading alone or watching a movie alone rarely creates the momentum for action whereas a group experience is more likely to inspire collective action.

Consider participating in, or even organizing, dialogue groups to share personal stories in groups that bring together people across roles, power, and identities in your neighborhood, workplace, school, or team. Dialogue groups are icebreakers, community builders, and friendship sparkers. They foster deeper connections among people instead of purely transactional interactions like the ones you might have when you're collaborating with someone at work to accomplish a task. By interacting with people in a dialogue group, you are likely to learn something new and meaningful about people you've known casually or others who you don't know in ways that humanize them, shine a light on shared experiences, and identify concerns that could be acted on together. Chapter 6 points to a resource that explains how to structure dialogue groups.

If you are a parent or teacher wanting to inspire young people, tell them stories of successful individuals who have struggled, not superstars who seem to have achieved easily and whose achievements appear unattainable. Relatable role models matter especially for young people who don't see others like themselves in influential roles in their local environment, as discussed in Chapter 5.

If you are savvy with streaming media on web platforms, create digital stories to uplift the narratives of people whose voices are less audible. It's cheap and sometimes even free.

Use Your Social Network to Promote Social Change

Most people find new jobs and other opportunities and learn the informal rules of getting ahead through people they know. This is the invisible social capital that some of us have more than others. Chapter 2 illustrates vividly how disparities in access to resource-rich networks magnify societal inequalities, allowing the privileged to increase their advantages over others with less privilege much like compound interest. This is where you come in. If you have experience and knowledge that would benefit someone with limited opportunities, be proactive in offering yourself as an informal resource, as suggested in Chapter 7. Remember from Chapter 4 that people who need help the most may not ask for it because of cultural mismatch. They may think that they have to figure it out independently and that asking for help shows weakness or is an imposition to the person being asked. So you need to step forward and offer advice and resources. Also, if your network includes people whose professional background, knowledge, and experience are valuable, be a connector and introduce people you know with limited resources to them. Be mindful to use your social network to connect and promote people with less opportunity more frequently than other people who already have a lot.

If you become aware of inequities at work, in your school, your neighborhood, or your community, use your network to find others who share your concerns, and band together to coordinate action and talk to people who can address the problem. Remember, ideas convert into action more effectively and spread more widely among people who know one another rather than among strangers on social media. Spreading the word can mobilize grassroots alliances when people act together to push for broader organizational or structural change.

If you are a person to whom people come for informal advice at work or in your social circle or community, it means that you're probably a central hub of a social network and well connected. You have special power to spread ideas, change norms, and start coordinated action because of your connection to others, as I show in Chapter 7. Use it for good. Speak up if you notice something unfair or unjust. Some may share your concern even if they have not voiced it publicly. Others who haven't thought about this issue before are more likely to pay attention and adopt your opinions. Your actions may get them to notice something that had previously been taken for granted as part of the wallpaper, and you might change their opinions and actions. This is an opportunity to create an alliance and build momentum for small-scale change locally.

Using your network to promote social justice in your local sphere starts with three intentional steps: notice, listen, and act with others. Notice people around you, how they relate to each other; pay attention to concerns that may be bubbling up. Listen to a wide range of people. Be curious, ask questions to deepen your understanding, listen more and speak less. Once you've identified key concerns, reach out and gather people to join a conversation and explore next steps. Injustices often hide in "3 Rs"—Rules, Resources, and Recognition. Sometimes formal rules or informal practices that function as de facto rules lead some people to have a seat at the decision-making table while others don't have a voice. On the resource front, sometimes only a select few get tapped for special opportunities for leadership development, such as invitations to serve on an important team, while others don't. In terms of recognition, some people's work may get elevated through awards much more often than others'. These inequities may be ripe for discussion and coordinated action.

If you care about a social justice issue and discover that it is supported by a candidate running for elected office, share your opinions on the issue and the candidate in person and online with people you know. There's good evidence that our ideas shape the opinions of people we know. Remember the study in Chapter 7 on a get-out-the-vote campaign in Virginia? It revealed that people's opinions influenced those of others who lived near them when they shared their opinion through door-knocking and postcard campaigns, even though these individuals didn't know each other personally. Applied to you, your social justice issue position and political candidate preference is more likely to stick if you find ways to share it with people who live nearby and with others in your personal network.

Prioritize Actions That Change the Realities of People's Lives

Support real changes through your actions by advocating for policies that improve the material conditions of people's lives. If the housing and rental market in your community is tight and highly priced, champion the changing of zoning laws to allow more affordable housing in your town or city. Support high-quality public education through taxes. Vote for and volunteer for political candidates who advocate for a living wage and universal healthcare. Although symbolic actions like posting lawn signs and wearing T-shirts that say we support diversity, equity, and inclusion may feel good, they are solely symbolic and do nothing to change structural inequalities between groups.

ACTIONS FOR PEOPLE IN LEADERSHIP ROLES

Hire and Promote People from Groups That Have Been Left Behind

Diverse representation in mid- and upper-level leadership roles in organizations pays dividends by attracting diverse people in entry-level roles. If you are a hiring manager, understand that the best way to recruit and retain diverse talent is to ensure that new people see others like them in the organization. Seeing homogeneous teams in a workplace is a red flag for prospective jobseekers from under-represented groups, making them cautious about accepting a position in your organization or increasing the chance that even if they come in they are likely to leave through a revolving door. If you are a hiring manager in a predominantly homogeneous organization, this may create a chicken-and-egg problem for you. One solution is cluster hiring. Recruit a cluster of new employees from underrepresented groups who are brought into different organizational units but join as a cohort and are all at similar ranks. Create opportunities for this group of diverse employees to connect, form relationships, and be mutual mentors to one another, strengthening their sense of belonging within the cohort and within the organization. As I show in Chapter 5, seeing diverse people matters not just when people are looking for jobs. It also matters to customers looking for services from a business.

As a leader you should know that for people who have been systematically excluded, seeing people in the organization who look like them matters far more than symbolic statements affirming diversity, equity, and inclusion. Diversity statements may make organizational leaders feel good, but they are less important to people who have been historically left behind and not seen as central to organizational success. To them, the proof is in the people they see much more than in symbolic and suspiciously performative statements.

On the topic of diversity mission statements, if you are an organizational leader remember that a "business case" for diversity is unlikely to appeal to people who are Black, gay, lesbian, or transgender: the focus on "the bottom line" can make them feel as if they are being used as tools for profit. In contrast, encountering a social justice rationale for the importance of diversity and inclusion in an organization is far more effective. For more on this, see Chapter 8.

Evaluate Your Organization's Physical Design

Whose portraits are on the wall? Ensure that you are elevating diverse people's successes and contributions in a visible and visual way, not only celebrating a homogeneous few. Pay attention to the accessibility of your physical space so that it can be navigated by people with disabilities.

Create space for people to mingle across organizational roles and seniority so that people with power share physical space with others who have less power, promoting casual social interactions. You might create a communal lounge to break down silos where people across role hierarchies gather informally as equals for coffee and lunch breaks or to refill their water bottles. If you have leadership clout, consider placing your office near your associates and support staff to allow casual hallway conversations across rank and role from which genuine relationships grow bridging social divides. You will learn firsthand what your employees care about. Spatial proximity allows people in diverse roles with differing degrees of power to have meaningful exchanges, some of which will evolve into friendships.

A wallpaper of visibly diverse people, intentional spatial design, and opportunities to connect across role divides shifts the local culture toward greater inclusion. This may involve informal interactions between junior employees and organizational leaders like David Cancel, the CEO of Drift, mentioned in Chapter 5, who intentionally hangs out in the same workspace as his employees. It might prompt a chance to form an authentic relationship with an admired peer. By making such opportunities frequent, redesigned physical spaces and their local cultures provide a safe haven for people to develop a sense of belonging, confidence, and professional identity.

Scrutinize Your Assumptions About Talent

When we think of talent as inner brilliance waiting to be discovered, we tend to hire and admit people from elite institutions who appear polished and confident, qualities associated with economic privilege, numerous prior opportunities, extra coaching paid for by affluent families, and advice from family and friends on how to navigate college admission and job interviews. This definition of talent is heavily biased against poor and working-class individuals, some of whom are racial and ethnic minorities. Race-conscious affirmative action policies were one way that organizations tried to offset such bias. However, a Supreme Court decision in summer 2023 effectively ended race-conscious affirmative action in college and university admission in the United States.[1] Although the Court's decision was specific to higher education, not employment, the ruling has opened the door to other lawsuits contesting race-conscious hiring and other pipeline programs in employment. If universities and employers want to live up to their diversity and inclusion mission, they will need alternative strategies that comply with the Court's ruling.

Although the Court's decision significantly weakened affirmative action, the ruling allows colleges and universities to consider other factors to increase diversity if it is central to their educational mission. One way to stay true to the diversity mission of higher education is to define talent in terms of applicants' potential rather than current prowess. If talent is conceived as an individual's potential to achieve in the future given the right opportunities, as I described in Chapter 8, universities could calibrate candidate evaluations based on what the student has achieved relative to the barriers they faced as well as the opportunities they received. By this measure, an applicant whose achievement is, say, in the top 25 percent despite social and economic barriers and limited opportunity may be more deserving of admission than another applicant whose achievement is in the top 10 percent after having received many opportunities and resources and having experienced few barriers. Barriers and opportunities could be measured by asking applicants to self-report their family circumstances and also by gathering publicly available data about the wealth and resources of their schools, neighborhoods, and counties.

A second way to reduce bias is by scrutinizing the validity of college admission criteria that are strongly correlated with affluence, such as high scores on the standardized Scholastic Aptitude Test, costly extracurricular activities, and unpaid internships. Do these metrics speak to applicants' intelligence and potential or are they mostly proxies for privilege? Are there alternate criteria that are less affected by economic affluence?

Third, colleges and universities could create academic programs connected to their diversity and inclusion mission. Consider the example of University of California Davis, which has one of the most diverse medical schools in the nation. The UC Davis School of Medicine developed medical specialties focused on the needs of underserved communities—tribal medicine, rural medicine, and primary care. They found that by emphasizing these social justice–oriented medical specialties, they attract large numbers of well-qualified diverse applicants, changing the demographics of their student body.

Another instance is the Institute of Diversity Sciences at the University of Massachusetts Amherst, whose mission is to connect STEM to social justice through research and education. It does so by prioritizing STEM research on topics related to social inequalities, disparities, or human diversity.[2] I founded this institute in 2017, when it dawned on me that two long-standing challenges related to STEM in the United States were not separate and unrelated, but instead were intimately connected. One intractable challenge is the gap between rising diversity in the national population and the limited diversity in the people who graduate with STEM college degrees and who pursue STEM careers. A second challenge is the disconnection between a very active research enterprise in the United States that pursues fundamental discoveries in STEM and the inconsistent application of these discoveries to address social problems in the real world. I realized that these two challenges are mutually reinforcing and that understanding the connection between them can unlock innovative solutions to both. I noticed a consistent pattern in my and others' research showing that students who see the successful pursuit of STEM education and careers as contributing meaningfully to disadvantaged communities are more likely to be attracted to the subject matter and persist in it, especially if they belong to groups underrepresented in STEM degree programs and the STEM workforce. Today, the Institute of Diversity Sciences attracts large numbers of diverse students and faculty who are engaged in research targeting issues related to healthy equity, environmental justice, diversity in learning styles, disparities in civic engagement and criminal justice, and much more. Collectively, their research is helping illuminate important social problems using rigorous science, engineering, and technology tools. The people in our institute's ecosystem are far more diverse than the larger population of science, engineering, and computer science faculty and students at our university and many other universities around the nation. The commonality between the

UC Davis medical school and the UMass Institute of Diversity Sciences is that both places center social justice research topics in the academic curriculum, allowing the institutions to live up to their diversity mission while staying within the constraints of the law.[3]

Back to scrutinizing our assumptions about talent, I encourage you to think of talent as a quality to be developed, not perfection waiting to be discovered. Developmental talent is shaped by the quality of the training ground—something you can enrich through three types of actions. First, make the effort to build strong relationships among individuals in your environment, to create a norm of giving back, and to foster sensitivity to others' feelings. Second, adopt a collaborative style that brings together people across skill levels, and recognize that the evolution of skills requires normalizing failure and encouraging consistent effort, which together lead to mastery over time. Third, help people connect their work to issues that are personally important to them to keep them motivated and engaged. Prioritizing these actions will attract and retain diverse people by fulfilling their need to belong, to feel competent, and to pursue something that is personally meaningful.

Some teams and organizations are oriented toward talent development, while others are oriented toward talent discovery. This is a way individual action influences organizational culture. Reflect on your team's or organization's assumptions about talent—does it implicitly view talent as a quality to be developed? If this is the case, you and your team are likely to reward improvement in employees' abilities through practice, process improvement, and an emphasis on collaboration, mentoring, and coaching. That's what the Wang School of Elite Sports in Norway and the Meyerhoff Scholars Program in Baltimore have in common, as I discuss in Chapter 8. Each takes a holistic approach to talent development—one that creates the right local environment rather than fixating on individual brilliance. Teams and organizations that value talent development satisfy the need for belonging and purpose, and boost motivation for mastery, especially among people who feel isolated, have been historically excluded, or are new to a field. In contrast, if you and your teams or organization view talent as innate and fixed within individuals, you're likely to place greater emphasis on recruiting individuals who appear polished, while weeding out others who are less so. This will result in elevating a homogeneous group of people who have had multiple privileges through their lives while inadvertently discarding others who didn't have those privileges but who have plenty of potential that needs cultivation.

Create Teams with Collective Intelligence

If you are a leader responsible for creating teams, try to create intelligent teams, which is more than the sum of intelligent individuals, as discussed in Chapter 8. To maximize collective intelligence, align your team members' skills with their contribution, ensure the strategic sharing of responsibilities, encourage frequent communication within the team without a few people dominating, and encourage team members to be attuned and responsive to one another's feelings. This type of social perceptiveness is a key ingredient of collective intelligence. It allows everyone on a team to feel psychologically safe taking risks to speak up, ask for help, and admit mistakes with confidence that their team won't embarrass, reject, or punish them. It is particularly important to people working in environments where few others share their identity.

DEVELOPING A PLAN OF ACTION

It's hard for insiders to see the wallpaper. If the room was built for us, its ways feel natural and invisible. If you are an insider, look for people for whom the room wasn't built. Create a culture that invites the voices of outsiders and people in the corners of the room. They will notice the wallpaper more easily because they are like travelers to a foreign land. Then, use their insights to rearrange the room to meet the needs of people whose experiences are invisible and others waiting outside.

Changing the wallpaper requires coordinated action by multiple people over time. One-shot individual action, without coordination, rarely produces culture change. The effort also requires coalition building and acting in solidarity with others. Solidarity is more likely when you develop relationships with people who are different, which increases issue awareness, empathy, trust, and a desire to help. So when you learn about actionable issues, act in support of other people even if you don't personally benefit from it.

Finally, timing matters. Changed wallpaper is more easily accepted by people who are new to an environment, like new employees joining an organization, or new students entering high school or college. They are more open to new experiences. These transition periods are often the first time people meet peers and coworkers of diverse races and ethnicities, social class backgrounds, religions, nationalities, abilities, and sexualities. Changing wallpaper may also be easier when internal or external events shake things up, creating windows of opportunity.

NOTES

Preface

1. For examples of science-based diversity training programs and their effects, see Carnes et al., "Effect of an Intervention to Break the Gender Bias Habit"; Devine et al., "Gender Bias Habit-Breaking Intervention"; Devine et al., "Long-Term Reduction in Implicit Race Bias"; Chang et al., "Mixed Effects of Online Diversity Training"; and Stone et al., "Testing Active Learning Workshops for Reducing Implicit Stereotyping." While these studies found that diversity training increased people's awareness and knowledge about bias, they did not produce reliable changes in behavior.
2. For reviews of research showing the limited impacts of diversity training, see Bezrukova et al., "Meta-Analytical Integration of over 40 Years of Research"; Dobbin and Kalev, *Getting to Diversity;* Dobbin, Kim, and Kalev, "You Can't Always Get What You Need"; Greenwald et al., "Implicit-Bias Remedies"; Kalev, Dobbin, and Kelly, "Best Practices or Best Guesses?"; Kalinoski et al., "Meta-Analytic Evaluation of Diversity Training Outcomes"; Anan and Winters, "Retrospective View of Corporate Diversity Training"; and Paluck and Green, "Prejudice Reduction: What Works?"

Introduction

1. Pinnamaneni, "The Test Kitchen"; Kimball, "Yewande Komolafe's Nigerian Kitchen"; Komolafe, Yewande Komolafe homepage; Li, Hello Artists page; Li, LinkedIn page, https://www.linkedin.com/in/sue-li-63383b56/.
2. Davis, "We're Pretty Sure."

3. Abad-Santos, "Food World Is Imploding"; Chung, "Bon Appétit Issues 'Long-Overdue Apology.'"
4. Dasgupta, "Implicit Attitudes and Beliefs"; Dasgupta and Greenwald, "On the Malleability of Automatic Attitudes"; Dasgupta and Asgari, "Seeing Is Believing"; Dasgupta and Rivera, "When Social Context Matters"; Cialdini and Goldstein, "Social Influence."
5. Cialdini and Trost, "Social Influence"; Guinote, "Power and Affordances."
6. Bou Zeineddine and Leach, "Feeling and Thought in Collective Action"; van Zomeren et al., "Put Your Money Where Your Mouth Is!"; Selvanathan, Lickel, and Dasgupta, "An Integrative Framework on the Impact of Allies."
7. Bohnet, *What Works;* Thaler and Sunstein, *Nudge;* Chetty, Hendren, and Katz, "Effects of Exposure to Better Neighborhoods"; Perez, *Invisible Women.*

Chapter 1. The Rooms in Which We Live

1. Purdie-Vaughns et al., "Social Identity Contingencies."
2. Marshburn et al., "Workplace Anger Costs Women"; Motro et al., "Race and Reactions to Women's Expressions of Anger at Work."
3. Ridgeway et al., "How Do Status Beliefs Develop?"
4. Ridgeway and Correll, "Consensus and the Creation of Status Beliefs."
5. Ray, "A Theory of Racialized Organizations."
6. Khan, "Accent Bias and the Myth of Comprehensibility."
7. Kraus et al., "Evidence for the Reproduction of Social Class in Brief Speech."
8. Saegert et al., *Final Report of the APA Task Force on Socioeconomic Status;* Diemer et al., "Best Practices in Conceptualizing and Measuring Social Class in Psychological Research." The study by Michael Kraus used a combination of education and occupation to measure social class. Many studies measure social class by combining three factors: education, income, and occupation, which together capture individuals' financial, social, cultural, and human capital resources. Most social class calculations that use occupation compute occupational prestige rankings based on analyses of national surveys.
9. Yogeeswaran and Dasgupta, "National Identity in a Globalized World."
10. Cheryan and Monin, "'Where Are You Really From?'"; Devos and Banaji, "American = White?"; Devos, Gavin, and Quintana, "Say 'Adios' to the American Dream?"; Devos and Ma, "Is Kate Winslet More American than Lucy Liu?"
11. Devos and Banaji, "American = White?"
12. Yogeeswaran and Dasgupta, "The Devil Is in the Details."
13. Purdy, "The Making of a Suspect"; Qiang, "21 Years After the Arrest of Dr. Wen."
14. Yogeeswaran and Dasgupta, "Will the 'Real' American Please Stand Up?"
15. Yogeeswaran, Dasgupta, and Gomez, "A New American Dilemma?"
16. Yogeeswaran et al., "To Be or Not to Be (Ethnic)"; Yogeeswaran et al., "In the Eyes of the Beholder."

17. Bertrand and Mullainathan, "Are Emily and Greg More Employable Than Lakisha and Jamal?"

18. For a quantitative analysis aggregating multiple similar studies, see Quillian et al., "Meta-Analysis of Field Experiments."

19. Quillian, Lee, and Oliver, "Evidence from Field Experiments in Hiring."

20. Rooth, "Automatic Associations and Discrimination in Hiring."

21. To learn about the Implicit Association Test, visit Project Implicit at https://www.projectimplicit.net/.

22. Banerjee et al., "Labor Market Discrimination in Delhi."

23. Imana, Korolova, and Heidemann, "Auditing for Discrimination in Algorithms Delivering Job Ads."

24. Chen, "AI Hiring Industry Is Under Scrutiny"; Engler, "For Some Employment Algorithms, Disability Discrimination by Default"; Harwell, "Rights Group Files Federal Complaint Against AI-Hiring Firm HireVue."

25. Biernat, Fuegen, and Kobrynowicz, "Shifting Standards and the Inference of Incompetence." Also see Biernat and Fuegen, "Shifting Standards and the Evaluation of Competence"; Foschi, "Double Standards for Competence."

26. Sauer, Thomas-Hunt, and Morris, "Too Good to Be True?"

27. Dasgupta, "Ingroup Experts and Peers as Social Vaccines"; Emerson and Murphy, "Identity Threat at Work"; Spencer, Logel, and Davies, "Stereotype Threat"; Steele, Spencer, and Aronson, "Contending with Group Image."

28. Cozzarelli and Major, "Exploring the Validity of the Impostor Phenomenon"; Kumar and Jagacinski, "Imposters Have Goals Too"; Thompson, Davis, and Davidson, "Attributional and Affective Responses."

29. Ewing et al., "Relationship Between Racial Identity Attitudes"; Crocker et al., "When Grades Determine Self-Worth"; Dasgupta, Scircle, and Hunsinger, "Female Peers in Small Work Groups."

30. Hall, Schmader, and Croft, "Engineering Exchanges"; Bedyńska and Żołnierczyk-Zreda, "Stereotype Threat as a Determinant of Burnout"; van Veelen, Derks, and Endedijk, "Double Trouble."

31. Cheryan et al., "Ambient Belonging"; Walton and Cohen, "A Question of Belonging"; Walton and Cohen, "A Brief Social-Belonging Intervention"; von Hippel et al., "Stereotype Threat."

32. Aguado and Porras, "Building a Virtual Community"; Klassen et al., "More Than a Modern Day Green Book"; Welbourne, Rolf, and Schlachter, "The Case for Employee Resource Group."

33. Duckworth et al., "Grit"; Southwick et al., "Resilience Definitions, Theory, and Challenges."

34. McCluney et al., 2021, "To Be, or Not to Be . . . Black"; Koch, Gross, and Kolts, "Attitudes Toward Black English and Code Switching"; McCluney et al., 2019, "Costs of Code-Switching"; Boulton, "Black Identities Inside Advertising"; Dickens and Chavez, "Navigating the Workplace."

35. Kamin, "Black Homeowners Face Discrimination in Appraisals."
36. Ibid.
37. Perry, Rothwell, and Harshbarger, "Devaluation of Assets in Black Neighborhoods."
38. Bonam, Bergsieker, and Eberhardt, "Polluting Black Space."
39. Sampson and Raudenbush, "Seeing Disorder."
40. Krysan et al., "Does Race Matter in Neighborhood Preferences?"
41. Havekes, Bader, and Krysan, "Realizing Racial and Ethnic Neighborhood Preferences?"
42. Anicich et al., "Structuring Local Environments to Avoid Racial Diversity."
43. Anderson and Plaut, "Property Law."

Chapter 2. Chutes and Ladders

1. Waldinger and Lichter, *How the Other Half Works,* 83–140; Corcoran, Datcher, and Duncan, "Most Workers Find Jobs Through Word of Mouth."
2. Fernandez, Castilla, and Moore, "Social Capital at Work"; Granovetter, "Strength of Weak Ties"; Castilla, Lan, and Rissing, "Social Networks and Employment," part 1; Castilla, Lan, and Rissing, "Social Networks and Employment," part 2; Trimble and Kmec, "Role of Social Networks."
3. Obukhova and Lan, "Do Job Seekers Benefit from Contacts?"
4. Granovetter, *Getting a Job,* 41–50, 73–84; Lin, *Social Capital,* 19–54.
5. McDonald, "What's in the 'Old Boys' Network?"
6. Pedulla and Pager, "Race and Networks in the Job Search Process."
7. Abraham, "Gender-Role Incongruity and Audience-Based Gender Bias."
8. DeVaro, "Employer Recruitment Strategies."
9. Smith, "'Don't Put My Name on It'"; Marin, "Don't Mention It."
10. Rubineau and Fernandez, "Missing Links."
11. Kahlenberg, *Affirmative Action for the Rich,* 101–118; Pinsker, "The Real Reasons Legacy Preferences Exist"; Binkley, "Legacy College Admissions Under Scrutiny." Without an affirmative-action preference based on race to counterbalance it, opponents argue that legacy preference is no longer defensible.
12. DiPrete and Eirich, "Cumulative Advantage as a Mechanism for Inequality"; Mayer and Jencks, "Growing up in Poor Neighborhoods"; O'Rand, "Cumulative Processes in the Life Course"; Dannefer, "Cumulative Advantage/ Disadvantage."
13. Massey and Denton, *American Apartheid,* 83–114; Peach, "Social Geography"; Peach, "Good Segregation, Bad Segregation"; Simpson, "Statistics of Racial Segregation"; Musterd, "Social and Ethnic Segregation in Europe."
14. Iceland, Mateos, and Sharp, "Ethnic Residential Segregation by Nativity."
15. Tóth et al., "Inequality Is Rising Where Social Network Segregation Interacts with Urban Topology."

16. Marmaros and Sacerdote, "Peer and Social Networks in Job Search."
17. Granovetter, "The Strength of Weak Ties"; Putnam, *Bowling Alone*, 93–115.
18. Rajkumar et al., "A Causal Test of the Strength of Weak Ties."
19. Li, Savage, and Pickles, "Social Change, Friendship, and Civic Participation"; Bennett, Emmison, and Frow, *Accounting for Tastes*, 24–56, 87–114.
20. Bourdieu, *Distinction*, 257–370; DiMaggio and Garip, "Network Effects and Social Inequality."

Chapter 3. Analyzing Myths

1. Leslie et al., "Expectations of Brilliance."
2. Storage et al., "Frequency of 'Brilliant' and 'Genius' in Teaching Evaluations."
3. Muradoglu et al., "Underrepresented Minority Women and Early-Career Academics"; Bian et al., "Messages About Brilliance Undermine Women's Interest."
4. Ford, "Defeating the Inner Imposter"; Pain, "Forging the Way for Other Minority Scientists."
5. Malcom and Feder, *Barriers and Opportunities*, 21–54; Chen, "STEM Attrition."
6. Cvencek, Meltzoff, and Greenwald, "Math-Gender Stereotypes"; Ambady et al., "Stereotype Susceptibility in Children"; Herbert and Stipek, "Emergence of Gender Differences."
7. Bian, Leslie, and Cimpian, "Gender Stereotypes About Intellectual Ability."
8. Bian, Leslie, and Cimpian, "Evidence of Bias Against Girls and Women."
9. National Center for Education Statistics, "Types of State and District Requirements."
10. Bian, Leslie, and Cimpian, "Gender Stereotypes About Intellectual Ability."
11. Napp and Breda, "The Stereotype That Girls Lack Talent: A Worldwide Investigation."
12. O'Donnell et al., "Is Difficulty Mostly About Impossibility?"
13. Gagnon, "The Forgotten Life of Einstein's First Wife"; Popović, *In Albert's Shadow*, 1–24; Renn and Schulmann, *Albert Einstein/Mileva Marić*, xi–xxi; Esterson, Cassidy, and Sime, *Einstein's Wife*, 1–88, 99–263.
14. Motiani, "The Million Dollar Question."
15. See, for example, Frank, *Success and Luck;* Mauboussin, *The Success Equation.*
16. Pluchino, Biondo, and Rapisarda, "Talent vs. Luck."
17. Pew Research Center, *Partisan Polarization Surges.*
18. Harvey, *A Brief History of Neoliberalism.*
19. Ibid.; Monbiot, *How Did We Get into This Mess?*
20. Adams et al., "Psychology of Neoliberalism and the Neoliberalism of Psychology"; Azevedo et al., "Neoliberal Ideology and the Justification of Inequality"; Sandel, *Tyranny of Merit.*
21. Goudarzi, Badaan, and Knowles, "Neoliberalism and the Ideological Construction of Equity Beliefs."

22. Azevedo et al., "Neoliberal Ideology and the Justification of Inequality."
23. Goudarzi et al., "Economic System Justification."
24. Meindl, Iyer, and Graham, "Distributive Justice Beliefs."
25. Census Organization of India, "Most Educated States."
26. Brody et al., "Is Resilience Only Skin Deep?"; Brody, Yu, and Beach, "Resilience to Adversity and the Early Origins of Disease."
27. James, "John Henryism and the Health of African-Americans."
28. Miller et al., "Self-Control Forecasts Better Psychosocial Outcomes."
29. Geronimus et al., "'Weathering' and Age Patterns of Allostatic Load Scores."

Chapter 4. Incompatible Patterns

1. Lareau, *Unequal Childhoods,* 1–32, 165–181; Lareau, "Cultural Knowledge and Social Inequality."
2. Bourdieu and Passeron, *Reproduction in Education, Society, and Culture,* 141–220.
3. Lareau, "Concerted Cultivation and the Accomplishment of Natural Growth."
4. Piff et al., "Having Less, Giving More"; Stephens, Markus, and Phillips, "Social Class Culture Cycles"; Miller, Cho, and Bracey, "Working-Class Children's Experience"; Snibbe and Markus, "You Can't Always Get What You Want."
5. Stephens et al., "Unseen Disadvantage."
6. Phillips et al., "Access Is Not Enough."
7. Stephens et al., "A Cultural Mismatch."
8. Chang et al., "The Complexity of Cultural Mismatch."
9. Sharps and Anderson, "Social Class Background, Disjoint Agency, and Hiring Decisions."
10. Chua, "Clash of Cultures in Elite Hiring."
11. Stephens, Markus, and Phillips, "Social Class Culture Cycles"; Lareau, *Unequal Childhoods,* 1–32.
12. Gelfand, Harrington, and Jackson, "The Strength of Social Norms Across Human Groups"; Gelfand et al., "Differences Between Tight and Loose Cultures."
13. Chua, "Clash of Cultures in Elite Hiring."
14. Harrington, "Worlds unto Themselves"; Harrington and Gelfand, "Tightness-Looseness Across the 50 United States."
15. Chetty, Hendren, and Katz, "Effects of Exposure to Better Neighborhoods."
16. Steinberg, "A Social Neuroscience Perspective on Adolescent Risk-Taking."
17. Guinote et al., "Social Status Modulates Prosocial Behavior."
18. Overbeck and Park, "Powerful Perceivers, Powerless Objects."
19. Fiske, "Controlling Other People"; Fiske and Dépret, "Control, Interdependence, and Power,"
20. Guinote and Phillips, "Power Can Increase Stereotyping."

21. Sawaoka, Hughes, and Ambady, "Power Heightens Sensitivity to Unfairness Against the Self."

22. Liu, Yang, and Nauta, "Examining the Mediating Effect of Supervisor Conflict."

23. Tamborini, Kim, and Sakamoto, "Education and Lifetime Earnings in the United States"; Case and Deaton, "Life Expectancy in Adulthood."

24. Haveman and Smeeding, "The Role of Higher Education in Social Mobility."

Chapter 5. Seeing Is Believing

1. Kliman, "Coding and Decoding Dinner."

2. Shallal, "Bridging Race and Culture."

3. Cheryan et al., "Ambient Belonging."

4. Comparably, "Drift Awards."

5. Richeson and Shelton, "Negotiating Interracial Interactions"; Richeson and Sommers, "Toward a Social Psychology of Race and Race Relations"; Shelton, Richeson, and Vorauer, "Threatened Identities and Interethnic Interactions"; Vorauer, "An Information Search Model."

6. Bergsieker, Shelton, and Richeson, "To Be Liked Versus Respected."

7. Trawalter, Richeson, and Shelton, "Predicting Behavior During Interracial Interactions."

8. Gaither and Sommers, "Living with an Other-Race Roommate"; Shook and Fazio, "Interracial Roommate Relationships."

9. Mousa, "Building Social Cohesion Between Christians and Muslims"; Grady et al., "How Contact Can Promote Societal Change."

10. Jahoda and West, "Race Relations in Public Housing."

11. Oliver and Wong, "Intergroup Prejudice in Multiethnic Settings."

12. Hartman, "Widow Who Was Invited to Eat with Strangers."

13. Piekut and Valentine, "Spaces of Encounter and Attitudes Towards Difference."

14. Stout et al., "STEMing the Tide."

15. Asgari, Dasgupta, and Stout, "When Do Counterstereotypic Ingroup Members Inspire Versus Deflate?"

16. Dennehy and Dasgupta, "Female Peer Mentors"; Wu, Thiem, and Dasgupta, "Female Peer Mentors."

17. Note that the percentage difference between having no mentor versus having a male mentor is too small to be statistically significant; this difference is within the margin of error and should not be interpreted to mean that having no mentor is better than having a male mentor. The correct interpretation is that there is no statistical difference between these two conditions. However, the percentage difference between having a female mentor versus the other two conditions is indeed statistically significant.

18. Glassdoor, "Job Search."

19. Purdie-Vaughns et al., "Social Identity Contingencies."

20. Wilton et al., "Show Don't Tell."

21. Cipollina and Sanchez, "Identity Cues Influence Sexual Minorities' Anticipated Treatment."

22. Dixon, "Contact and Boundaries"; Bulger et al., "Social Inclusion Through
Mixed-Income Development."

23. Jacobs, *Death and Life,* 143–320.

Chapter 6. Tap into Emotions

1. Jayadev, Participatory Defense, "Origin Story."

2. Jayadev, "How Community Transforms the Courts."

3. Gerrig, *Experiencing Narrative Worlds,* 1–25; Green, Brock, and Kaufman, "Understanding Media Enjoyment"; Green and Brock, "Role of Transportation."

4. Perner, *Understanding the Representational Mind;* Ziv and Frye, "Relation Between Desire and False Belief."

5. Mar and Oatley, "Function of Fiction."

6. Grall et al., "Stories Collectively Engage Listeners' Brains."

7. Nummenmaa et al., "Emotions Promote Social Interaction."

8. Mar, Oatley, and Peterson, "Exploring the Link Between Reading Fiction and
Empathy."

9. Mar, "Neural Bases of Social Cognition."

10. Murrar and Brauer, "Entertainment-Education Effectively Reduces Prejudice."

11. Braddock and Dillard, "Meta-Analytic Evidence for the Persuasive Effect of
Narratives"; Moyer-Gusé, "Toward a Theory of Entertainment Persuasion";
Murrar and Brauer, "Overcoming Resistance to Change."

12. Dasgupta and Rivera, "When Social Context Matters."

13. Fernandez and Jordan, "3-Year-Old Found Alone at Border"; Lankford, Ernst,
and Cassidy, "Senators: Abolishing ICE Would Worsen Child Smuggling";
Singman, "Hundreds of Migrant Caravan Members Found to Have US Criminal Histories."

14. Sanchez and Tran, "It Took This Mother 55 Days to Be Reunited with Her
Young Daughter."

15. Moore-Berg, Hameiri, and Bruneau, "Empathy, Dehumanization, and
Misperceptions."

16. Barraza and Zak, "Empathy Toward Strangers Triggers Oxytocin."

17. Barraza et al., "Heart of the Story"; Lin et al., "Oxytocin Increases the Influence of Public Service Advertisements"; Zak, "Why Inspiring Stories Make Us
React."

18. Moyer-Gusé and Nabi, "Explaining the Effects of Narrative."

19. Paluck, "Reducing Intergroup Prejudice and Conflict."

20. Ramasubramanian, "Racial/Ethnic Identity."
21. Kim and Ball-Rokeach, "Community Storytelling Network."
22. Silicon Valley De-Bug, "About SV De-Bug."
23. Zadbood et al., "How We Transmit Memories to Other Brains."
24. Honey et al., "Not Lost in Translation."
25. Lockhart, "#WakandaTheVote."
26. Organizing Engagement, "Principles."

Chapter 7. Network for Social Justice

1. Bond et al., "61-Million-Person Experiment."
2. Handan-Nader et al., "Effectiveness of a Neighbor-to-Neighbor Get-Out-the-Vote Program."
3. Fowler and Christakis, "Cooperative Behavior Cascades."
4. Rand, Arbesman, and Christakis, "Dynamic Social Networks Promote Cooperation."
5. Chwe, "Structure and Strategy in Collective Action"; Rolfe, "Conditional Choice"; Watts and Dodds, "Influentials, Networks, and Public Opinion Formation."
6. Brands and Rattan, "Perceived Centrality in Social Networks"; Brands and Rattan, "Use Your Social Network as a Tool for Social Justice."
7. Ibarra and Andrews, "Power, Social Influence, and Sense Making."
8. Lamertz, "Social Construction of Fairness."
9. Corazzini et al., "Influential Listeners."
10. Ames, Maissen, and Brockner, "Role of Listening in Interpersonal Influence."
11. Bergsieker, Shelton, and Richeson, "To Be Liked Versus Respected"; Shnabel et al., "Promoting Reconciliation Through the Satisfaction of the Emotional Needs of Victimized and Perpetrating Group Members."
12. Dovidio, Gaertner, and Kawakami, "Contact Hypothesis"; Swart et al., "Impact of Cross-Group Friendships."
13. Cakal et al., "Investigation of the Social Identity Model of Collective Action"; Dixon et al., "Paradox of Integration?"; Hässler et al., "Large-Scale Test of the Link Between Intergroup Contact and Support for Social Change"; Saguy et al., "Irony of Harmony"; Selvanathan et al., "Whites for Racial Justice."
14. Cakal et al., "Investigation of the Social Identity Model of Collective Action." See also Dixon et al., "Paradox of Integration?"; Saguy et al., "Irony of Harmony."
15. Tropp and Dehrone, "Prejudice Reduction and Social Change"; Tropp et al., "How Intergroup Contact and Communication About Group Differences Predict Collective Action Intentions."

Chapter 8. Talent Is Made, Not Born

1. Hansen, "Kizzmekia Corbett '08 Talks to CNN."
2. Maton et al., "Outcomes and Processes in the Meyerhoff Scholars Program"; Maton et al., "Enhancing the Number of African Americans Who Pursue STEM PhDs."
3. Rentz, "'Agents of Change.'"
4. Sto. Domingo et al., "Replicating Meyerhoff for Inclusive Excellence in STEM"; Stolle-McAllister, Sto. Domingo, and Carrillo, "The Meyerhoff Way."
5. Wu et al., "An Identity-Based Learning Community for First-Generation College Students."
6. Soldner et al., "Supporting Students' Intentions to Persist"; Inkelas et al., "Living-Learning Programs."
7. Ashley et al., "Building Better Bridges into STEM"; Bradford, Beier, and Oswald, "Meta-Analysis of University STEM Summer Bridge Program Effectiveness."
8. Ramirez et al., "Making Hidden Resources Visible."
9. Stephens, Hamedani, and Destin, "Closing the Social-Class Achievement Gap."
10. Welbourne, Rolf, and Schlachter, "Case for Employee Resource Groups"; Slootman, "Affinity Networks as Diversity Instruments"; Briscoe and Safford, "Employee Affinity Groups."
11. Friedman, Kane, and Cornfield, "Social Support and Career Optimism"; Friedman and Craig, "Predicting Joining and Participating"; Friedman and Holtom, "Effects of Network Groups."
12. Githens and Aragon, "LGBT Employee Groups."
13. Creed and Scully, "Songs of Ourselves"; Briscoe and Safford, "The Nixon-in-China Effect."
14. Moseley, "Why a Social Cause Is Often the Best Motivation."
15. Burrage, Dasgupta, and Ganguli, "Gender Diversity in Academic Entrepreneurship."
16. Guzman, Oh, and Sen, "What Motivates Innovative Entrepreneurs?"
17. Georgeac and Rattan, "Business Case for Diversity Backfires."
18. Dasgupta et al., "Impact of Communal Learning Contexts."
19. Henriksen, Stambulova, and Roessler, "Riding the Wave of an Expert."
20. Martindale, Collins, and Abraham, "Effective Talent Development"; Henriksen, Stambulova, and Roessler, "Successful Talent Development in Track and Field"; Henriksen, Stambulova, and Roessler, "Holistic Approach to Athletic Talent Development Environments"; Larsen et al., "Successful Talent Development in Soccer."
21. Woolley et al., "Evidence for a Collective Intelligence Factor"; Woolley, Aggarwal, and Malone, "Collective Intelligence and Group Performance."

22. Edmondson, "Psychological Safety and Learning Behavior"; Edmondson and Lei, "Psychological Safety"; Baer and Frese, "Innovation Is Not Enough"; Kirkman et al., "Global Organizational Communities of Practice."

23. Singh, Winkel, and Selvarajan, "Managing Diversity at Work."

24. Ashford et al., "Out on a Limb."

25. Yu, Kreijkes, and Salmela-Aro, "Students' Growth Mindset."

26. Yeager et al., "Teacher Mindsets Help Explain Where a Growth-Mindset Intervention Does and Doesn't Work."

27. Yeager et al., "National Experiment Reveals Where a Growth Mindset Improves Achievement."

28. Canning et al., "STEM Faculty Who Believe Ability Is Fixed."

29. Canning et al., "Cultures of Genius at Work."

Epilogue

1. Totenberg, "Supreme Court Guts Affirmative Action."

2. University of Massachusetts Amherst, Institute of Diversity Sciences homepage, https://www.umass.edu/diversitysciences/.

3. Dasgupta, "To Make Science and Engineering More Diverse."

BIBLIOGRAPHY

Abad-Santos, Alex. "The Food World Is Imploding Over Structural Racism. The Problems Are Much Bigger Than Bon Appétit." *Vox*, June 11, 2020. https://www.vox.com/the-goods/21287732/bon-appetit-sohla-adam-rapoport-resigned-duckor-food-racism.

Abraham, Mabel. "Gender-Role Incongruity and Audience-Based Gender Bias: An Examination of Networking Among Entrepreneurs." *Administrative Science Quarterly* 65, no. 1 (2020): 151–180. https://doi.org/10.1177/0001839219832813.

Adams, Glenn, Sara Estrada-Villalta, Daniel Sullivan, and Hazel Rose Markus. "The Psychology of Neoliberalism and the Neoliberalism of Psychology." *Journal of Social Issues* 75, no. 1 (2019): 189–216. https://doi.org/10.1111/josi.12305.

Aguado, Brian A., and Ana M. Porras. "Building a Virtual Community to Support and Celebrate the Success of Latinx Scientists." *Nature Reviews Materials* 5, no. 12 (2020): 862–864. https://doi.org/10.1038/s41578-020-00259-8.

Ambady, Nalini, Margaret Shih, Amy Kim, and Todd L. Pittinsky. "Stereotype Susceptibility in Children: Effects of Identity Activation on Quantitative Performance." *Psychological Science* 12, no. 5 (2001): 385–390. https://doi.org/10.1111/1467-9280.00371.

Ames, Daniel, Lily Benjamin Maissen, and Joel Brockner. "The Role of Listening in Interpersonal Influence." *Journal of Research in Personality* 46, no. 3 (2012): 345–349. https://doi.org/10.1016/j.jrp.2012.01.010.

Anand, Rohini, and Mary-Frances Winters. "A Retrospective View of Corporate Diversity Training from 1964 to the Present." *Academy of Management Learning and Education* 7, no. 3 (2008): 356–372. https://doi.org/10.5465/AMLE.2008.34251673.

Anderson, Michelle Wilde, and Victoria C. Plaut. "Property Law: Implicit Bias and the Resilience of Spatial Colorlines." In *Implicit Racial Bias Across the Law,* ed.

Justin D. Levinson and Robert J. Smith, 25–44. Cambridge: Cambridge University Press, 2012.

Anicich, Eric M., Jon M. Jachimowicz, Merrick R. Osborne, and L. Taylor Phillips. "Structuring Local Environments to Avoid Racial Diversity: Anxiety Drives Whites' Geographical and Institutional Self-Segregation Preferences." *Journal of Experimental Social Psychology* 95 (2021): 104117. https://doi.org/10.1016/j.jesp.2021.104117.

Asgari, Shaki, Nilanjana Dasgupta, and Jane G. Stout. "When Do Counterstereotypic Ingroup Members Inspire Versus Deflate? The Effect of Successful Professional Women on Young Women's Leadership Self-Concept." *Personality and Social Psychology Bulletin* 38, no. 3 (2012): 370–383. https://doi.org/10.1177/0146167211431968.

Ashford, Susan J., Nancy P. Rothbard, Sandy K. Piderit, and Jane E. Dutton. "Out on a Limb: The Role of Context and Impression Management in Selling Gender-Equity Issues." *Administrative Science Quarterly* 43, no. 1 (1998): 23–57. https://doi.org/10.2307/2393590.

Ashley, Michael, Katelyn M. Cooper, Jacqueline M. Cala, and Sara E. Brownell. "Building Better Bridges into STEM: A Synthesis of 25 Years of Literature on STEM Summer Bridge Programs." *CBE Life Sciences Education* 16, no. 4 (2017): es3, 1–18. https://www.lifescied.org/doi/10.1187/cbe.17-05-0085.

Azevedo, Flavio, John T. Jost, Tobias Rothmund, and Joanna Sterling. "Neoliberal Ideology and the Justification of Inequality in Capitalist Societies: Why Social and Economic Dimensions of Ideology Are Intertwined." *Journal of Social Issues* 75, no. 1 (2019): 49–88. https://doi.org/10.1111/josi.12310.

Baer, Markus, and Michael Frese. "Innovation Is Not Enough: Climates for Initiative and Psychological Safety, Process Innovations, and Firm Performance." *Journal of Organizational Behavior* 24, no. 1 (2002): 45–88. https://doi.org/10.1002/job.179.

Banerjee, Abhijit, Marianne Bertrand, Saugato Datta, and Sendhil Mullainathan. "Labor Market Discrimination in Delhi: Evidence from a Field Experiment." *Journal of Comparative Economics* 37, no. 1 (2009): 14–27. https://doi.org/10.1016/j.jce.2008.09.002.

Barraza, Jorge A., Veronika Alexander, Laura E. Beavin, Elizabeth T. Terris, and Paul J. Zak. "The Heart of the Story: Peripheral Physiology During Narrative Exposure Predicts Charitable Giving." *Biological Psychology* 105, no. 1 (2015): 138–143. https://doi.org/10.1016/j.biopsycho.2015.01.008.

Barraza, Jorge A., and Paul J. Zak. "Empathy Toward Strangers Triggers Oxytocin Release and Subsequent Generosity." *Annals of the New York Academy of Sciences* 1167, no. 1 (2009): 182–189. https://doi.org/10.1111/j.1749-6632.2009.04504.x.

Bedyńska, Sylwia, and Dorota Żołnierczyk-Zreda. "Stereotype Threat as a Determinant of Burnout or Work Engagement. Mediating Role of Positive and Negative Emotions." *International Journal of Occupational Safety and Ergonomics* 21, no. 1 (2015): 1–8. https://doi.org/10.1080/10803548.2015.1017939.

Bennett, Tony, Michael Emmison, and John Frow. *Accounting for Tastes: Australian Everyday Cultures.* Cambridge: Cambridge University Press, 2001.

Bergsieker, Hilary B., J. Nicole Shelton, and Jennifer A. Richeson. "To Be Liked Versus Respected: Divergent Goals in Interracial Interactions." *Journal of Personality and Social Psychology* 99, no. 2 (2010): 248–264. https://doi.org/10.1037/a0018474.

Bertrand, Marianne, and Sendhil Mullainathan. "Are Emily and Greg More Employable Than Lakisha and Jamal? A Field Experiment on Labor Market Discrimination." *American Economic Review* 94, no. 4 (2004): 991–1013. https://doi.org/10.1257/0002828042002561.

Bezrukova, Katerina, Chester S. Spell, Jamie L. Perry, and Karen A. Jehn. "A Meta-Analytical Integration of over 40 Years of Research on Diversity Training Evaluation." *Psychological Bulletin* 142, no. 11 (2016): 1227–1274. https://doi.org/10.1037/bul0000067.

Bian, Lin, Sarah-Jane Leslie, and Andrei Cimpian. "Gender Stereotypes About Intellectual Ability Emerge Early and Influence Children's Interests," *Science* 355, no. 6323 (2017): 389–391. https://doi.org/10.1126/science.aah6524.

———. "Evidence of Bias Against Girls and Women in Contexts That Emphasize Intellectual Ability." *American Psychologist* 73, no. 9 (2018): 1139–1153. https://doi.org/10.1037/amp0000427.

Bian, Lin, Sarah-Jane Leslie, Mary C. Murphy, and Andrei Cimpian. "Messages About Brilliance Undermine Women's Interest in Educational and Professional Opportunities." *Journal of Experimental Social Psychology* 76 (2018): 404–420. https://doi.org/10.1016/j.jesp.2017.11.006.

Biernat, Monica, and Kathleen Fuegen. "Shifting Standards and the Evaluation of Competence: Complexity in Gender-Based Judgment and Decision Making." *Journal of Social Issues* 57, no. 4 (2002): 707–724. https://doi.org/10.1111/0022-4537.00237.

Biernat, Monica, Kathleen Fuegen, and Diane Kobrynowicz. "Shifting Standards and the Inference of Incompetence: Effects of Formal and Informal Evaluation Tools." *Personality and Social Psychology Bulletin* 36, no. 7 (2010): 855–868. https://doi.org/10.1177/0146167210369483.

Binkley, Collin. "Legacy College Admissions Under Scrutiny Again After Supreme Court Ruling on Affirmative Action." *PBS NewsHour,* July 1, 2023. https://www.pbs.org/newshour/education/legacy-college-admissions-under-scrutiny-again-after-supreme-court-ruling-on-affirmative-action.

Bohnet, Iris. *What Works: Gender Equality by Design.* Cambridge: Harvard University Press, 2016.

Bonam, Courtney M., Hilary B. Bergsieker, and Jennifer L. Eberhardt. "Polluting Black Space." *Journal of Experimental Psychology: General* 145, no. 11 (2016): 1561–1582. https://doi.org/10.1037/xge0000226.

Bond, Robert M., Christopher J. Fariss, Jason D. Jones, Adam D. I. Kramer, Cameron Marlow, Jaime E. Settle, and James H. Fowler. "A 61-Million-Person Experiment in Social Influence and Political Mobilization." *Nature* 489, no. 7415 (2012): 295–298. https://doi.org/10.1038/nature11421.

Boulton, Christopher. "Black Identities Inside Advertising: Race Inequality, Code Switching, and Stereotype Threat." *Howard Journal of Communications* 27, no. 2 (2016): 130–144. https://doi.org/10.1080/10646175.2016.1148646.

Bourdieu, Pierre. *Distinction: A Social Critique of the Judgement of Taste,* trans. Richard Nice. New York: Routledge and Kegan Paul, 1984.

Bourdieu, Pierre, and Jean-Claude Passeron. *Reproduction in Education, Society, and Culture,* trans. Richard Nice. New York: Sage, 1990.

Bourdieu, Pierre, and Loïc J. D. Wacquant. *An Invitation to Reflexive Sociology.* Chicago: University of Chicago Press, 1992.

Bou Zeineddine, F., and Colin W. Leach. "Feeling and Thought in Collective Action on Social Issues: Toward a Systems Perspective." *Social and Personality Psychology Compass* 15, no. 7 (2021): e12622. https://doi.org/10.1111/spc3.12622.

Braddock, Kurt, and James Price Dillard. "Meta-Analytic Evidence for the Persuasive Effect of Narratives on Beliefs, Attitudes, Intentions, and Behaviors." *Communication Monographs* 83, no. 4 (2016): 446–467. https://doi.org/10.1080/03637751.2015.1128555.

Bradford, Brittany C., Margaret E. Beier, and Frederick L. Oswald. "A Meta-Analysis of University STEM Summer Bridge Program Effectiveness." *CBE Life Sciences Education* 20, no. 2 (2021): ar21, 1–14. https://doi.org/10.1187/cbe.20-03-0046.

Brands, Raina A., and Aneeta Rattan. "Perceived Centrality in Social Networks Increases Women's Expectations of Confronting Sexism." *Personality and Social Psychology Bulletin* 46, no. 12 (March 2020): 1682–1701. https://doi.org/10.1177/0146167220912621.

———. "Use Your Social Network as a Tool for Social Justice." *Harvard Business Review,* July 13, 2020, 1–8. https://hbr.org/2020/07/use-your-social-network-as-a-tool-for-social-justice.

Briscoe, Forrest, and Sean Safford. "The Nixon-in-China Effect: Activism, Imitation, and the Institutionalization of Contentious Practices." *Administrative Science Quarterly* 53, no. 3 (2008): 460–491. https://doi.org/10.2189/asqu.53.3.460.

———. "Employee Affinity Groups: Their Evolution from Social Movement Vehicles to Employer Strategies." *Perspectives on Work* 14, no. 1 (2010): 42–45. https://sciencespo.hal.science/hal-01052900/.

Brody, Gene H., Tianyi Yu, and Steven R. H. Beach. "Resilience to Adversity and the Early Origins of Disease." *Development and Psychopathology* 28, no. 4, part 2 (2016): 1347–1365. https://doi.org/10.1017/S0954579416000894.

Brody, Gene H., Tianyi Yu, Edith Chen, Gregory E. Miller, Steven M. Kogan, and Steven R. H. Beach. "Is Resilience Only Skin Deep? Rural African Americans' Socioeconomic Status—Related Risk and Competence in Preadolescence and Psychological Adjustment and Allostatic Load at Age 19." *Psychological Science* 24, no. 7 (2013): 1285–1293. https://doi.org/10.1177/0956797612471954.

Bulger, Morgan, Mark Joseph, Sherise McKinney, and Diana Bilimoria. "Social Inclusion Through Mixed-Income Development: Design and Practice in the Choice Neighborhoods Initiative." *Journal of Urban Affairs* 45, no. 2 (2023): 168–190. https://doi.org/10.1080/07352166.2021.1898283.

Burrage, A., Nilanjana Dasgupta, and Ina Ganguli. "Gender Diversity in Academic Entrepreneurship: Social Impact Motives and the NSF I-Corps Program." Unpublished manuscript. November 19, 2023.

Cakal, H., M. Hewstone, G. Schwär, and A. Heath. "An Investigation of the Social Identity Model of Collective Action and the 'Sedative' Effect of Intergroup Contact Among Black and White Students in South Africa." *British Journal of Social Psychology* 50 (2011): 606–627.

Canning, Elizabeth A., Katherine Muenks, Dorainne J. Green, and Mary C. Murphy. "STEM Faculty Who Believe Ability Is Fixed Have Larger Racial Achievement Gaps and Inspire Less Student Motivation in Their Classes." *Science Advances* 5, no. 2 (2019). https://doi.org/10.1126/sciadv.aau4734.

Canning, Elizabeth A., Mary C. Murphy, Katherine T. U. Emerson, Jennifer A. Chatman, Carol S. Dweck, and Laura J. Kray. "Cultures of Genius at Work: Organizational Mindsets Predict Cultural Norms, Trust, and Commitment." *Personality and Social Psychology Bulletin* 46, no. 4 (2019): 626–642. https://doi.org/10.1177/0146167219872473.

Carnes, Molly, Patricia G. Devine, Linda Baier Manwell, Angela Byars-Winston, Eve Fine, Cecilia E. Ford, Patrick Forscher, et al. "Effect of an Intervention to Break the Gender Bias Habit for Faculty at One Institution: A Cluster Randomized, Controlled Trial." *Academic Medicine: Journal of the Association of American Medical Colleges* 90, no. 2 (2015): 221. https://doi.org/10.1097/ACM.0000000000000552.

Case, Anne, and Angus Deaton. "Life Expectancy in Adulthood Is Falling for Those Without a BA Degree, But as Educational Gaps Have Widened, Racial Gaps Have Narrowed." *Proceedings of the National Academy of Sciences* 118, no. 11 (2021): e2024777118. https://doi.org/10.1073/pnas.2024777118.

Castilla, Emilio J., George J. Lan, and Ben A. Rissing. "Social Networks and Employment," part 1, "Mechanisms." *Sociology Compass* 7, no. 12 (2013): 999–1012. https://doi.org/10.1111/soc4.12096.

———. "Social Networks and Employment," part 2, "Outcomes." *Sociology Compass* 7, no. 12 (2013): 1013–1026. https://doi.org/10.1111/soc4.12095.

Census Organization of India. "Most Educated States in India." https://www.census2011.co.in/facts/highstateliteracy.html.

Chang, Edward H., Katherine L. Milkman, Dena M. Gromet, Robert W. Rebele, Cade Massey, Angela L. Duckworth, and Adam M. Grant. "The Mixed Effects of Online Diversity Training." *Proceedings of the National Academy of Sciences* 116, no. 16 (2019): 7778–7783. https://doi.org/10.1073/pnas.1816076116.

Chang, Janet, Shu-wen Wang, Colin Mancini, Brianna McGrath-Mahrer, and Sujey Orama de Jesus. "The Complexity of Cultural Mismatch in Higher Education: Norms Affecting First-Generation College Students' Coping and Help-Seeking Behaviors." *Cultural Diversity and Ethnic Minority Psychology* 26, no. 3 (2020): 280–294. https://doi.org/10.1037/cdp0000311.

Chen, Angela. "The AI Hiring Industry Is Under Scrutiny—But It'll Be Hard to Fix." *MIT Technology Review,* November 7, 2019. https://www.technologyreview .com/2019/11/07/75194/hirevue-ai-automated-hiring-discrimination-ftc-epic -bias/.

Chen, Xianglei. "STEM Attrition Among High-Performing College Students: Scope and Potential Causes." *Journal of Technology and Science Education* 5, no. 1 (2015). https://doi.org/10.3926/jotse.136.

Cheryan, Sapna, and B. Monin. "'Where Are You Really From?': Asian-Americans and Identity Denial." *Journal of Personality and Social Psychology* 89 (2005): 717–730.

Cheryan, Sapna, Victoria C. Plaut, Paul G. Davies, and Claude M. Steele. "Ambient Belonging: How Stereotypical Cues Impact Gender Participation in Computer Science." *Journal of Personality and Social Psychology* 97, no. 6 (2009): 1045–1060. https://doi.org/10.1037/a0016239.

Chetty, Raj, Nathaniel Hendren, and Lawrence F. Katz. "The Effects of Exposure to Better Neighborhoods on Children: New Evidence from the Moving to Opportunity Experiment." *American Economic Review* 106, no. 4 (2016): 855–902. https://doi.org/10.1257/aer.20150572.

Chua, Phoebe, K. "Clash of Cultures in Elite Hiring: How Social Class Background Shapes the Hiring Process of Large Technology Companies." PhD diss., University of California Irvine, 2022.

Chung, Gabrielle. "Bon Appétit Issues 'Long-Overdue Apology' amid Accusations of Racial Discrimination." *People,* June 10, 2020. https://people.com/food/bon -appetit-issues-apology-amid-racial-discrimination/.

Chwe, Michael Suk-Young. "Structure and Strategy in Collective Action." *American Journal of Sociology* 105, no. 1 (1999): 128–156. https://doi.org/10.1086/210269.

Cialdini, Robert B., and Noah J. Goldstein. "Social Influence: Compliance and Conformity." *Annual Review of Psychology* 55, no. 1 (2004): 591–621. https://doi.org /10.1146/annurev.psych.55.090902.142015.

Cialdini, Robert B., and Melanie R. Trost. "Social Influence: Social Norms, Conformity, and Compliance." In *The Handbook of Social Psychology,* ed. Daniel T. Gilbert, Susan T. Fiske, and G. Lindzey, 151–192. New York: McGraw-Hill, 1998.

Cipollina, Rebecca, and Diana T. Sanchez. "Identity Cues Influence Sexual Minorities' Anticipated Treatment and Disclosure Intentions in Healthcare Settings: Exploring a Multiple Pathway Model." *Journal of Health Psychology* 27, no. 7 (2021): 1569–1582. https://doi.org/10.1177/1359105321995984.

Comparably. "Drift Awards." https://www.comparably.com/companies/drift/awards.

Corazzini, Luca, Filippo Pavesi, Beatrice Petrovich, and Luca Stanca. "Influential Listeners: An Experiment on Persuasion Bias in Social Networks," *European Economic Review* 56, no. 6 (2012): 1276–1288. https://doi.org/10.1016/j.euroeco rev.2012.05.005.

Corcoran, Mary, Linda Datcher, and Greg J. Duncan. "Most Workers Find Jobs Through Word of Mouth." *Monthly Labor Review* 103, no. 8 (1980): 33–35. https://www.jstor.org/stable/41841304.

Cozzarelli, Catherine, and Brenda Major. "Exploring the Validity of the Impostor Phenomenon." *Journal of Social and Clinical Psychology* 9, no. 4 (1990): 401–417. https://doi.org/10.1521/jscp.1990.9.4.401.

Creed, W. E. Douglas, and Maureen A. Scully. "Songs of Ourselves: Employees' Deployment of Social Identity in Workplace Encounters." *Journal of Management Inquiry* 20, no. 4 (2011): 408–429. https://doi.org/10.1177/1056492611432810.

Crocker, Jennifer, Andrew Karpinski, Diane M. Quinn, and Sara K. Chase. "When Grades Determine Self-Worth: Consequences of Contingent Self-Worth for Male and Female Engineering and Psychology Majors." *Journal of Personality and Social Psychology* 85, no. 3 (2003): 507–516. https://doi.org/10.1037/0022 -3514.85.3.507.

Cvencek, Dario, Andrew N. Meltzoff, and Anthony G. Greenwald. "Math-Gender Stereotypes in Elementary School Children." *Child Development* 82, no. 3 (2011): 766–779. https://doi.org/10.1111/j.1467-8624.2010.01529.x.

Dannefer, Dale. "Cumulative Advantage/Disadvantage and the Life Course: Cross-Fertilizing Age and Social Science Theory." *Journal of Gerontology* 58, no. 6 (2003): 327–337. https://doi.org/10.1093/geronb/58.6.s327.

Dasgupta, Nilanjana. "Ingroup Experts and Peers as Social Vaccines Who Inoculate the Self-Concept: The Stereotype Inoculation Model." *Psychological Inquiry* 22, no. 4 (2011): 231–246. https://doi.org/10.1080/1047840x.2011.607313.

———. "Implicit Attitudes and Beliefs Adapt to Situations: A Decade of Research on the Malleability of Implicit Prejudice, Stereotypes, and the Self-Concept." *Advances in Experimental Social Psychology* 47 (2013): 233–279. https://doi.org /10.1016/b978-0-12-407236-7.00005-x.

———. "To Make Science and Engineering More Diverse, Make Research Socially Relevant." *Issues in Science and Technology* 40 (2023): 76–79. https://doi.org/10 .58875/MAAC9457.

Dasgupta, Nilanjana, and Shaki Asgari. "Seeing Is Believing: Exposure to Counter-stereotypic Women Leaders and Its Effect on the Malleability of Automatic Gender Stereotyping." *Journal of Experimental Social Psychology* 40, no. 5 (2004): 642–658. https://doi.org/10.1016/j.jesp.2004.02.003.

Dasgupta, Nilanjana, and Anthony G. Greenwald. "On the Malleability of Auto-
    matic Attitudes: Combating Automatic Prejudice with Images of Admired
    and Disliked Individuals." *Journal of Personality and Social Psychology* 81, no. 5
    (2001): 800–814. https://doi.org/10.1037/0022-3514.81.5.800.
Dasgupta, Nilanjana, and Luis M. Rivera. "When Social Context Matters: The In-
    fluence of Long-Term Contact and Short-Term Exposure to Admired Out-
    group Members on Implicit Attitudes and Behavioral Intentions." *Social Cog-
    nition* 26, no. 1 (2008): 112–123. https://doi.org/10.1521/soco.2008.26.1.112.
Dasgupta, Nilanjana, Melissa M. Scircle, and Matthew Hunsinger. "Female Peers
    in Small Work Groups Enhance Women's Motivation, Verbal Participation,
    and Career Aspirations in Engineering." *Proceedings of the National Academy of
    Sciences* 112, no. 16 (2015): 4988–4993. https://doi.org/10.1073/pnas.1422822112.
Dasgupta, Nilanjana, Kelsey C. Thiem, Alice E. Coyne, Holly Laws, Marielena
    Barbieri, and Ryan S. Wells. "The Impact of Communal Learning Contexts
    on Adolescent Self-Concept and Achievement: Similarities and Differences
    Across Race and Gender." *Journal of Personality and Social Psychology* 123, no. 3
    (2022): 537–558. https://doi.org/10.1037/pspi0000377.
Davis, Noah. "We're Pretty Sure Adam Rapoport Is the Coolest Editor in NYC."
    Business Insider, April 21, 2011. https://www.businessinsider.com/demi-glace
    -drinks-and-designer-socks-a-candid-conversation-with-bon-appetit-eic
    -adam-rapoport-2011-4.
Dennehy, Tara C., and Nilanjana Dasgupta. "Female Peer Mentors Early in College
    Increase Women's Positive Academic Experiences and Retention in Engineer-
    ing." *Proceedings of the National Academy of Sciences* 114, no. 23 (2017): 5964–
    5969. https://doi.org/10.1073/pnas.1613117114.
DeVaro, Jed. "Employer Recruitment Strategies and the Labor Market Outcomes
    of New Hires." *Economic Inquiry* 43, no. 2 (2007): 263–282. https://doi.org/10
    .1093/ei/cbi018.
Devine, Patricia G., Patrick S. Forscher, Anthony J. Austin, and William T. L. Cox.
    "Long-Term Reduction in Implicit Race Bias: A Prejudice Habit–Breaking In-
    tervention." *Journal of Experimental Social Psychology* 48, no. 6 (2012): 1267–
    1278. https://doi.org/10.1016/j.jesp.2012.06.003.
Devine, Patricia G., Patrick S. Forscher, William T. L. Cox, Anna Kaatz, Jennifer
    Sheridan, and Molly Carnes. "A Gender Bias Habit-Breaking Intervention Led
    to Increased Hiring of Female Faculty in STEMM Departments." *Journal of
    Experimental Social Psychology* 73 (2017): 211–215. https://doi.org/10.1016/j.jesp
    .2017.07.002.
Devos, T., and M. Banaji. "American = White?" *Journal of Personality and Social Psy-
    chology* 88 (2005): 447–466.
Devos, T., K. Gavin, and F. Quintana. "Say 'Adios' to the American Dream? The In-
    terplay Between Ethnic and National Identity Among Latino and Caucasian
    Americans." *Cultural Diversity and Ethnic Minority Psychology* 16 (2010): 37–49.

Devos, T., and D. Ma. "Is Kate Winslet More American than Lucy Liu? The Impact of Construal Processes on the Implicit Ascription of a National Identity." *British Journal of Social Psychology* 47 (2008): 191–215.

Dickens, Danielle D., and Ernest L. Chavez. "Navigating the Workplace: The Costs and Benefits of Shifting Identities at Work Among Early Career U.S. Black Women." *Sex Roles* 78, no. 1 (2018): 760–774. https://doi.org/10.1007/s11199-017-0844-x.

Diemer, Matthew A., Rashmita S. Mistry, Martha E. Wadsworth, Irene López, and Faye Reimers. "Best Practices in Conceptualizing and Measuring Social Class in Psychological Research." *Analyses of Social Issues and Public Policy* 13, no. 1 (2013): 77–113. https://doi.org/10.1111/asap.12001.

DiMaggio, Paul, and Filiz Garip. "Network Effects and Social Inequality." *Annual Review of Sociology* 38, no. 1 (2012): 93–118. https://doi.org/10.1146/annurev.soc.012809.102545.

DiPrete, Thomas A., and Gregory M. Eirich. "Cumulative Advantage as a Mechanism for Inequality: A Review of Theoretical and Empirical Developments." *Annual Review of Sociology* 32, no. 1 (2006): 271–297. https://doi.org/10.1146/annurev.soc.32.061604.123127.

Dixon, John. "Contact and Boundaries: 'Locating' the Social Psychology of Intergroup Relations." *Theory and Psychology* 11, no. 5 (2001): 587–608. https://doi.org/10.1177/0959354301115001.

Dixon, John, Kevin Durrheim, Colin Tredoux, Linda Tropp, Beverly Clack, and Liberty Eaton. "A Paradox of Integration? Interracial Contact, Prejudice Reduction, and Perceptions of Racial Discrimination." *Journal of Social Issues* 66 (2010): 401–416.

Dobbin, Frank, and Alexandra Kalev. *Getting to Diversity: What Works and What Doesn't.* Cambridge: Harvard University Press, 2022.

Dobbin, Frank, Soohan Kim, and Alexandra Kalev. "You Can't Always Get What You Need: Organizational Determinants of Diversity Programs." *American Sociological Review* 76, no. 3 (2011): 386–411. https://doi.org/10.1177/0003122411409704.

Dovidio, J. F., S. L. Gaertner, and K. Kawakami. "The Contact Hypothesis: The Past, Present, and the Future." *Group Processes and Intergroup Relations* 6 (2003): 5–21.

Duckworth, Angela L., Christopher Peterson, Michael D. Matthews, and Dennis R. Kelly. "Grit: Perseverance and Passion for Long-Term Goals." *Journal of Personality and Social Psychology* 92, no. 6 (2007): 1087–1101. https://doi.org/10.1037/0022-3514.92.6.1087.

Edmondson, Amy. "Psychological Safety and Learning Behavior in Work Teams." *Administrative Science Quarterly* 44, no. 2 (1999): 350–383. https://doi.org/10.2307/2666999.

Edmondson, Amy C., and Zhike Lei. "Psychological Safety: The History, Renais-

sance, and Future of an Interpersonal Construct." *Annual Review of Organizational Psychology and Organizational Behavior* 1 (2014): 23–43. https://doi.org/10
.1146/annurev-orgpsych-031413-091305.

Emerson, Katherine T. U., and Mary C. Murphy. "Identity Threat at Work: How
Social Identity Threat and Situational Cues Contribute to Racial and Ethnic
Disparities in the Workplace." *Cultural Diversity and Ethnic Minority Psychol-
ogy* 20, no. 4 (2014): 508–520. https://doi.org/10.1037/a0035403.

Engler, Alex. "For Some Employment Algorithms, Disability Discrimination by
Default." Brookings Institution, October 31, 2019. https://www.brookings
.edu/articles/for-some-employment-algorithms-disability-discrimination-by
-default/.

Esterson, Allen, David Cassidy, and Ruth Lewin Sime. *Einstein's Wife: The Real Story
of Mileva Einstein-Marić.* Cambridge: MIT Press, 2019.

Ewing, Kimberly M., Tina Q. Richardson, Linda James-Myers, and Richard K. Russell. "The Relationship Between Racial Identity Attitudes, Worldview, and African American Graduate Students' Experience of the Imposter Phenomenon." *Journal of Black Psychology* 22, no. 1 (1996): 53–66. https://doi.org/10.1177
/00957984960221005.

Fernandez, Manny, and Miriam Jordan. "3-Year-Old Found Alone at Border Is One
of the Many 'Heartbreaking' Migrant Cases." *New York Times,* April 24, 2019.
https://www.nytimes.com/2019/04/24/us/toddler-border-patrol-migrant
-children.html.

Fernandez, Robert M., Emilio J. Castilla, and Paul Moore. "Social Capital at Work:
Networks and Employment at a Phone Center." *American Journal of Sociology*
105, no. 5 (2000): 1288–1356. https://www.jstor.org/stable/3003768.

Fiske, Susan T. "Controlling Other People: The Impact of Power on Stereotyping
Tales of Two Women." *American Psychologist* 48, no. 6 (1993): 621–628. https://
doi.org/10.1037/0003-066x.48.6.621.

Fiske, Susan T., and Eric Dépret. "Control, Interdependence, and Power: Understanding Social Cognition in Its Social Context." *European Review of Social
Psychology* 7, no. 1 (1996): 31–61. https://doi.org/10.1080/14792779443000094.

Ford, Knatokie. "Defeating the Inner Imposter That Keeps Us from Being Successful." TEDxMidAtlantic video, October 2016, 14:25. https://www.youtube.com
/watch?v=J9PgY1mbPgM.

Foschi, Martha. "Double Standards for Competence: Theory and Research." *Annual Review of Sociology* 26 (2000): 21–42. https://doi.org/10.1146/annurev.soc
.26.1.21.

Fowler, James H., and Nicholas A. Christakis. "Cooperative Behavior Cascades in
Human Social Networks." *Proceedings of the National Academy of Sciences of
the United States of America* 107, no. 12 (2010): 5334–5538. https://doi.org/10.1073
/pnas.0913149107.

Frank, Robert H. *Success and Luck: Good Fortune and the Myth of Meritocracy.* Princeton: Princeton University Press, 2016.

Friedman, Raymond A., and Kellina M. Craig. "Predicting Joining and Participating in Minority Employee Network Groups." *Industrial Relations: A Journal of Economy and Society* 43, no. 4 (2004): 793–816. https://doi.org/10.1111/j.0019-8676.2004.00362.x.

Friedman, Raymond A., and Brooks Holtom. "The Effects of Network Groups on Minority Employee Turnover Intentions." *Human Resource Management* 41, no. 4 (2002): 405–421. https://doi.org/10.1002/hrm.10051.

Friedman, Raymond A., Melinda Kane, and Daniel B. Cornfield. "Social Support and Career Optimism: Examining the Effectiveness of Network Groups Among Black Managers." *Human Relations* 51, no. 9 (1998): 1155–1177. https://doi.org/10.1023/A:1016973611184.

Gagnon, Pauline. "The Forgotten Life of Einstein's First Wife." Guest Blog. *Scientific American,* December 19, 2016. https://blogs.scientificamerican.com/guest-blog/the-forgotten-life-of-einsteins-first-wife/.

Gaither, Sarah E., and Samuel R. Sommers. "Living with an Other-Race Roommate Shapes Whites' Behavior in Subsequent Diverse Settings." *Journal of Experimental Social Psychology* 49, no. 2 (2013): 272–276. https://doi.org/10.1016/j.jesp.2012.10.020.

Gelfand, Michele J., Jesse R. Harrington, and Joshua Conrad Jackson. "The Strength of Social Norms Across Human Groups." *Perspectives on Psychological Science* 12, no. 5 (2017): 800–809. https://doi.org/10.1177/1745691617708631.

Gelfand, Michele J., Jana L. Raver, Lisa Nishii, Lisa M. Leslie, Janetta Lun, Beng Chong Lim, Lili Duan, Assaf Almaliach, Soon Ang, Jakobina Arnadottir, et al. "Differences Between Tight and Loose Cultures: A 33-Nation Study." *Science* 332, no. 6033 (2011): 1100–1104. https://doi.org/10.1126/science.1197754.

Georgeac, Oriane A., and Aneeta Rattan. "The Business Case for Diversity Backfires: Detrimental Effects of Organizations' Instrumental Diversity Rhetoric for Underrepresented Group Members' Sense of Belonging." *Journal of Personality and Social Psychology* 124, no. 1 (2023): 69–108. https://doi.org/10.1037/pspi0000394.

Geronimus, Arline T., Margaret Hicken, Danya Keene, and John Bound. "'Weathering' and Age Patterns of Allostatic Load Scores Among Blacks and Whites in the United States." *American Journal of Public Health* 96, no. 5 (2006): 826–833. https://doi.org/10.2105/ajph.2004.060749.

Gerrig, Richard. *Experiencing Narrative Worlds: On the Psychological Activities of Reading.* New York: Routledge, 2018.

Githens, Rod P., and Steve R. Aragon. "LGBT Employee Groups: Goals and Organizational Structures." *Advances in Developing Human Resources* 11, no. 1 (2009): 121–135. https://doi.org/10.1177/1523422308329200.

Glassdoor. "Job Search." https://www.glassdoor.com/Job/index.htm.

Goudarzi, Shahrzad, Vivienne Badaan, and Eric D. Knowles. "Neoliberalism and the Ideological Construction of Equity Beliefs." *Perspectives on Psychological Science* 17, no. 5 (2022): 1431–1451. https://doi.org/10.1177/1745691621105331.

Goudarzi, Shahrzad, Ruthie Pliskin, John T. Jost, and Eric D. Knowles. "Economic System Justification Predicts Muted Emotional Responses to Inequality." *Nature Communications* 11, no. 383 (2020). https://doi.org/10.1038/s41467-019-14193-z.

Grady, Christopher, Rebecca Wolfe, Danjuma Dawop, and Lisa Inks. "How Contact Can Promote Societal Change amid Conflict: An Intergroup Contact Field Experiment in Nigeria." *Proceedings of the National Academy of Sciences of the United States of America* 120, no. 43 (2023): e2304882120. https://doi.org/10.1073/pnas.2304882120.

Grall, Clare, Ron Tamborini, René Weber, and Ralf Schmälzle. "Stories Collectively Engage Listeners' Brains: Enhanced Intersubject Correlations During Reception of Personal Narratives." *Journal of Communication* 71, no. 2 (2021): 332–355. https://doi.org/10.1093/joc/jqab004.

Granovetter, Mark S. "The Strength of Weak Ties." *American Journal of Sociology* 78, no. 6 (1973): 1360–1380. http://www.jstor.org/stable/2776392.

———. *Getting a Job: A Study of Contacts and Careers.* Chicago: University of Chicago Press, 1995.

Green, Melanie C., and Timothy C. Brock. "The Role of Transportation in the Persuasiveness of Public Narratives." *Journal of Personality and Social Psychology* 79, no. 5 (2000): 701–721. https://doi.org/10.1037/0022-3514.79.5.701.

Green, Melanie C., Timothy C. Brock, and Geoff F. Kaufman. "Understanding Media Enjoyment: The Role of Transportation into Narrative Worlds." *Communication Theory* 14, no. 4 (2004): 311–327. https://doi.org/10.1111/j.1468-2885.2004.tb00317.x.

Greenwald, Anthony G., Nilanjana Dasgupta, John F. Dovidio, Jerry Kang, Corinne A. Moss-Racusin, and Bethany A. Teachman. "Implicit-Bias Remedies: Treating Discriminatory Bias as a Public-Health Problem." *Psychological Science in the Public Interest* 23, no. 1 (2022): 7–40. https://doi.org/10.1177/15291006211070781.

Guillén, Manuel, and González, Tomas F. "The Ethical Dimension of Managerial Leadership: Two Illustrative Case Studies in TQM." *Journal of Business Ethics* 34 (2001): 175–189. https://doi.org/10.1023/A:1012569609275.

Guinote, Ana. "Power and Affordances: When the Situation Has More Power Over Powerful Than Powerless Individuals." *Journal of Personality and Social Psychology* 95, no. 2 (2008): 237–252. https://doi.org/10.1037/a0012518.

Guinote, Ana, Ioanna Cotzia, Sanpreet Sandhu, and Pramila Siwa. "Social Status Modulates Prosocial Behavior and Egalitarianism in Preschool Children and

Adults." *Proceedings of the National Academy of Sciences* 112, no. 3 (2015): 731–736. https://doi.org/10.1073/pnas.1414550112.

Guinote, Ana, and Adele Phillips. "Power Can Increase Stereotyping: Evidence from Managers and Subordinates in the Hotel Industry." *Social Psychology* 41, no. 1 (2010): 3–9. https://doi.org/10.1027/1864-9335/a000002.

Guzman, Jorge, Jean Joohyun Oh, and Ananya Sen. "What Motivates Innovative Entrepreneurs? Evidence from a Global Field Experiment." *Management Science* 66, no. 10 (2020): 4808–4819. https://doi.org/10.1287/mnsc.2020.3612.

Hall, William M., Toni Schmader, and Elizabeth Croft. "Engineering Exchanges: Daily Social Identity Threat Predicts Burnout Among Female Engineers." *Social Psychological and Personality Science* 6, no. 5 (2015): 528–534. https://doi.org/10.1177/1948550615572637.

Handan-Nader, Cassandra, Daniel E. Ho, Alison Morantz, and Tom A. Rutter. "The Effectiveness of a Neighbor-to-Neighbor Get-Out-the-Vote Program: Evidence from the 2017 Virginia State Elections." *Journal of Experimental Political Science* 8, no. 2 (2021): 145–160. https://doi.org/10.1017/XPS.2020.11.

Hansen, Sarah. "Kizzmekia Corbett '08 Talks to CNN About Meyerhoff Scholars, Vaccine Hesitancy." UMBC News. University of Maryland Baltimore County, April 5, 2021. https://umbc.edu/stories/kizzmekia-corbett-08-talks-to-cnn-about-meyerhoff-scholars-vaccine-hesitancy/.

Harrington, Jesse R. "Worlds unto Themselves: Tightness-Looseness and Social Class." PhD diss., University of Maryland, College Park, 2017.

Harrington, Jesse R., and Michele J. Gelfand. "Tightness-Looseness Across the 50 United States." *Proceedings of the National Academy of Sciences* 111, no. 22 (2014): 7990–7995. https://doi.org/10.1073/pnas.1317937111.

Hartman, Steve. "Widow Who Was Invited to Eat with Strangers: 'I Think God Sent Me There.'" *CBS Evening News*, April 26, 2019, 2:47. https://www.youtube.com/watch?v=xyhQyi_KrWE.

Harvey, David. *A Brief History of Neoliberalism.* Oxford: Oxford University Press, 2005.

Harwell, Drew. "Rights Group Files Federal Complaint Against AI-Hiring Firm HireVue, Citing 'Unfair and Deceptive' Practices." *Washington Post,* November 6, 2019. https://www.washingtonpost.com/technology/2019/11/06/prominent-rights-group-files-federal-complaint-against-ai-hiring-firm-hirevue-citing-unfair-deceptive-practices/.

Hässler, T., J. Ullrich, M. Bernardino, N. Shnabel, C. V. Laar, D. Valdenegro, and L. M. Ugarte. "A Large-Scale Test of the Link Between Intergroup Contact and Support for Social Change." *Nature Human Behaviour* 4 (2020): 380–386.

Havekes, Esther, Michael Bader, and Maria Krysan. "Realizing Racial and Ethnic Neighborhood Preferences? Exploring the Mismatches Between What People Want, Where They Search, and Where They Live." *Population Research and Policy Review* 35, no. 1 (2015): 101–126. https://doi.org/10.1007/s11113-015-9369-6.

Haveman, Robert H., and Timothy M. Smeeding. "The Role of Higher Education in Social Mobility." *Future of Children* 16, no. 2 (2006): 125–150. https://doi.org /10.1353/foc.2006.0015.

Henriksen, Kristoffer, Natalia Stambulova, and Kirsten K. Roessler. "Holistic Approach to Athletic Talent Development Environments: A Successful Sailing Milieu." *Psychology of Sport and Exercise* 11, no. 3 (2010): 212–222. https://doi.org /10.1016/j.psychsport.2009.10.005.

———. "Successful Talent Development in Track and Field: Considering the Role of Environment." *Scandinavian Journal of Medicine and Science in Sports* 20, no. 2 (2010): 122–132. https://doi.org/10.1111/j.1600-0838.2010.01187.x.

———. "Riding the Wave of an Expert: A Successful Talent Development Environment in Kayaking." *Sport Psychologist* 25, no. 3 (2011): 341–362. https://doi.org /10.1123/tsp.25.3.341.

Herbert, Jennifer, and Deborah Stipek. "The Emergence of Gender Differences in Children's Perceptions of Their Academic Competence." *Journal of Applied Developmental Psychology* 26, no. 3 (2005): 276–295. https://doi.org/10.1016/j .appdev.2005.02.007.

Honey, Christopher J., Christopher R. Thompson, Yulia Lerner, and Uri Hasson. "Not Lost in Translation: Neural Responses Shared Across Languages." *Journal of Neuroscience* 32, no. 44 (2012): 15277–15283. https://doi.org/10.1523 /JNEUROSCI.1800-12.2012.

Ibarra, Herminia, and Steven B. Andrews. "Power, Social Influence, and Sense Making: Effects of Network Centrality and Proximity on Employee Perceptions." *Administrative Science Quarterly* 38, no. 2 (1993): 277–303. https://doi.org /10.2307/2393414.

Iceland, John, Pablo Mateos, and Gregory Sharp. "Ethnic Residential Segregation by Nativity in Great Britain and the United States." *Journal of Urban Affairs* 33, no. 4 (2011): 409–429. https://doi.org/10.1111/j.1467-9906.2011.00555.x.

Imana, Basileal, Aleksandra Korolova, and John Heidemann. "Auditing for Discrimination in Algorithms Delivering Job Ads." In *Proceedings of the Web Conference, Association for Computing Machinery,* Ljubljana, Slovenia, 2021, 3767–3778. https://doi.org/10.1145/3442381.3450077.

Inkelas, Karen K., Zaneeta E. Daver, Kristen E. Vogt, and Jeannie B. Leonard. "Living-Learning Programs and First-Generation College Students' Academic and Social Transition to College." *Research in Higher Education* 48 (2007): 403–434. https://doi.org/10.1007/s11162-006-9031-6.

Jacobs, Jane. *The Death and Life of Great American Cities.* New York: Random House, 1961.

Jahoda, Marie, and Patricia Salter West. "Race Relations in Public Housing." *Journal of Social Issues* 7, nos. 1–2 (1951): 132–139. https://doi.org/10.1111/j.1540-4560 .1951.tb02227.x.

James, Sherman A. "John Henryism and the Health of African-Americans." *Culture, Medicine, and Psychiatry* 18, no. 2 (1994): 163–182. https://doi.org/10.1007/bf01379448.

Jayadev, Raj. "How Community Transforms the Courts." TEDxBinghamtonUniversity video, March 2018, 14:08. https://www.ted.com/talks/raj_jayadev_how_community_transforms_the_courts.

———. "The Origin Story of Participatory Defense." Participatory Defense. https://www.participatorydefense.org/about.

Kahlenberg, Richard D., ed. *Affirmative Action for the Rich: Legacy Preferences in College Admissions.* Washington, DC: Century Foundation Press, 2010.

Kalev, A., F. Dobbin, and E. Kelly. "Best Practices or Best Guesses? Assessing the Efficacy of Corporate Affirmative Action and Diversity Policies." *American Sociological Review* 71, no. 4 (2006): 589–617. https://doi.org/10.1177/000312240607100404.

Kalinoski, Zachary T., Debra Steele-Johnson, Elizabeth J. Peyton, Keith A. Leas, Julie Steinke, and Nathan A. Bowling. "A Meta-Analytic Evaluation of Diversity Training Outcomes." *Journal of Organizational Behavior* 34, no. 8 (2012): 1076–1104. https://doi.org/10.1002/job.1839.

Kamin, Debra. "Black Homeowners Face Discrimination in Appraisals." *New York Times,* January 26, 2023. https://www.nytimes.com/2020/08/25/realestate/blacks-minorities-appraisals-discrimination.html.

Khan, Saadia. "Accent Bias and the Myth of Comprehensibility." *YES!* September 14, 2022. https://www.yesmagazine.org/opinion/2022/09/14/accent-bias-english.

Kim, Yong-Chan, and Sandra J. Ball-Rokeach. "Community Storytelling Network, Neighborhood Context, and Civic Engagement: A Multilevel Approach." *Human Communication Research* 32, no. 4 (2006): 411–439. https://doi.org/10.1111/j.1468-2958.2006.00282.x.

Kimball, Christopher. "Yewande Komolafe's Nigerian Kitchen." *Christopher Kimball's Milk Street,* September 27, 2019. Podcast, MP3 audio, 22:03. https://www.177milkstreet.com/radio/yewande-komolafes-nigerian-kitchen.

Kirkman, Bradley L., John L. Cordery, John Mathieu, Benson Rosen, and Michael Kukenberger. "Global Organizational Communities of Practice: The Effects of Nationality Diversity, Psychological Safety, and Media Richness on Community Performance." *Human Relations* 66, no. 3 (2013): 333–362. https://doi.org/10.1177/0018726712464076.

Klassen, Shamika, Sara Kingsley, Kalyn McCall, Joy Weinberg, and Casey Fiesler. "More Than a Modern Day Green Book: Exploring the Online Community of Black Twitter." *Proceedings of the ACM on Human-Computer Interaction* 5, no. 458 (2021): 1–29. https://doi.org/10.1145/3479602.

Kliman, Todd. "Coding and Decoding Dinner." *Oxford American,* May 13, 2015.

https://oxfordamerican.org/magazine/issue-88-spring-2015/coding-and-de
coding-dinner.

Koch, Lisa M., Alan M. Gross, and Russell Kolts. "Attitudes Toward Black English
and Code Switching." *Journal of Black Psychology* 27, no. 1 (2001): 29–42. https://
doi.org/10.1177/0095798401027001002.

Komolafe, Yewande. Yewande Komolafe webpage. https://www.yewandekomolafe
.com/.

Kraus, Michael W., Brittany Torrez, Jun Won Park, and Fariba Ghayebi. "Evidence
for the Reproduction of Social Class in Brief Speech." *Proceedings of the National Academy of Sciences* 116, no. 46 (2012): 22998–23003. https://doi.org/10
.1073/pnas.1900500116.

Krysan, Maria, Mick P. Couper, Reynolds Farley, and Tyrone A. Forman. "Does
Race Matter in Neighborhood Preferences? Results from a Video Experiment." *American Journal of Sociology* 115, no. 2 (2009): 527–559. https://doi.org
/10.1086/599248.

Kumar, Shamala, and Carolyn M. Jagacinski. "Imposters Have Goals Too: The Imposter Phenomenon and Its Relationship to Achievement Goal Theory." *Personality and Individual Differences* 40, no. 1 (2006): 147–157. https://doi.org/10
.1016/j.paid.2005.05.014.

Lamertz, Kai. "The Social Construction of Fairness: Social Influence and Sense
Making in Organizations." *Journal of Organizational Behavior* 23, no. 1 (2001):
19–37. https://doi.org/10.1002/job.128.

Lankford, James, Joni Ernst, and Bill Cassidy. "Senators: Abolishing ICE Would
Worsen Child Smuggling and Other US-Mexico Border Problems." *USA Today*, August 17, 2019. https://www.usatoday.com/story/opinion/2019/08/14
/us-mexico-border-problems-childsmuggling-ice-needed-senators-column
/1902206001/.

Lareau, Annette. *Unequal Childhoods: Class, Race, and Family Life,* 2nd ed. Berkeley:
University of California Press, 2011.

———. "Cultural Knowledge and Social Inequality." *American Sociological Review*
80, no. 1 (2015): 1–27. https://doi.org/10.1177/0003122414565814.

———. "Concerted Cultivation and the Accomplishment of Natural Growth." In
Childhood Socialization, ed. Theron Alexander, 335–344. New York: Routledge,
2017. https://doi.org/10.4324/9781315081427.

Larsen, Carsten H., Dorothee Alfermann, Kristoffer Henriksen, and Mette K.
Christensen. "Successful Talent Development in Soccer: The Characteristics
of the Environment." *Sport, Exercise, and Performance Psychology* 2, no. 3 (2013):
190–206. https://doi.org/10.1037/a0031958.

Leslie, Sarah-Jane, Andrei Cimpian, Meredith Meyer, and Edward Freeland. "Expectations of Brilliance Underlie Gender Distributions Across Academic Disciplines." *Science* 347, no. 6219 (2015): 262–265. https://doi.org/10.1126/science
.1261375.

Li, Sue. Hello Artists page. https://www.helloartists.com/stylists/sue-li/.
———. LinkedIn page. https://www.linkedin.com/in/sue-li-63383b56/.
Li, Yaojun, Mike Savage, and Andrew Pickles. "Social Change, Friendship, and Civic Participation." *Sociological Research Online* 8, no. 4 (2003): 111–127. https://doi.org/10.5153/sro.863.
Lin, Nan. *Social Capital: A Theory of Social Structure and Action.* Cambridge: Cambridge University Press, 2002.
Lin, Pei-Ying, Naomi Sparks Grewal, Christophe Morin, Walter D. Johnson, and Paul J. Zak. "Oxytocin Increases the Influence of Public Service Advertisements." *Public Library of Science* 8, no. 2 (2013). https://doi.org/10.1371/journal.pone.0056934.
Liu, Cong, Liu-Qin Yang, and Margaret M. Nauta. "Examining the Mediating Effect of Supervisor Conflict on Procedural Injustice–Job Strain Relations: The Function of Power Distance." *Journal of Occupational Health Psychology* 18, no. 1 (2013): 64–74. https://doi.org/10.1037/a0030889.
Lockhart, P. R. "#WakandaTheVote: How Activists Are Using Black Panther Screenings to Register Voters." *Vox,* February 21, 2018. https://www.vox.com/policy-and-politics/2018/2/21/17033644/black-panther-screenings-voter-registration-wakanda-the-vote.
Malcom, Shirley, and Michael Feder, eds. *Barriers and Opportunities for 2-Year and 4-Year STEM Degrees: Systemic Change to Support Students' Diverse Pathways.* Washington, DC: National Academies Press: 2016.
Mar, Raymond A. "The Neural Bases of Social Cognition and Story Comprehension." *Annual Review of Psychology* 62 (2011): 103–134. https://doi.org/10.1146/annurev-psych-120709-145406.
Mar, Raymond A., and Keith Oatley. "The Function of Fiction Is the Abstraction and Simulation of Social Experience." *Perspectives on Psychological Science: A Journal of the Association for Psychological Science* 3, no. 3 (2008): 173–192. https://doi.org/10.1111/j.1745-6924.2008.00073.x.
Mar, Raymond A., Keith Oatley, and Jordan B. Peterson. "Exploring the Link Between Reading Fiction and Empathy: Ruling Out Individual Differences and Examining Outcomes." *Communications* 34, no. 4 (2009): 407–428. https://doi.org/10.1515/COMM.2009.025.
Marin, Alexandra. "Don't Mention It: Why People Don't Share Job Information, When They Do, and Why It Matters." *Social Networks* 34, no. 2 (2012): 181–192. https://doi.org/10.1016/j.socnet.2011.11.002.
Marmaros, David, and Bruce Sacerdote. "Peer and Social Networks in Job Search." *European Economic Review* 46, nos. 4–5 (2002): 870–879. https://doi.org/10.1016/S0014-2921(01)00221-5.
Marshburn, Christopher K., Kevin J. Cochran, Elinor Flynn, and Linda J. Levine. "Workplace Anger Costs Women Irrespective of Race." *Frontiers in Psychology* 11 (2020). https://doi.org/10.3389/fpsyg.2020.579884.

Martindale, Russell J., Dave Collins, and Andy Abraham. "Effective Talent Development: The Elite Coach Perspective in UK Sport." *Journal of Applied Sport Psychology* 19, no. 2 (2007): 187–206. https://doi.org/10.1080/10413200701188944.

Massey, Douglas, and Nancy A. Denton. *American Apartheid: Segregation and the Making of the Underclass.* Cambridge: Harvard University Press, 1998.

Maton, Kenneth I., Tiffany S. Beason, Surbhi Godsay, Mariano R. Sto. Domingo, TaShara C. Bailey, Shuyan Sun, and Freeman A. Hrabowski III. "Outcomes and Processes in the Meyerhoff Scholars Program: STEM PhD Completion, Sense of Community, Perceived Program Benefit, Science Identity, and Research Self-Efficacy." *CBE Life Sciences Education* 15, no. 3 (2017): 1–11. https://doi.org/10.1187/cbe.16-01-0062.

Maton, Kenneth I., Mariano R. Sto. Domingo, Kathleen E. Stolle-McAllister, J. Lynn Zimmerman, and Freeman A Hrabowski III. "Enhancing the Number of African Americans Who Pursue STEM PhDs: Meyerhoff Scholarship Program Outcomes, Processes, and Individual Predictors." *Journal of Women and Minorities in Science and Engineering* 15, no. 1 (2009): 15–37. https://doi.org/10.1615/JWomenMinorScienEng.v15.i1.20.

Mauboussin, Michael J. *The Success Equation: Untangling Skill and Luck in Business, Sports, and Investing.* Cambridge: Harvard Business Review Press, 2012.

Mayer, Susan E., and Christopher Jencks. "Growing Up in Poor Neighborhoods: How Much Does It Matter?" *Science* 243, no. 4897 (1989): 1441–1445. https://doi.org/10.1126/science.243.4897.1441.

McCluney, Courtney L., Myles I. Durkee, Richard E. Smith II, Kathrina J. Robotham, and Serenity Sai-Lee Lee. "To Be, or Not to Be . . . Black: The Effects of Racial Codeswitching on Perceived Professionalism in the Workplace." *Journal of Experimental Social Psychology* 97 (2021): 104199. https://doi.org/10.1016/j.jesp.2021.104199.

McCluney, Courtney L., Kathrina Robotham, Serenity Lee, Richard Smith, and Myles Durkee. "The Costs of Code-Switching." *Harvard Business Review* 11 (2019): 1–16. https://hbr.org/2019/11/the-costs-of-codeswitching?ab=seriesnav-bigidea.

McDonald, Steve. "What's in the 'Old Boys' Network? Accessing Social Capital in Gendered and Racialized Networks." *Social Networks* 33, no. 4 (2011): 317–330. https://doi.org/10.1016/j.socnet.2011.10.002.

Meindl, Peter, Ravi Iyer, and Jesse Graham. "Distributive Justice Beliefs Are Guided by Whether People Think the Ultimate Goal of Society Is Well-Being or Power." *Basic and Applied Social Psychology* 41, no. 6 (2019): 359–385. https://doi.org/10.1080/01973533.2019.1663524.

Miller, Gregory E., Tianyi Yu, Edith Chen, and Gene H. Brody. "Self-Control Forecasts Better Psychosocial Outcomes but Faster Epigenetic Aging in Low-SES Youth." *Proceedings of the National Academy of Sciences* 112, no. 33 (2015): 10325–10330. https://doi.org/10.1073/pnas.1505063112.

Miller, Peggy J., Grace E. Cho, and Jeana R. Bracey. "Working-Class Children's Experience Through the Prism of Personal Storytelling." *Human Development* 48, no. 3 (2005): 115–135. https://doi.org/10.1159/000085515.

Monbiot, George. *How Did We Get into This Mess? Politics, Equality, Nature.* New York: Verso Books, 2016.

Moore-Berg, Samantha, Boaz Hameiri, and Emile G. Bruneau. "Empathy, Dehumanization, and Misperceptions: A Media Intervention Humanizes Migrants and Increases Empathy for their Plight but Only if Misinformation About Migrants Is Also Corrected." *Social Psychological and Personality Science* 13 (2021): 645–655.

Moseley, Jessica. "Why a Social Cause Is Often the Best Motivation a Founder Can Tap Into." YEC Women Council Post. *Forbes*, October 4, 2018. https://www.forbes.com/sites/yec/2018/10/04/why-a-social-cause-is-often-the-best-motivation-a-founder-can-tap-into/?sh=62a3ff803624.

Motiani, Ansh. "The Million Dollar Question: Merit or Luck?" TEDxStJohnsPrep video, May 2021, 8:28. https://www.youtube.com/watch?v=geVfnF9FHR4.

Motro, Daphna, Jonathan B. Evans, Aleksander P. J. Ellis, and Lehman Benson III. "Race and Reactions to Women's Expressions of Anger at Work: Examining the Effects of the 'Angry Black Woman' Stereotype." *Journal of Applied Psychology* 107, no. 1 (2021): 142–152. https://doi.org/10.1037/apl0000884.

Mousa, Salma. "Building Social Cohesion Between Christians and Muslims Through Soccer in Post-ISIS Iraq." *Science* 369, no. 6505 (2020): 866–870. https://doi.org/10.1126/science.abb3153.

Moyer-Gusé, Emily. "Toward a Theory of Entertainment Persuasion: Explaining the Persuasive Effects of Entertainment-Education Messages." *Communication Theory* 18, no. 3 (2008): 407–425. https://doi.org/10.1111/j.1468-2885.2008.00328.x.

Moyer-Gusé, Emily, and Robin L. Nabi. "Explaining the Effects of Narrative in an Entertainment Television Program: Overcoming Resistance to Persuasion." *Human Communication Research* 36, no. 1 (2010): 26–52. https://doi.org/10.1111/j.1468-2958.2009.01367.x.

Muradoglu, Melis, Zachary Horne, Matthew D. Hammond, Sarah-Jane Leslie, and Andrei Cimpian. "Women—Particularly Underrepresented Minority Women—and Early-Career Academics Feel Like Impostors in Fields That Value Brilliance." *Journal of Educational Psychology* 114, no. 5 (2022): 1086–1100. https://doi.org/10.1037/edu0000669.

Murrar, Sohad, and Markus Brauer. "Entertainment-Education Effectively Reduces Prejudice." *Group Processes and Intergroup Relations* 21, no. 7 (2018): 1053–1077. https://doi.org/10.1177/1368430216682350.

———. "Overcoming Resistance to Change: Using Narratives to Create More Positive Intergroup Attitudes." *Current Directions in Psychological Science* 28, no. 2 (2019): 164–169. https://doi.org/10.1177/0963721418818552.

Musterd, Sako. "Social and Ethnic Segregation in Europe: Levels, Causes, and Effects." *Journal of Urban Affairs* 27, no. 3 (2005): 331–348. https://doi.org/10.1111/j.0735-2166.2005.00239.x.

Napp, Clotilde, and Thomas Breda. "The Stereotype That Girls Lack Talent: A Worldwide Investigation." *Science Advances* 8 (2022): eabm3689. https://doi.org/10.1126/sciadv.abm3689.

National Center for Education Statistics. "Types of State and District Requirements for Kindergarten Entrance and Attendance, Waivers, and Exemptions for Kindergarten Entrance, by State." 2018. https://nces.ed.gov/programs/statereform/tab5_3.asp.

Newkirk, Pamela. *Diversity, Inc: The Failed Promise of a Billion-Dollar Business.* New York: Hachette Book Group, 2019.

Nummenmaa, Lauri, Enrico Glerean, Mikko Viinikainen, Iiro P. Jääskeläinen, Riitta Hari, and Mikko Sams. "Emotions Promote Social Interaction by Synchronizing Brain Activity Across Individuals." *Proceedings of the National Academy of Sciences* 109, no. 24 (2012): 9599–9604. https://doi.org/10.1073/pnas.1206095109.

Obukhova, Elena, and George Lan. "Do Job Seekers Benefit from Contacts? A Direct Test with Contemporaneous Searches." *Management Science* 59, no. 10 (2013): 2204–2016. https://doi.org/10.1287/mnsc.1120.1701.

O'Donnell, S. Casey, Veronica X. Yan, Chongzeng Bi, and Daphna Oyserman. "Is Difficulty Mostly About Impossibility? What Difficulty Implies May Be Culturally Variant." *Personality and Social Psychology Bulletin* 49, no. 2 (2021): 309–328. https://doi.org/10.1177/01461672211065595.

Oliver, J. Eric, and Janelle Wong. "Intergroup Prejudice in Multiethnic Settings." *American Journal of Political Science* 47, no. 4 (2003): 567–582. https://doi.org/10.2307/3186119.

O'Rand, Angela M. "Cumulative Processes in the Life Course." In *The Craft of Life Course Research,* ed. Glen H. Elder and Janet Z. Giele, 121–140. New York: Guilford Press, 2009.

Organizing Engagement. "Principles: Dialogue." https://organizingengagement.org/principles/dialogue/.

Overbeck, Jennifer R., and Bernadette Park. "Powerful Perceivers, Powerless Objects: Flexibility of Powerholders' Social Attention." *Organizational Behavior and Human Decision Processes* 99, no. 2 (2006): 227–243. https://doi.org/10.1016/j.obhdp.2005.10.003.

Pain, Elisabeth. "Forging the Way for Other Minority Scientists." *Science,* May 22, 2013. https://www.science.org/content/article/forging-way-other-minority-scientists.

Paluck, Elizabeth L. "Reducing Intergroup Prejudice and Conflict Using the Media: A Field Experiment in Rwanda." *Journal of Personality and Social Psychology* 96, no. 3 (2009): 574–587. https://doi.org/10.1037/a0011989.

Paluck, Elizabeth L., and Donald P. Green. "Prejudice Reduction: What Works? A Review and Assessment of Research and Practice." *Annual Review of Psychology* 60 (2009): 339–367. https://doi.org/10.1146/annurev.psych.60.110707.163607.

Peach, Ceri. "Social Geography." *Progress in Human Geography* 23, no. 2 (1999): 282–288. https://doi.org/10.1177/030913259902300208.

———. "Good Segregation, Bad Segregation," *Planning Perspectives* 11, no. 4 (2010): 379–398. https://doi.org/10.1080/026654396364817.

Pedulla, David S., and Devah Pager. "Race and Networks in the Job Search Process." *American Sociological Review* 84, no. 6 (2019): 983–1012. https://doi.org/10.1177/0003122419883255.

Perez, Caroline Criado. *Invisible Women: Exposing Data Bias in a World Designed for Men.* London: Penguin Random House, 2019.

Perner, Josef. *Understanding the Representational Mind.* Cambridge: MIT Press, 1993.

Perry, Andre M., Jonathan Rothwell, and David Harshbarger. "The Devaluation of Assets in Black Neighborhoods." Brookings Institution, November 27, 2018. https://www.brookings.edu/articles/devaluation-of-assets-in-black-neighborhoods/.

Pew Research Center. *Partisan Polarization Surges in Bush, Obama Years: Trends in American Values: 1987–2012.* Washington, DC: Pew, 2012. https://www.pewresearch.org/politics/2012/06/04/partisan-polarization-surges-in-bush-obama-years/.

Phillips, L. Taylor, Nicole M. Stephens, Sarah S. M. Townsend, and Sébastien Goudeau. "Access Is Not Enough: Cultural Mismatch Persists to Limit First-Generation Students' Opportunities for Achievement throughout College." *Journal of Personality and Social Psychology* 119, no. 5 (2020): 1112–1131. https://doi.org/10.1037/pspi0000234.

Piekut, A., and G. Valentine. "Spaces of Encounter and Attitudes Towards Difference: A Comparative Study of Two European Cities." *Social Science Research* 62 (2017): 175–188.

Piff, Paul K., Michael W. Kraus, Stéphane Côté, Bonnie Hayden Cheng, and Dacher Keltner. "Having Less, Giving More: The Influence of Social Class on Prosocial Behavior." *Journal of Personality and Social Psychology* 99, no. 5 (2010): 771–784. https://doi.org/10.1037/a0020092.

Pinnamaneni, Sruthi. "The Test Kitchen, Chapter 1." *Reply All,* no. 172, February 4, 2021. Podcast, 59:20. https://gimletmedia.com/shows/reply-all/dvhzkdo.

Pinsker, Joe. "The Real Reasons Legacy Preferences Exist." *Atlantic,* April 4, 2019. https://www.theatlantic.com/education/archive/2019/04/legacy-admissions-preferences-ivy/586465/.

Pluchino, Alessandro, Alessio E. Biondo, and Andrea Rapisarda. "Talent vs. Luck: The Role of Randomness in Success and Failure." *Advances in Complex Systems* 21, nos. 3–4 (2018): 107–137. https://doi.org/10.48550/arXiv.1802.07068.

Popović, Milan, ed. *In Albert's Shadow: The Life and Letters of Mileva Marić, Einstein's First Wife.* Baltimore: John Hopkins University Press, 2003.

244

BIBLIOGRAPHY

Project Implicit. "What Is Implicit Bias?" https://www.projectimplicit.net/.

Purdie-Vaughns, Valerie, Claude M. Steele, Paul G. Davies, Ruth Ditlmann, and Jennifer Randall Crosby. "Social Identity Contingencies: How Diversity Cues Signal Threat or Safety for African Americans in Mainstream Institutions." *Journal of Personality and Social Psychology* 94, no. 4 (2008): 615–630. https://doi.org/10.1037/0022-3514.94.4.615.

Purdy, Matthew. "The Making of a Suspect: The Case of Wen Ho Lee." *New York Times,* February 4, 2001. https://www.nytimes.com/2001/02/04/us/the-mak ing-of-a-suspect-the-case-of-wen-ho-lee.html.

Putnam, Robert D. *Bowling Alone: The Collapse and Revival of American Community.* New York: Simon and Schuster, 2000.

Qiang, Vivin. "21 Years After the Arrest of Dr. Wen." *Advancing Justice—AAJC,* December 10, 2020. https://medium.com/advancing-justice-aajc/21-years-after -the-arrest-of-dr-6098b921589a.

Quillian, Lincoln, John J. Lee, and Mariana Oliver. "Evidence from Field Experiments in Hiring Shows Substantial Additional Racial Discrimination After the Callback." *Social Forces* 99, no. 2 (2020): 732–759. https://doi.org/10.1093 /sf/soaa026.

Quillian, Lincoln, Devah Pager, Ole Hexel, and Arnfinn H. Midtbøen. "Meta-Analysis of Field Experiments Shows No Change in Racial Discrimination in Hiring Over Time." *Proceedings of the National Academy of Sciences* 114, no. 41 (2017): 10870–10875. https://doi.org/10.1073/pnas.1706255114.

Rajkumar, Karthik, Guillaume Saint-Jacques, Iavor Bojinov, Erik Brynjolfsson, and Sinan Aral. "A Causal Test of the Strength of Weak Ties." *Science* 377, no. 6612 (2022): 1304–1310. https://doi.org/10.1126/science.abl4476.

Ramasubramanian, Srividya. "Racial/Ethnic Identity, Community-Oriented Media Initiatives, and Transmedia Storytelling." *Information Society* 32, no. 5 (2016): 333–342. https://doi.org/10.1080/01972243.2016.1212618.

Ramirez, Gerardo, Rebecca Covarrubias, Matthew Jackson, and Ji Y Son. "Making Hidden Resources Visible in a Minority Serving College Context." *Cultural Diversity and Ethnic Minority Psychology* 27, no. 2 (2021): 256–268. https://doi.org /10.1037/cdp0000423.

Rand, David G., Samuel Arbesman, and Nicholas A. Christakis. "Dynamic Social Networks Promote Cooperation in Experiments with Humans." *Proceedings of the National Academy of Sciences* 108, no. 48 (2011): 19193–19198. https://doi .org/10.1073/pnas.1108243108.

Ray, Victor. "A Theory of Racialized Organizations." *American Sociological Review* 84, no. 1 (2019): 26–53. https://doi.org/10.1177/0003122418822335.

Renn, Jürgen, and Robert Schulmann, eds. *Albert Einstein/Mileva Marić: The Love Letters.* Princeton: Princeton University Press, 1992.

Rentz, Catherine. "'Agents of Change': A Year with the UMBC Program Shaping Some of the Nation's Best and Most Diverse Scientists." *Baltimore Sun,* May 18,

2018. https://www.baltimoresun.com/education/bs-md-meyerhoff-scholars -20170907-story.html.

Richeson, Jennifer A., and J. Nicole Shelton. "Negotiating Interracial Interactions: Costs, Consequences, and Possibilities." *Current Directions in Psychological Science* 16, no. 6 (2007): 316–320. https://doi.org/10.1111/j.1467-8721.2007.00528.x.

Richeson, Jennifer A., and Samuel R. Sommers. "Toward a Social Psychology of Race and Race Relations for the Twenty-First Century." *Annual Review of Psychology* 67, no. 1 (2016): 439–463. https://doi.org/10.1146/annurev-psych-010213 -115115.

Ridgeway, Cecilia L., Elizabeth H. Boyle, Kathy J. Kuipers, and Dawn T. Robinson. "How Do Status Beliefs Develop? The Role of Resources and Interactional Experience." *American Sociological Review* 63, no. 3 (1998): 331–350. https://doi.org /10.2307/2657553.

Ridgeway, Cecilia L., and Shelley J. Correll. "Consensus and the Creation of Status Beliefs." *Social Forces* 85, no. 1 (2006): 431–453. https://doi.org/10.1353/sof .2006.0139.

Rolfe, Meredith. "Conditional Choice." In *The Oxford Handbook of Analytical Sociology*, ed. Peter Bearman and Peter Hedström, 419–446. Oxford: Oxford University Press, 2011. https://doi.org/10.1093/oxfordhb/9780199215362.013.18.

Rooth, Dan-Olof. "Automatic Associations and Discrimination in Hiring: Real World Evidence." *Labour Economics* 17, no. 3 (2010): 523–534. https://doi.org/10 .1016/j.labeco.2009.04.005.

Rubineau, Brian, and Roberto M. Fernandez. "Missing Links: Referrer Behavior and Job Segregation." *Management Science* 59, no. 11 (2013): 2470–2489. https:// doi.org/10.1287/mnsc.2013.1717.

Saegert, Susan, Nancy E. Adler, Heather E. Bullock, Ana Mari Cauce, William Ming Lui, and Karen F. Wyche. *Final Report of the APA Task Force on Socioeconomic Status*. Washington, DC: American Psychological Association, 2006.

Saguy, Tamar, Nicole Tausch, John F. Dovidio, and Felicia Pratto. "The Irony of Harmony: Intergroup Contact Can Produce False Expectations for Equality." *Psychological Science* 20 (2009): 114–121.

Sampson, Robert J., and Stephen W. Raudenbush. "Seeing Disorder: Neighborhood Stigma and the Social Construction of 'Broken Windows.'" *Social Psychology Quarterly* 67, no. 4 (2004): 319–342. https://doi.org/10.1177/019027250 406700401.

Sanchez, Ray, and Linh Tran. "It Took This Mother 55 Days to Be Reunited with Her Young Daughter." CNN.com. https://www.cnn.com/2018/07/05/us/mas sachusetts-separated-families-reunification/index.html.

Sandel, Michael J. *The Tyranny of Merit: What's Become of the Common Good*. New York: Farrar, Straus and Giroux, 2020.

Sauer, Stephen J., Melissa C. Thomas-Hunt, and Patrick A. Morris. "Too Good to Be True? The Unintended Signaling Effects of Educational Prestige on External Expectations of Team Performance." *Organization Science* 21, no. 5 (2010): 1108–1120. https://doi.org/10.1287/orsc.1090.0523.

Sawaoka, Takuya, Brent L. Hughes, and Nalini Ambady. "Power Heightens Sensitivity to Unfairness Against the Self." *Personality and Social Psychology Bulletin* 41, no. 8 (2015): 1023–1035. https://doi.org/10.1177/0146167215588755.

Selvanathan, Hema Preya, Brian Lickel, and Nilanjana Dasgupta. "An Integrative Framework on the Impact of Allies: How Identity-Based Needs Influence Intergroup Solidarity and Social Movements." *European Journal of Social Psychology* 50, no. 6 (2020): 1344–1361. https://doi.org/10.1002/ejsp.2697.

Selvanathan, Hema Preya, Pirathat Techakesari, Linda R. Tropp, and Fiona Kate Barlow. "Whites for Racial Justice: How Contact with Black Americans Predicts Support for Collective Action Among White Americans." *Group Processes and Intergroup Relations* 21 (2018): 893–912.

Settles, Isis H. "When Multiple Identities Interfere: The Role of Identity Centrality." *Personality and Social Psychology Bulletin* 30, no. 4 (2004): 487–500. https://doi.org/10.1177/0146167203261885.

Shallal, Andy. "Bridging Race and Culture—the Story of Busboys and Poets." TEDxMidAtlantic video, May 2014, 10:28. https://www.youtube.com/watch?v=a5bpaTl0ELM.

Sharps, Daron L., and Cameron Anderson. "Social Class Background, Disjoint Agency, and Hiring Decisions." *Organizational Behavior and Human Decision Processes* 167 (2021): 129–143. https://doi.org/10.1016/j.obhdp.2021.08.003.

Shelton, J. Nicole, Jennifer A. Richeson, and Jacquie D. Vorauer. "Threatened Identities and Interethnic Interactions." *European Review of Social Psychology* 17, no. 1 (1, 2006): 321–358. https://doi.org/10.1080/10463280601095240.

Shnabel, N., A. Nadler, J. Ullrich, J. F. Dovidio, and D. Carmi. "Promoting Reconciliation Through the Satisfaction of the Emotional Needs of Victimized and Perpetrating Group Members: The Needs-Based Model of Reconciliation." *Personality and Social Psychology Bulletin* 35 (2009): 1021–1030.

Shook, Natalie J., and Russell H. Fazio. "Interracial Roommate Relationships: An Experimental Field Test of the Contact Hypothesis." *Psychological Science,* 19, no. 7 (2008): 717–723. https://doi.org/10.1111/j.1467-9280.2008.02147.x.

Silicon Valley De-Bug. "About SV De-Bug." https://www.siliconvalleydebug.org/about.

Simpson, Ludi. "Statistics of Racial Segregation: Measures, Evidence, and Policy." *Urban Studies* 41, no. 3 (2004): 661–681. https://doi.org/10.1080/0042098042000178735.

Singh, Barjinder, Doan E. Winkel, and T. T. Selvarajan. "Managing Diversity at Work: Does Psychological Safety Hold the Key to Racial Differences in Employee Performance?" *Journal of Occupational and Organizational Psychology* 86, no. 2 (2013): 242–263. https://doi.org/10.1111/joop.12015.

Singman, Brooke. "Hundreds of Migrant Caravan Members Found to Have US

Criminal Histories: DHS File." Fox News, June 20, 2019. https://www.foxnews
.com/politics/hundreds-of-migrant-caravan-found-to-have-criminal-histo
ries-dhs-files.

Slootman, Marieke. "Affinity Networks as Diversity Instruments. Three Sociological Dilemmas." *Scandinavian Journal of Management* 38, no. 3 (2022). https://
doi.org/10.1016/j.scaman.2022.101217.

Smith, Sandra S. "'Don't Put My Name on It': Social Capital Activation and Job-
Finding Assistance Among the Black Urban Poor." *American Journal of Sociology* 111, no. 1 (2005). https://doi.org/10.1086/428814.

Snibbe, Alana C., and Hazel R. Markus. "You Can't Always Get What You Want:
Educational Attainment, Agency, and Choice." *Journal of Personality and Social Psychology* 88, no. 4 (2005): 703–720. https://doi.org/10.1037/0022-3514.88
.4.703.

Soldner, Matthew, Heather Rowan-Kenyon, Karen K. Inkelas, Jason Garvey, and
Claire Robbins. "Supporting Students' Intentions to Persist in STEM Disciplines: The Role of Living-Learning Programs Among Other Social-Cognitive
Factors." *Journal of Higher Education* 83, no. 3 (2012): 311–336. https://doi.org/10
.1080/00221546.2012.11777246.

Southwick, Steven M., George A. Bonanno, Ann S. Masten, Catherine Panter-
Brick, and Rachel Yehuda. "Resilience Definitions, Theory, and Challenges:
Interdisciplinary Perspectives." *European Journal of Psychotraumatology* 5,
no. 1 (2014). https://doi.org/10.3402/ejpt.v5.25338.

Spencer, Steven J., Christine Logel, and Paul G. Davies. "Stereotype Threat." *Annual Review of Psychology* 67 (2016): 415–437. https://doi.org/10.1146/annurev
-psych-073115-103235.

Steele, Claude M., Steven J. Spencer, and Joshua Aronson. "Contending with Group
Image: The Psychology of Stereotype and Social Identity Threat." *Advances
in Experimental Social Psychology* 34 (2002): 379–440. https://doi.org/10.1016
/S0065-2601(02)80009-0.

Steinberg, Laurence. "A Social Neuroscience Perspective on Adolescent Risk-
Taking." *Developmental Review* 28, no. 1 (2008): 78–106. https://doi.org/10.1016
/j.dr.2007.08.002.

Stephens, Nicole M., Stephanie A. Fryberg, Hazel R. Markus, Camille S. Johnson,
and Rebecca Covarrubias. "Unseen Disadvantage: How American Universities' Focus on Independence Undermines the Academic Performance of First-
Generation College Students." *Journal of Personality and Social Psychology* 102,
no. 6 (2012): 1178–1197. https://doi.org/10.1037/a0027143.

Stephens, Nicole M., MaryAm G. Hamedani, and Mesmin Destin. "Closing the
Social-Class Achievement Gap: A Difference-Education Intervention Improves First-Generation Students' Academic Performance and All Students'
College Transition." *Psychological Science* 25, no. 4 (2014): 943–953. https://doi
.org/10.1177/0956797613518349.

Stephens, Nicole M., Hazel Rose Markus, and L. Taylor Phillips. "Social Class Culture Cycles: How Three Gateway Contexts Shape Selves and Fuel Inequality." *Annual Review of Psychology* 65 (2014): 611–634. https://doi.org/10.1146/annurev-psych-010213-115143.

Stephens, Nicole M., Sarah S. M. Townsend, Hazel R. Markus, and L. Taylor Phillips. "A Cultural Mismatch: Independent Cultural Norms Produce Greater Increases in Cortisol and More Negative Emotions Among First-Generation College Students." *Journal of Experimental Social Psychology* 48, no. 6 (2012): 1389–1393. https://doi.org/10.1016/j.jesp.2012.07.008.

Sto. Domingo, Mariano R., Starlette Sharp, Amy Freeman, Thomas Freeman Jr., Keith Harmon, Mitsue Wiggs, Vigi Sathy, et al. "Replicating Meyerhoff for Inclusive Excellence in STEM." *Science* 364, no. 6438 (2019): 335–337. https://doi.org/10.1126/science.aar5540.

Stolle-McAllister, Kathy, Mariano R. Sto. Domingo, and Amy Carrillo. "The Meyerhoff Way: How the Meyerhoff Scholarship Program Helps Black Students Succeed in the Sciences." *Journal of Science Education and Technology* 20, no. 1 (2011): 5–16. https://doi.org/10.1007/s10956-010-9228-5.

Stone, Jeff, Gordon B. Moskowitz, Colin A. Zestcott, and Katherine J. Wolsiefer. "Testing Active Learning Workshops for Reducing Implicit Stereotyping of Hispanics by Majority and Minority Group Medical Students." *Stigma and Health* 5, no. 1 (2020): 94–103. https://doi.org/10.1037/sah0000179.

Storage, Daniel, Zachary Horne, Andrei Cimpian, and Sarah-Jane Leslie. "The Frequency of 'Brilliant' and 'Genius' in Teaching Evaluations Predicts the Representation of Women and African Americans Across Fields." *PLos One* 11, no. 3 (2016): e0150194. https://doi.org/10.1371/journal.pone.0150194.

Stout, Jane G., Nilanjana Dasgupta, Matthew Hunsinger, and Melissa A. McManus. "STEMing the Tide: Using Ingroup Experts to Inoculate Women's Self-Concept in Science, Technology, Engineering, and Mathematics (STEM)." *Journal of Personality and Social Psychology* 100, no. 2 (2011): 255–270. https://doi.org/10.1037/a0021385.

Swart, Hermann, Miles Hewstone, Oliver Christ, and Alberto Voci. "The Impact of Crossgroup Friendships in South Africa: Affective Mediators and Multigroup Comparisons." *Journal of Social Issues* 66, no. 2 (2010): 309–333.

Tamborini, Christopher R., ChangHwan Kim, and Arthur Sakamoto. "Education and Lifetime Earnings in the United States." *Demography* 52, no. 4 (2015): 1383–1407. https://doi.org/10.1007/s13524-015-0407-0.

Thaler, Richard H., and Cass R. Sunstein. *Nudge: Improving Decisions About Health, Wealth, and Happiness.* New York: Penguin, 2009.

Thompson, Ted, Helen Davis, and John Davidson. "Attributional and Affective Responses of Impostors to Academic Success and Failure Outcomes." *Personality and Individual Differences* 25, no. 2 (1998): 381–396. https://doi.org/10.1016/S0191-8869(98)00065-8.

Totenberg, Nina. "Supreme Court Guts Affirmative Action, Effectively Ending Race-Conscious Admissions." National Public Radio, June 29, 2023. https://www.npr.org/2023/06/29/1181138066/affirmative-action-supreme-court-decision.

Tóth, Gergő, Johannes Wachs, Riccardo Di Clemente, Ákos Jakobi, Bence Ságvári, János Kertész, and Balázs Lengyel. "Inequality Is Rising Where Social Network Segregation Interacts with Urban Topology." *Nature Communications* 12, no. 1143 (2021). https://doi.org/10.1038/s41467-021-21465-0.

Trawalter, Sophie, Jennifer A. Richeson, and J. Nicole Shelton. "Predicting Behavior During Interracial Interactions: A Stress and Coping Approach." *Personality and Social Psychology Review* 13, no. 4 (1, 2009): 243–268. https://doi.org/10.1177/1088868309345850.

Trimble, Lindsey B., and Julie A. Kmec. "The Role of Social Networks in Getting a Job." *Sociology Compass* 5, no. 2 (2011): 165–178. https://doi.org/10.1111/j.1751-9020.2010.00353.x.

Tropp, Linda R., and Trisha A. Dehrone. "Prejudice Reduction and Social Change: Dual Goals to Be Pursued in Tandem." In *The Oxford Handbook of Political Psychology,* 3rd ed., ed. L. Huddy, D. O. Sears, J. S. Levy, and J. Jerit, 1062–1094. New York: Oxford University Press, 2023.

Tropp, Linda R., Özden Melis Uluğ, and Mete Sefa Uysal. "How Intergroup Contact and Communication About Group Differences Predict Collective Action Intentions Among Advantaged Groups." *International Journal of Intercultural Relations* 80 (2021): 7–16.

University of Massachusetts Amherst. Institute of Diversity Sciences homepage. https://www.umass.edu/diversitysciences/.

van Veelen, Ruth, Belle Derks, and Maaike D. Endedijk. "Double Trouble: How Being Outnumbered and Negatively Stereotyped Threatens Career Outcomes of Women in STEM." *Frontiers in Psychology* 10 (2019): 1–18. https://doi.org/10.3389/fpsyg.2019.00150.

van Zomeren, Martijn, Russell Spears, Agneta H. Fischer, and Colin W. Leach. "Put Your Money Where Your Mouth Is! Explaining Collective Action Tendencies Through Group-Based Anger and Group Efficacy." *Journal of Personality and Social Psychology* 87, no. 5 (November 2004): 649–664. https://doi.org/10.1037/0022-3514.87.5.649.

von Hippel, Courtney, Mona Issa, Roslyn Ma, and Abby Stokes. "Stereotype Threat: Antecedents and Consequences for Working Women." *European Journal of Social Psychology* 41, no. 2 (2011): 151–161. https://doi.org/10.1002/ejsp.749.

Vorauer, Jacquie D. "An Information Search Model of Evaluative Concerns in Intergroup Interaction." *Journal of Personality and Social* Psychology 113, no. 4 (2006): 862–886. https://psycnet.apa.org/doi/10.1037/0033-295X.113.4.862.

Vorauer, Jacquie D., and Yumiko Sakamoto. "Who Cares What the Outgroup Thinks? Testing an Information Search Model of the Importance Individu-

als Accord to an Outgroup Member's View of Them During Intergroup Interaction." *Journal of Personality and Social Psychology* 95, no. 6 (2008): 1467–1480.
https://doi.org/10.1037/a0012631.

Waldinger, Roger, and Michael I. Lichter. *How the Other Half Works: Immigration
and the Social Organization of Labor.* Berkeley: University of California Press,
2003.

Walton, Gregory M., and Geoffrey L. Cohen. "A Brief Social-Belonging Intervention Improves Academic and Health Outcomes of Minority Students." *Science*
331, no. 6023 (2011): 1447–1451. https://doi.org/10.1126/science.1198364.

———. "A Question of Belonging: Race, Social Fit, and Achievement." *Journal of
Personality and Social Psychology* 92, no. 1 (2007): 82–96. https://doi.org/10.1037
/0022-3514.92.1.82.

Watts, Duncan J., and Peter Sheridan Dodds. "Influentials, Networks, and Public
Opinion Formation." *Journal of Consumer Research* 34, no. 4 (2007): 441–458.
https://doi.org/10.1086/518527.

Welbourne, Theresa M., Skylar Rolf, and Steven Schlachter. "The Case for Employee Resource Groups: A Review and Social Identity Theory–Based Research Agenda." *Personnel Review* 46, no. 8 (2017): 1816–1834. https://doi.org/10
.1108/PR-01-2016-0004.

Wilton, Leigh S., Ariana N. Bell, Mariam Vahradyan, and Cheryl R. Kaiser. "Show
Don't Tell: Diversity Dishonesty Harms Racial/Ethnic Minorities at Work."
Personality and Social Psychology Bulletin 46, no. 8 (2020): 1171–1185. https://doi
.org/10.1177/0146167219897149.

Woolley, Anita W., Ishani Aggarwal, and Thomas W. Malone. "Collective Intelligence and Group Performance." *Current Directions in Psychological Science* 24,
no. 6 (2015): 420–424. https://doi.org/10.1177/0963721415599543.

Woolley, Anita W., Christopher F. Chabris, Alex Pentland, Nada Hashmi, and
Thomas W. Malone. "Evidence for a Collective Intelligence Factor in the Performance of Human Groups." *Science* 330, no. 6004 (2010): 686–688. https://
doi.org/10.1126/science.1193147.

Wu, Deborah J., Tracie Gibson, Linda M. Ziegenbein, Randall W. Phillis, Caralyn
B. Zehnder, Elizabeth A. Connor, and Nilanjana Dasgupta. "An Identity-Based
Learning Community Intervention Enhances the Lived Experience and Suc-
cess of First-Generation College Students in the Biological Sciences." *Scientific
Reports* 14, article 10163 (2024). https://doi.org/10.1038/s41598-024-60650-1.

Wu, Deborah J., Kelsey C. Thiem, and Nilanjana Dasgupta. "Female Peer Mentors
Early in College Have Lasting Positive Impacts on Female Engineering Students That Persist Beyond Graduation." *Nature Communications* 13, article
6837 (2022): 1–12. https://doi.org/10.1038/s41467-022-34508-x.

Yeager, David S., Jamie M. Carroll, Jenny Buontempo, Andrei Cimpian, Spencer
Woody, Robert Crosnoe, Chandra Muller, et al. "Teacher Mindsets Help Ex-

plain Where a Growth-Mindset Intervention Does and Doesn't Work." *Psychological Science* 33, no. 1 (2021): 18–32. https://doi.org/10.1177/09567976211028984.

Yeager, David S., Paul Hanselman, Gregory M. Walton, Jared S. Murray, Robert Crosnoe, Chandra Muller, Elizabeth Tipton, et. al. "A National Experiment Reveals Where a Growth Mindset Improves Achievement." *Nature* 573, no. 7774 (2019): 364–369. https://doi.org/10.1038/s41586-019-1466-y.

Yogeeswaran, K., L. Adelman, M. Parker, and N. Dasgupta. "In the Eyes of the Beholder: White Americans' National Identification Predicts Differential Reactions to Ethnic Identity Expressions." *Cultural Diversity and Ethnic Minority Psychology* 20 (2014): 362–369.

Yogeeswaran, K., and N. Dasgupta. "Will the 'Real' American Please Stand Up? The Effect of Implicit Stereotypes About Nationality on Discriminatory Behavior." *Personality and Social Psychology Bulletin* 36 (2010): 1332–1345.

———. "The Devil Is in the Details: Abstract Versus Concrete Construals of Multiculturalism Differentially Impact Intergroup Relations." *Journal of Personality and Social Psychology* 106 (2014): 772–789.

———. "National Identity in a Globalized World: Psychological Processes and Implications." *European Review of Social Psychology* 25 (2017): 189–227.

Yogeeswaran, K., N. Dasgupta, L. Adelman, A. Eccleston, and M. Parker. "To Be or Not to Be (Ethnic): The Hidden Cost of Ethnic Identification for Americans of European and Non-European Origin." *Journal of Experimental Social Psychology* 47 (2011): 908–914.

Yogeeswaran, K., N. Dasgupta, and C. Gomez. "A New American Dilemma? The Effect of Ethnic Identification and Public Service on the National Inclusion of Ethnic Minorities." *European Journal of Social Psychology* 42 (2012): 691–705.

Yu, Junlin, Pia Kreijkes, and Katariina Salmela-Aro. "Students' Growth Mindset: Relation to Teacher Beliefs, Teaching Practices, and School Climate." *Learning and Instruction* 80 (2022): 101616. https://doi.org/10.1016/j.learninstruc.2022.101616.

Zadbood, Asieh, Janice Chen, Yuan Chang Leong, Kenneth A. Norman, and Uri Hasson. "How We Transmit Memories to Other Brains: Constructing Shared Neural Representations Via Communication." *Cerebral Cortex* 27, no. 10 (2017): 4988–5000. https://doi.org/10.1093/cercor/bhx202.

Zak, Paul J. "Why Inspiring Stories Make Us React: The Neuroscience of Narrative." *Cerebrum* 2 (2015): 2. https://pubmed.ncbi.nlm.nih.gov/26034526/.

Ziv, Margalit, and Douglas Frye. "The Relation Between Desire and False Belief in Children's Theory of Mind: No Satisfaction?" *Developmental Psychology* 39, no. 5 (2003): 859–876. https://doi.org/10.1037/0012-1649.39.5.859.

INDEX

markers and self-doubt, 19; names, 27–32; nationality, 22–27; and the presumption of competence, 32–33

Stephens, Nicole, 95–96, 179

stereotypes: of Americanness, 23–27; of brilliance, 68–73; caste, 30; of girls learning math, 68; and power, 106–107; racial, 17–18, 28, 38–39, 107; status, 38–39

Storage, Daniel, 65

storytelling: arousing empathy and reducing bias, 140–146; creating conditions for structural change, 153–156; creating social glue, 148–150; effect on mind and brain, 138–140; grassroots, 147–148; illuminating systemic inequalities, 150–153; increasing social acceptance, 146–148; power of, 137–138; to promote social change, 199–200

Stout, Jane, 126

stress, 82–84

structural change, 132–135, 152, 153–156, 169–171, 180–182, 195–196, 201. See also social change

students: Africana studies majors, 93; athletes, 50–51, 187–189; in the Bio-Pioneers program, 174–178, 179; Black and Hispanic, 82–84, 172–173, 178, 186, 189, 194; business majors, 137; and classroom culture, 193–194; cohort-based programs for, 173–179; diversity in, 206–208; first-generation, 82–84, 97, 128, 178–179; forensic psychology majors, 59; gifted, 63, 84–85; in mathematics classrooms, 186, 189; in the Meyerhoff Scholars Program, 172–174; from middle- and upper-middle-class families, 34, 58, 87, 89–90, 94, 96, 97, 99–100, 101, 108, 109, 128, 177; Native American, 194; premed

majors, 92; psychology majors, 137; reasons for pursuing college, 96; STEM majors, 118–119, 137, 176–177, 207; women as, 66–68, 70–71, 90–93, 125, 127–130; from working-class families, 43, 59, 89–90, 94, 95–96, 98–100, 105, 108, 127, 128, 174, 177–179, 205. See also education

success: and hard work, 7, 74, 76, 80, 84, 86; and luck, 73–76, 86; recognition of, 16; and talent, 68–73, 86

summer bridge programs, 178

Sunstein, Cass, 8

symbolic (nonmaterial) culture, 6–7. See also culture

systemic, 42, 77, 84, 86, 150–152, 155, 181–182. See also structural change

talent: assumptions about, 205–209; developmental, 72, 194, 208; discovery of, 208–209; encouragement of, 173–174; failure as lack of, 70, 85; and growth potential, 192–195; myths about, 62–63, 63; natural, 72, 194. See also brilliance

Thaler, Richard, 8

Thatcher, Margaret, 77

theory of mind, 138

Thiem, Kelsey, 129

Torres, Elias, 131

Tóth, Gergő, 53

trust, 60, 119, 120, 121, 131–132, 145, 160, 167, 175, 190, 191, 195, 196, 210

Tufts University, 105

Turkey, 169

U Street (Washington, DC), 115, 116

University of Alabama, 148

University of British Columbia, 150

University of California Davis School of Medicine, 206, 208

University of California Irvine, 99